TAKING THE LAW INTO THEIR OWN HANDS

The Making of Modern Africa
Series Editors: Abebe Zegeye and John Higginson

From Dictatorship to Democracy
Economic policy in Malawi 1964-2000
Jane Harrigan

Manoeuvring in an Environment of Uncertainty
Structural change and social action in sub-Saharan Africa
Edited by Boel Berner and Per Trulsson

Gender, Family and Work in Tanzania
Edited by Colin Creighton and C.K. Omari

Contesting Forestry in West Africa
Edited by Reginald Cline-Cole and Clare Madge

Electoral Territoriality in Southern Africa
Stephen Rule

Community Health Needs in South Africa
Ntombenhle Protasia Khoti Torkington

Consolidation of Democracy in Africa
A view from the South
Edited by Hussein Solomon and Ian Liebenberg

Ghana in Search of Development
The challenge of governance, economic management and institution building
Dan-Bright S. Dzorgbo

Regional and Local Economic Development in South Africa
The experience of the Eastern Cape
Etienne Louis Nel

Agrarian Economy, State and Society in Contemporary Tanzania
Edited by Peter G. Forster and Sam Maghimbi

Taking the Law into Their Own Hands
Lawless law enforcers in Africa

BRUCE BAKER
African Studies Centre
Coventry University

ASHGATE

© Bruce Baker 2002

All rights reserved. No part of this publication may be reproduced, stored in a retrieval system or transmitted in any form or by any means, electronic, mechanical, photocopying, recording or otherwise without the prior permission of the publisher.

The Author hereby asserts his moral right to be identified as the Author of this Work, in accordance with the Copyright, Designs and Patents Act, 1988.

Published by
Ashgate Publishing Limited
Gower House
Croft Road
Aldershot
Hampshire GU11 3HR
England

Ashgate Publishing Company
Suite 420
101 Cherry St
Burlington, VT 05401-4405 USA

Ashgate website: http://www.ashgate.com

British Library Cataloguing in Publication Data
Baker, Bruce
 Taking the law into their own hands : lawless law enforcers
 in Africa. - (The making of modern Africa)
 1. Law enforcement - Africa 2. Vigilantes - Africa
 3. Political violence - Africa 4. Democracy - Africa
 I. Title
 363.2'3'096

Library of Congress Cataloging-in-Publication Data
Baker, Bruce.
 Taking the law into their own hands : lawless law enforcers in Africa / Bruce Baker.
  p. cm. -- (The making of modern Africa)
 Includes bibliographical references and index.
 ISBN 0-7546-1884-6 (alk.paper)
 1. Vigilance committees--Africa. 2. Death squads--Africa. 3. Crime prevention--Africa--Citizen participation. 4. Government, Resistance to--Africa--Prevention. 5. Law enforcement--Africa. I. Title. II. Series.

HV6322.3.A35 B35 2002
364.1'32'0967--dc21

2002074715

ISBN 0 7546 1884 6
Printed and bound by Athenaeum Press, Ltd.,
Gateshead, Tyne & Wear.

Contents

List of Figures vii
Acknowledgements ix

Introduction 1

PART I: LAWLESSNESS AND DEMOCRACY IN AFRICA

1 The Importance of the Rule of Law in Democracy 9
2 The Construction of Attitudes Towards the Law 27

PART II: THE ARMY TAKES THE LAW INTO ITS OWN HANDS

3 The Ugandan Peoples Defence Force and the Northern Rebellion 55
4 The Senegalese Army and the Casamance Secessionists 81

PART III: THE POLICE AND STATE MILITIA TAKE THE LAW INTO THEIR OWN HANDS

5 The Mozambican National Police and Crime 107
6 Anambra State Vigilante Service (Nigeria) and Crime 129

PART IV: THE PEOPLE TAKE THE LAW INTO THEIR OWN HANDS

7 Vigilantes and Crime in South Africa 153
8 East Africa's Vigilantes and Cattle Rustling 179

PART V: THE IMPLICATIONS FOR DEMOCRACY

9 Sustaining Democracy in a Context of Lawless Law Enforcement 205

Bibliography 221
Index 231

List of Figures

Figure 1.1 The parallels between the rule of law and democracy   19

Figure 3.1 Northern Uganda   54

Figure 4.1 Casamance, Senegal   80

Figure 6.1 Anambra State, Nigeria   128

Figure 8.1 East African Pastoralists   178

Acknowledgements

This book emerged from my post-doctoral research into the relationship between democracy and violence and in particular from four months spent at Rhodes University, South Africa as a visiting Research Fellow and research time in Uganda, Senegal and Mozambique. I am grateful to Coventry University and especially the African Studies Centre for funding to go to South Africa and Senegal. Professor Roy May, the director of the African Studies Centre has, as ever, encouraged me on the way, although he was partly to blame that I visited the bed of the Nile rather than its source. Gideon Baker was invaluable in his criticisms and encouragement as usual and Marcie Edwards was indispensable in getting the text camera ready.

Introduction

This is a book about policing in Africa. It is about policing as an activity rather than being confined to the police as an organisation. It is about policing, whether by state or non-state groups, and its response to challenges to internal order and security from both serious crime and from rebellion. It is a deliberate attempt to bring together what are normally separate, namely state *and* non-state law enforcement and criminal *and* rebel lawlessness. Not that those divisions are not useful, but here the choice is to consider the similarities, rather than the differences. In the course of the book it will be seen that, in practice, the boundaries are not so clear-cut as often imagined.

Policing personnel collaborate and even interchange, not only across the army/gendarmerie/police divides, but also across state/non-state ones. The relationship self-defence groups have with state security forces, the police, local politicians, regional power brokers and the local community is complex. For instance, many popular responses to lawlessness, like vigilantism, are tolerated by the authorities or even sponsored by them, despite their illegal nature.

Again, serious crime and rebellion not only exploit one another's presence, but also can have unholy alliances or even merge. Many rebels now live by looting and some have ambitions that are far more concerned with personal enrichment than political power or social revolution. On the other hand, criminals may seek political influence to further their success. Certainly both serious crime and rebellion create similar terror and social chaos on the local communities where they operate.

On the ground, Africans want protection from this threat of violence, whatever it is called and whoever is causing it; and care more about the effectiveness of the protection than whether the security agents that are providing it are state or non-state employees. Some would even argue that they care little how the security agencies contain and ultimately dismantle the threat. If that is too sweeping, it does raise the other blurred boundary that is at the centre of this book, that is the one between the methods employed by law breakers and law enforcers. The text unfolds how the various agencies of law enforcement and internal security counter the threats to social order. It is at this level that the supposed distinction between the law breakers and the law enforcers looks least relevant, for in tackling their common 'enemies' they use remarkably similar methods, which can only be described as outside of national and international law. The tragic irony is that much of law enforcement in Africa is lawless. It breaks the law to uphold the law.

There has been no shortage of criticisms of the quality and breadth of Africa's new democracies, both by the African public and by political analysts. Most of the assessment has been in terms of examining the performance of democratic institutions and processes such as the fairness of elections, the accountability of governments, the freedom of the press, the integrity of the bureaucracy, the impartiality of the judiciary and the respect for human rights (e.g. Diamond and Plattner, 1999; Bratton and Van de Walle, 1997; Ottaway, 1997; Joseph, 1998; Villalon and Huxtable, 1998; Widner, 1994; Freedom House yearly reports). In addition, some published research has examined how this variable performance has impacted on the attitudes of people towards democracy (Gibson and Gouws, 1997; Mattes and Thiele, 1999; Bratton, and Mattes, 2001; Bratton and Lambright, 2001). This book contributes to the debate on democratic quality by examining policing. This has largely been neglected, despite the fact that state security agents alone in a democracy have the right of exercising the state's claim to the monopoly of violence. These state agents and their non-state counterparts determine how citizens enjoy the privileges and freedoms of the law and also how they are restrained from breaking it and treated when they do. They are thus central to the democratic processes.

The book also examines popular attitudes, but reverses the usual order of enquiry. It looks, not at how the performance of democratic institutions impact on people's attitudes, but how people's attitudes (democratic or non-democratic) impact on democratic institutions. In particular, it considers the attitude to the rule of law when faced with lawlessness, particularly those of law enforcers.

The premise of the book is that the rule of law is a central element of democracy. In a polity that upholds popular control and political equality, citizens are bound by collective decisions. Before those democratically determined laws, all are equal, whether calling upon it to accuse or to excuse. To ensure equal and just treatment, trials are required to be conducted by a public authority and to be held in public before lay juries and impartial judges. It is manifestly not a right of citizens or agents of the state to conduct trials and mete out punishment outside the criminal justice system. From this normative base line the book makes an assessment of the actual methods of law enforcement in Africa and weighs the implications of what it finds for the new democracies.

The book shows that the reality in much of Africa is very different from democratic theory. Though democratically elected legislatures, rather than the politburos or the military committees, now make the law, that law is not consistently enforced throughout the whole of the national territory. Much of this inconsistency has to do, both with the limited resources available for state administration and policing, and the inadequate training and supervision of those personnel. It does mean, however, that over large swathes of Africa, particularly the peripheral provinces and informal settlements, the rule of law does not run consistently. In addition to, or because of, this weak state provision of security, crime and insurgency are widely regarded by African populations and by academics as a serious and growing problem (Zolberg, 1992; Callaghy, 1994; Kaplan, 1994) and there have been repeated calls for more attention to be directed towards them (Joseph, 1998; Mbembe, 1990). Across Africa there are reports of widespread banditry and a high incidence of violent urban crime. Further, many professing democratic states are confronted with civil war (e.g. Sierra Leone, Angola), rebellions (Uganda, Liberia, Guinea, Chad), armed secessionist groups (e.g. Senegal, Cameroon, Ethiopia, Namibia) and 'warlord' militias (e.g. Chad, Central African Republic, henceforth, CAR).

Tragic though this lawlessness is, it in turn frequently provokes unlawful and undemocratic responses. Left without the protection of the police and the security forces and with the courts often physically and financially inaccessible, the people have continued with (or resorted to) their own methods of maintaining communal order, preserving life and property, and of punishing those who threaten it. Anti-crime groups and vigilantes, often armed, defend persons, property and stock and hunt down alleged criminals. Some may choose to hand them over to the public authorities for trial, but others mete out their own punishment, that may or may not be sanctioned by the community. And in response to rebel groups that seriously threaten lives and livelihoods, militias may be formed to drive them away. In all these examples of insecurity, there is always the likelihood of the situation being exploited by authoritarian political 'saviours', warlords and mafia elements.

Unlawful responses are not, however, confined to citizens. The coercive forces of the state itself are also implicated. Under pressure from governments to cut crime, terrorism, banditry and rebel activity, and with the limited resources available to them, the temptation is to discard democratic procedures as too cumbersome and too lenient. Under torture, suspects talk more readily and opponents give more leads, whilst extrajudicial executions save the need to go through the prolonged and uncertain criminal justice system.

It is contested as to how much the state is aware of its security forces acting outside of the law, suspending legal processes and undertaking extrajudicial executions and the torture of political opponents. Clearly much is done by personnel ignorant of, or indifferent to, human rights and legal requirements and without the knowledge or consent of their superiors. But other cases reveal complicity, or even instigation, by the highest authorities, which are fired by the political urgency of getting results. Cutting democratic corners can seem an attractive policy to a government under siege and well aware of their new exposure to regular elections on their performance.

The book is set out in five sections: the rule of law and democracy; when the army takes the law into its own hands; when the police and state militias take the law into their own hands; when the people take the law into their own hands; and the implications for democracy.

The first section consists of two chapters that provide the theoretical and historical introduction to the subject. Chapter one focuses on defining what is meant by lawlessness and law enforcers, before going on to examine the role of law in democracy and the complex concept of the rule of law and its relationship to democracy. It emphasises how crucial the rule of law is to the functioning of democracy and that legal rights are as much a part of democracy as political rights. It is followed, in chapter 2, with an account of how attitudes to the rule of law have been constructed among law enforcers and the public at large. In particular, it examines how authoritarianism and what is called 'disciplinarianism' have developed. It then traces the practices based on these attitudes through history to the present time.

The following three sections of the book seek to capture the responses to crime and insurgency in six case studies. Each examines the interaction between economic restraints, political realities, cultural norms and democratic values and considers the difficulties of transforming security agencies that have often been partial, incompetent, corrupt and sometimes brutal. The case studies have been chosen for the contrasts they offer around the central theme and for their regional diversity.

The first two case studies, comprising section two, concern situations where a national army takes the law into its own hands. Chapter three is a study of the Ugandan Peoples Defence Force and their response to the Lord's Resistance Army in the north of the country. It demonstrates that, though facing a brutal and violent enemy, the army has itself ignored lawful procedures in its response. This has been to the detriment of democratic processes, not just in the north, but also on the whole country.

The second study, in chapter 4, relates to the Senegalese Army's handling of the secessionist rebellion in Casamance. It reveals a similar pattern to Uganda of lawless rebel action met by lawless army response. Violence by the MFDC rebels has been matched by summary sentences, extrajudicial killings and torture by the army. The effect on democratic procedures has likewise been negative.

The third section of the book turns to policing, both national police and regional state militias. Though human rights legislation is in place in Mozambique, chapter 5 reveals that the Mozambique Police is often unaware or indifferent to its restraints. In their attempt to control crime there have been innumerable cases of illegal arrests, torture, and the rape and deaths of those held in detention. Even more lawless have been the activities of the quasi-official militia in Anambra state in Nigeria, which is the subject of chapter 6. Both the Mozambican and the Nigerian police organisations have not only denied citizens their human and civil rights, but through their summary justice and complicity with criminals have discredited the criminal justice system. Yet the two organisations considered have had very different popular responses, with the Mozambican Police widely condemned, whilst the Anambra Vigilante Service has been extremely popular in the state. Both, however, show little evidence of accountability or transparency and are therefore at odds with democracy.

When citizens become disillusioned with official internal security agencies they frequently turn to self-policing. The subject of the fourth section of the book, therefore, is when people take the law into their own hands. Chapter 7 looks at non-state policing in South Africa such as formal and informal vigilante groups. Inevitably these involve personnel who are poorly trained and supervised and have little or no accountability to the general public. The result is that they commonly disregard the law in their methods of investigation, trials and sentencing. Yet despite widespread condemnation by politicians, they have substantial popular support. The second case study in the section, chapter 8, looks at how pastoral communities in East Africa seek to curtail cattle rustling. With the widespread availability of cheap modern weapons, village vigilante groups protect stock and hunt down and kill raiders with new levels of violence. However, the vigilantes are themselves often cattle thieves, so that the boundary between policing and crime becomes blurred.

The final section, chapter 9, considers the problem of sustaining democracy in a context of lawless law enforcement. It argues that it is not only serious crime and insurgency that threatens democracy by flouting the rule of law, creating insecurity, disrupting the political process, diverting resources and undermining the economy. The responses to crime and insurgency also damage democracy at every level. They encourage disrespect or even scorn for the state whose law officers, criminal justice system and security services are revealed to be manifestly inadequate for the task; provoke actions outside of the law that are frequently violent and entail miscarriages of justice; promote racial and class stereotypes about who the 'bandits' are and encourage social intolerance of these groups; and they sustain misinformation, cover-ups and censorship by allies wanting to protect the perpetrators of unlawful actions.

If democracy in Africa is to be sustained and deepened, then both the authoritarian and disciplinarian values that underlie much current policing, and the weak systems of control and accountability that account for lawless practices continuing unimpeded, must be tackled. Yet changing cultural values and finding finance for extra personnel and their training are both going to be tough challenges. They will yield only to governments and people with focus and patience. If unaddressed, then no matter how well established democratic institutions like fair elections, a free press, an impartial judiciary and executive accountability to parliament become, a fundamental element of democracy will be missing and one that is likely to undermine other institutions. In the view of many (e.g. Mbembe, 1992; Chabal, 1992; Joseph, 1998; Callaghy, 1994; Przeworski, 1995), violence may be the most significant factor currently threatening constitutional democracy. Zolberg speaks of 'the specter of anarchy' and Kaplan (1994) has achieved notoriety by spreading the view of a 'coming anarchy'. But the danger is not simply the lawlessness of various rebel movements, warlords and organised crime groups. There is the danger that the very response to them will be characterised by a violence and lawlessness that is equally threatening to the health and sustainability of democratic institutions and processes, such as state accountability and transparency, freedom of information, the free press, respect for human rights, a right to a fair trial and equality before law.

PART I
LAWLESSNESS AND DEMOCRACY IN AFRICA

1 The Importance of the Rule of Law in Democracy

Lawless law enforcement is a familiar feature throughout Africa. In their efforts to uphold the law and in their response to those who break it, state and non-state policing agencies use methods that are both contrary to national law and international law. According to the Human Rights Report of 2000, by the US State Department, police in Malawi 'continued to beat and otherwise abuse detainees and to use excessive force in handling criminal suspects... Police sometimes hide these abuses by keeping prisoners in police custody until wounds heal before turning them over to the prison system for remand'. To the south, members of the security forces in Namibia 'used excessive violence against citizens and Angolan civilians along the northern border of the country... Senior civilian and military government officials made public statements acknowledging that security forces abused and killed civilians in the Kavango and Caprivi regions during security operations'. To the north a mass grave was found near Lake Chad in Niger in 1999 'containing 149 bodies alleged to be those of missing Toubou former rebels... When last seen the Toubous were in the custody of the Nigerian armed forces'. To the west, in Benin, 'a rural popular leader, the self-styled Colonel Devi, incited mobs [in 1999] to lynch more than 100 suspected criminals in the southwestern part of the country. Most of the victims were burned alive, many after being abducted, beaten, and tortured by Devi's followers... Individual incidents of mob justice continued to occur nationwide, and police most often ignored vigilante attacks' (US Department of State, 2001).

This book is an examination of what happens to the polity in general and democratic institutions in particular when those who seek to enforce the state law, be they state security forces or local informal arrangements, do so with scant regard for state legal process. Often the abuses of law enforcers are borne of desperation to impose order when organised violence threatens social stability. When lawful methods fail to restrain the 'rebels', 'bandits', 'hoodlums' and 'thugs', then the temptation is to apply methods of detention, interrogation, trial and punishment that offer quick results or at least results more acceptable to the perpetrators. It is worth remembering

Tilly's observation that, 'Contrary to the image of dissidents lashing out at regimes – the great bulk of killing and wounding in the course of modern collective violence is done by troops, police, and other specialized repressive forces' (1975, p. 495). Beyond the violent aspect of law enforcement, however, is the issue of their lawlessness.

Lawlessness

By lawlessness is meant conduct by law enforcers that is not subject to or controlled by the national law. This has frequently been found to be closely related to the level of perceived domestic threat by the authorities, whether at national or village level. When the level of threat is high, as is the case in the examples chosen for this book, the greater their willingness to call upon security personnel to restore order and to nullify the threat, if necessary, through repression and unlawful methods. Measuring threat levels is not a scientific process, but authorities will take into account the target of the threat (the political system itself or material assets), support levels, use of violence, and the organisation level (Davenport, 2000, pp. 3-5).

It may well be that law enforcers are only enforcing the orders of those in power and that lawless law enforcement is the response of these leaders to a threat to destabilise or overthrow their rule. But law enforcers also act with varying degrees of independence and it is important to consider what reasons they might have themselves for lawless conduct, whether it be lack of supervision, frustration at the ineffectiveness of lawful procedures, the nature of the recruits, security group culture, revenge, non-liberal views of punishment, pressure for results, or social discrimination.

There is then, potentially, a multiplicity of causes behind lawlessness, both at the level of the political authorities and at the level of the security agents themselves. Can sociological theories of crime and deviancy provide any over-arching explanations of lawlessness among law enforcers? There are three perspectives that warrant consideration. The first is anomie theory, which proposes that people use alternative means, including deviant and illegal activities, to gain access to socially created needs that they are unable to obtain through legitimate behaviour. In societies, for instance, where there is an over-emphasis on the goal of achieving material wealth, but the approved institutional means of attaining it are restricted, this can lead to social strain or anomie. As a result some may embark on 'innovative' routes to acquire wealth which society regards as deviant. Lawlessness among law enforcers could therefore be seen as deviant behaviour arising where the societal goals of security from violence and crime cannot be attained through traditional legal methods of policing. This interpretation, however, makes the assumption that society is agreed on the institutional means of deterring and punishing violent crime and rebellion. Though law passed by parliament may represent the legally approved institutional means, in much of Africa there is a sharp division of popular opinion about the legitimacy of conferring human rights on criminals and rebels. It is this contested view of lawlessness that undergirds a second approach.

This is the victimised actor model, which questions how lawlessness and deviancy is defined. It notes that very often deviance is not a property inherent in certain forms of behaviour, but one that is conferred. It is the powerful who determine that elements of the behaviour of the poor and disadvantaged are deviant. They then impose the new rules upon the powerless against their will. Are, therefore, summary punishments, extrajudicial killings, illegal detentions, and similar such abuses by law enforcers, a case of national or international elite labelling of popularly accepted behaviour? Though it might be argued that there are degrees of lawlessness attracting differing levels of support, it does remind us not to view African policing through European spectacles. Actions may be lawless in the sense of being contrary to national law, but not illegitimate in the social context in which they occur.

A third perspective that has relevance to lawlessness is social control theory, which considers why people conform and how restraints on behaviour may break down. A number of circumstances have been explored that lower social constraint, such as periods of rapid modernisation and social change, when new forms of regulation cannot evolve quickly enough to replace the declining force of social integration. No one would doubt that African nations have undergone a severe economic crisis in the last ten years. Further, the states often have weak capacity and penetration and have been unable to inculcate norms of the rule of law. In practice, therefore, policing is not effectively controlled. State agencies and informal groups are allowed to get away with abuses, although whether this is always from ignorance of them or because they are excused for various reasons is disputed. With supervisory control of policing being in such a parlous state, policing has been allowed to become or remain inefficient, corrupt and lawless. Left, as they often are, to their own devices, law enforcement agencies, whether formal or informal, have a low stake in conformity.

None of these approaches provides a total explanation. They appear inadequate when it comes to explaining a specific form of deviance; or why lawless behaviour is undertaken by those who are otherwise lawful; or why not all those involved in policing resort to lawlessness, despite being exposed to similar pressures or the lack of them. Yet despite their limitations, each has something to say about lawless law enforcement; to what degree must be assessed chapter by chapter.

Law Enforcement

Law enforcement is a broad category associated with an array of functions, including regulating society and maintaining order, preserving security, preventing crime, responding to crime and restoring order, and the use where necessary of instruments of coercion to assist in any of these. The nature of these functions has caused it to be widely regarded in the West as an inherently public good, whose provision should reside in the hand of a single monopoly supplier, the democratic state. In the state's hands, it is argued, policing activities can be required to be accountable, consistent and humane. However, the reality on the ground is outstripping these common sentiments. Law enforcement is 'being reconstructed worldwide', with not only a separation between those who authorise it from those who provide the service, but a dispersal of both functions away from government (Bayley and Shearing, 2001). Policing for an array of authorities that includes business interests, residential communities, cultural communities, individuals as well as the state, is now provided by commercial security companies, formal voluntary non-governmental groups, individuals and even governments themselves as private suppliers of protection.

This reconstruction of policing is evident across Africa, where non-state agencies are found engaged in street patrolling, guarding private and public property, order maintenance, arrest, search, detection, surveillance, inspection and personal escort/protection. In fulfilling many of these duties they bear firearms and other means of coercion, such as handcuffs, truncheons and pepper spray to, if necessary, enforce their activities. In other words, such policing groups do everything that the public police force does and do it as the police do it. Or, put another way, law enforcement is a broader activity than simply what The Police do.

The reality, therefore, especially in Africa, is that law enforcement is being reconstructed. There is not only a separation between those who authorise it from those who provide the service, but the dispersal of both functions away from government. It is provided by commercial security companies, formal voluntary organisations, informal groups, individuals, as well as the state, for an array of authorities, formal and informal, that includes business interests (legal and illegal), residential communities, cultural communities, individuals and the state. As Bayley and Shearing note, the relationship between authorisers and providers can have several permutations: public/public, public/private, private/public, private/private:

> Without close scrutiny it has become difficult to tell whether policing is being done by a government using sworn personnel, by an agent using a private security company, by a private security company using civilian employees, by a private company using pubic police or by a government employing civilians (Bayley and Shearing, 2001).

The boundary between public and private has lost its distinctiveness. Both public and private entities authorise policing and both public and private entities provide services for those authorisers. Further blurring the divide, governments provide policing for private organisations and private providers offer services to governments. Bringing together into a single analytical category of law enforcement, activity by state and non-state agencies, is not, however, without its problems. Some would insist that collapsing the whole field of law enforcement is to merge phenomena that are inherently separate. It is true that the informal vigilantes, regional state vigilante services, national police and internal security forces that are considered in this book have significant differences in their authority, organisational structure, legality and how they define social deviance and the type of 'order' they wish to establish. Nevertheless they do have important features in common. They are all forces of coercion engaged to preserve internal social order, which they do either in co-operation, or in opposition or sometimes in isolation. That they all use similar methods is a reflection of the similar roles they perform. As Hills observes, in Africa at least, talking about policing is more helpful than talking about the police:

> policing in Africa goes beyond formal civilian groups... the focus should be on policing (as in the provision of order and enforcement) rather than on what organizations call themselves. How police style themselves is less important than what they do or do not do (Hills, 2000, p. 6).

Hills illustrates her point from Nigeria where, 'the military, some eight or more paramilitary units, various palace guards, numerous quasi-official units in various states, and miscellaneous thugs associated with strongmen' all engage at some time or other in what could be called policing (Hills, 2000, p.7). The fact is that the boundary between private and public has lost its clarity. Both public and private entities have assumed responsibility for authorising policing. And both public and private entities provide policing to those providers. Even the government's role is no longer exclusively public, for it authorises policing, encourages non-government groups to authorise policing and provides policing to specialised consumers on a fee basis. Similarly private providers are not exclusively private, since they sometimes work under public authorisers and are sometimes staffed by public police personnel. Law enforcement as an activity rather than an organisation is, therefore, the approach that will be followed. The book endorses the inclusive views of policing offered by McLean: 'Policing is an activity of enforcing the criminal law...Typically [the people doing the policing] have been the military, church officials and citizens taking their turn or persons hired by a magistrate' (McLean, 1996) or Hills, 'policing concerns the enforcement of a state's (or regime's) definition of appropriate public order and behaviour' (Hills, 2000, p. 7). Despite the rhetoric of governments, state as well as non-state law enforcers are controlled only poorly or not at all by state institutions. It is this minimal accountability to the public that explains their at times violent, self-regarding and lawless conduct.

The Role of the Law

Before the breakdown of law in parts of Africa's new democracies is examined, it is helpful to be clear about our ideas of what the role of law should be in a democracy and what its relationship with democracy consists of. Each individual in a community desires freedom, but paradoxically, to secure and preserve that freedom, a degree of freedom has to be relinquished. Living in a community there is always the danger of the strong members taking advantage of the weak ones. Binding communal rules, whether written or the standard established by reiterated human activity, can limit the strong, but at the same time, they limit all. The inescapable conclusion is that to maximise freedom of action for all, some actions have to be restricted. When it comes to organising the state, libertarians, who see freedom in terms of non-intervention, regard state law as a necessary evil to stop greater interference (Berlin, 1958). To republicans, who see freedom in terms of non-domination, state law is a vital good to maximise such freedom (Pettit, 1999). Whatever the preferred conceptualisation of freedom, however, both agree that freedom is preserved by state law. How can it be, asked Rousseau:

> That all should obey, yet nobody takes upon him to command, and that all should serve and yet have no masters?... these wonders are the work of the law. It is to law alone that men owe justice and liberty. It is this salutary organ of the will of all which establishes in civil right the natural equality between men...The first of all laws is to respect laws (Rousseau, 1973, p. 124).

As Kauper has said, 'Rule of law must mean freedom from private lawlessness and anarchy before it can mean anything at all' (quoted in Walker, 1988, p. 24). The alternative, of a law-less society, is an environment that allows the powerful to dominate and to use that domination to exploit the weak at will and with impunity (Pettit, 1999, p. 93). Such a community is undesirable whatever the character of the most powerful member. It gives space not just to the brute force of tyrants, but to the arbitrary and unexpected impositions of otherwise benevolent superiors. It creates a condition either of actual suffering, or at best, of living with the anxiety of possible loss that an individual is helpless to prevent and may only delay by subservience and obsequiousness.

Almost every political system establishes binding rules on the whole community, or what Rawls calls, 'a coercive order of public rules' to regulate conduct and facilitate co-operation (Rawls, 1971, p. 235). Yet the existence of such rules does not in and of itself provide a harmonious society. The question is the degree to which the rules are obeyed. Do the rules rule? Do they actually constrain the behaviour of the people and, in particular, of those who govern and who enforce the law? Is there a universal consensus, or do they contradict the established rules of minorities? These are questions that lead us from considering law, to considering the rule of law, that is the recognition by rulers and the ruled of the authority and superiority of a single body of law.

Defining the Rule of Law

Law is a code that sets down what is forbidden, whereas the rule of law is a principle of restraint and compliance entailing self-control and the absence of arbitrary coercion of others. Beyond that broad definition, however, there have been various distinct interpretations. One approach to understanding the principle of the rule of law is to see it as making a legal system user-friendly and effective. This is an instrumentalist view of the rule of law, recognising that rules work best when they are consistently applied. Whatever laws there are in a political community, they will be applied to all of its members (or all those specified in particular rules) by approved institutions. In this view of the rule of law there is no guarantee of good law free of discrimination, bias, and undue severity, nor does it relate to the way law is made. But what it does provide is the virtue of certainty. Ideally, according to functionalists, the rule of law should also have other virtues. Fuller lists generality, notice of publicity, prospectivity, clarity, non-contradictoriness, conformability, stability, and congruence (Fuller, 1969, pp. 33-94). In Radin's words what is required is 'know-ability' and 'perform-ability' (Radin, 1989, p. 786). Rules put together in this way constitute a system that is effective in inducing the desired behaviour of all. The 'rule of law' is the way to make rules work, of getting the most out of rules. Yet it says nothing about the relationship of rulers to the law, or of the content of the law, or of who makes the law. Indeed such a rule of law might be preserved just as well by an authoritarian or apartheid government as a democratic one. Both will prefer uniformity, regularity and stability to anarchy.

A second, though overlapping, approach to understanding the rule of law is to see it as 'government under law', moving away from a prime concern with how to control society, to how to control the state. With the government itself under the law, the government's actions can be tested by independent courts of law and are constrained by the law. The rule of law is recognised where all power in the state is derived from and exercised in accordance with the law. In the 1880s, in one of the first re-formations of the rule of law since the seventeenth century, Dicey wrote of the need for law to have absolute supremacy so that there could be no arbitrary power and no one punished unless there had been a breach of law. He also cited the necessity for equality before the law (Dicey, 1960, pp. 202-3). Similarly, for Hayek, the rule of law means:

> that government in all its actions is bound by rules fixed and announced beforehand – rules which make it possible to foresee with fair certainty how the authority will use its coercive powers in given circumstances, and to plan one's individual affairs on the basis of this knowledge (quoted in Raz, 1977, p. 195).

Raz, in much the same tradition, sees two under-girding principles to the rule of law, namely, that everyone should be ruled by law and obey it, and that the law should be knowable and performable. From these propositions he reasons that laws should be prospective, relatively stable, and consistent with general rules. Further, he argues that the judiciary should be independent and able to review other branches of government; the discretion of law enforcement agencies should not be allowed to pervert the law; courts should be accessible; and the rules of natural justice should be followed (Raz, 1977).

But is a government under law sufficient for it to be controlled? Mathews observed of his own South Africa in the 1980s that 'security laws have placed the ruling party in a position to make its own determination of what is legitimate political opposition to itself and its policies' (Mathews, 1986, p. 271). Should not government, therefore, also be circumscribed by law, so that space is left for individual liberty? Hayek argued that this was vital, since the rule of law:

> means not that everything is to be regulated by law, but, on the contrary, that the coercive power of the state can be used only in cases defined in advance by the law and in such a way that it can be foreseen how it will be used (Hayek, 1976, p. 63).

Clearly Hayek has in mind that even democratic states can alter and redefine the law to suit their own purposes and can even secure majority support for discriminatory law that denies certain rights to minorities (Michelman, 1998). It is a short step, therefore, to a third perspective that argues that the substance of the law is as important as its supremacy. This third perspective goes beyond a concern for administrative efficiency and restraint of government and introduces normative considerations. The rule of law from this perspective incorporates that body of inherited libertarian values such as presumption of innocence, non-retroactive law, jury trials, open courts and some would say political rights such as the right to vote. It holds that society should be just and fair and sees that the rule of law is what is required to achieve this. The rule of law, says John Rawls, is formal justice, 'the regular and impartial administration of public rules' applied to the legal system. It promotes (negative) liberty, the prime value in justice as fairness, for two reasons according to Rawls. First, because when rules and the consequences of breaking them are clear and when like cases are treated alike, then the boundaries are certain. It is when these boundaries are uncertain that 'liberty is restricted by reasonable fear of its exercise' (Rawls, 1971, p. 239). Second, it restrains states. Although state coercion is necessary to remove the incentive from those who reason that acting in self-interest is beneficial (so long as everybody else but them is co-operating with community rules), that state coercion itself needs restraint. Such power in the hands of the state threatens liberty, unless the state itself is compelled by law to act impartially and consistently. Justice requires liberty from an overbearing state. Those, like Rawls, who hold this 'rights view' of the rule of law see it as necessary for liberty; liberty from those who pursue self interest at the expense of others and from a state with powers (and a claimed monopoly) of coercion.

In practice, this third view of the rule of law necessitates adopting a package of principles to safeguard it and procedures to implement it. Different jurists have offered different inventories, but there is considerable agreement. In fact their lists are not dissimilar to the functionalists; it is the justification that is different. Rawl's list of the necessary virtues of the rule of law includes generality, consistency, notice, perform-ability, and congruence. In the light of his experience under the apartheid state of South Africa, Bienart calls for the standards of natural justice − such as the right of the accused to know the charges against them, to have access to counsel, to be tried before an unprejudiced judge, to give and introduce evidence and the like. In addition, he calls for a legal system which minimises official discretion (and possible arbitrariness) and for the law to be observed by government as much as citizens (Bienart, 1962). Walker is perhaps the most thorough in his rights definition of the rule of law. He concludes that the rule of law necessitates laws against private coercion, a government bound by the law, certainty, generality and equality of law, congruence with public opinion and values, independence of judiciary and legal profession, natural justice and an 'attitude of legality', that is, popular support for the rule of law (Walker, 1988).

The Relationship of the Rule of Law to Democracy

Though there is difference in the details, the general thrust of the rights approach to the rule of law is clear. While wanting to stay within the territory of a juridical concept they, and to a lesser extent the other views on the rule of law, have included much that is common ground with the political ideals of democracy. Most importantly is the commitment of both to equality. In terms of the rule of law, this translates into equality before the law and the insistence that no one is above the law or entitled to special treatment. All law is to be applied to all; laws should be specific about what they prohibit, they should not particularise the subjects to whom they apply. In terms of political democracy, the equality principle translates into equal political rights. There is similarity, too, in their positions on the status of governors and their insistence that the government is not 'above' the people. For the jurists this means that the government is not above the law, but accountable to it; for the democrats it means that they are not above the citizens, but accountable to them. There is also agreement on the significance of popular support. The rule of law requires not just a body of law, but its obedience. A legal system that is widely flouted is no rule of law. In other words, it is important to jurists to have a community culture that in general holds to obeying the law and in particular legitimates the specific laws and the way they are interpreted by the judiciary. Followers of Wittgenstein in particular stress the social context of law. They argue that it is not rules that cause agreement over conduct, rather the agreement that permits it to be said that there are rules. Rule can be promulgated by parliament, but what actually determines compliance is when there is reiterated human action, both in responding to the rule and in observing others respond. There has to be a social context in which an action seems a matter of course and disputes about it do not break out (Radin, 1989). Likewise democrats require law to have that popular support through a general consensus on accepting majority rule and because of the nature in which law is made through public debate and the legislation of elected representatives.

	Rule of law	**Democracy**
Equality	Equality before the law	Equal political rights
Accountability	Government not above the law, but accountable to it	Government not above citizens, but accountable to them
Popular support	Law upheld and largely obeyed by community	Majority decisions accepted as binding after public debate
Libertarian values	(In the case of 'rights-view') Law maintains libertarian values	State maintains libertarian values

Figure 1.1   The parallels between the rule of law and democracy

Both those who uphold the rule of law and democrats disdain anarchy, want binding community laws and (in the case of advocates of the rights approach to the rule of law) want those laws to maintain libertarian values (see summary, Figure 1.1). Yet democrats acknowledge that they depend on the rule of law since talk of political and civil rights is worthless unless the rule of law is first made to prevail. Commenting on the historical sequencing of the rule of law coming before liberal democracy, Kriegel writes:

> liberty begins with the protection of life secured by law. Consequently, subjective rights are directly linked to the conception of power that rejects slavery and dominion... The status of liberty also reinforces the point that without a political guarantee of legal recourse, there are no individual rights but only pious professions of the value of human beings. Without the rule of law, there are no human rights. It is, indeed, only in those states committed to the rule of law that liberal democracy has taken root, for a people can choose its own destiny, enjoy political liberties and civil rights, only if it is composed of free human beings (1995, pp. 37, 50).

This historical sequence of the rule of law preceding democracy is taken from the western experience. In England, for instance, the rule of law was established in the seventeenth century when the Crown became accountable to Parliament. The sovereignty of the state was to be based on the will of the people and no longer on divine right, natural right, custom or mere force. Independent institutions of civil society, both economic and political, developed in the late eighteenth century. Only from 1832 onwards did successive acts of parliament widen the franchise until universal suffrage was achieved in 1928. This pattern was so regular in the first wave of democracy that few thought it worthy of comment until the contradictions of the third wave of democracy. The rule of law was an indispensable condition of a modern state. Thus Weber, for instance, characterises the modern state as a *Rechtsstaat*, relying on the rule of law rather than rule by arbitrary decisions of a ruler or their agents.

Philosophical anarchists, of course, argue that law emanating from a centralised authority cannot be legitimate because there can be no meaningful consent to it. But democrats counter that this need not disqualify law as a violation of personal autonomy if the republican view of freedom as non-domination is followed. Even the non-interference freedom of libertarians concedes that 'freedom for the pike is death for the minnows'.

Where democrats go further than the jurists is in their concern not just that law exists, but with how those laws are arrived at. In effect they want to virtually equate self rule (or in practice, government only through collective agreement) with law-rule. Democrats are concerned with equality in the process of determining the law as well as in the nature of the laws themselves. In a debate which parallels that held among the jurists, political theorists have considered what is sufficient to secure negative liberty. Locke argued that the rule of law and limited government was enough, but the republicans Nedham, Harrington and Milton pointed out that the danger still remains of governments depriving individuals of their liberty and estates *legally*. They insisted that what was required was popular control of the government that makes the law (Skinner, 1998). Only when the government is accountable to the people can the people be sure that the rule of law guarantees liberty. Rousseau, going still further, argued that citizens should be the authors of the laws under which they live; that is, that there must be active participation by citizens and not just representation.

Liberal democracy's approach to governance rests on its shared belief with the rule of law in individual equality. Because every single person is viewed as having personal autonomy, they must be accorded the same worth, the same rights and for that matter the same duties. The equality offered by democracy takes two forms. First, there is political equality, or the right (and some would say, the duty) to debate and choose law and/or lawmakers. Law is made only at the behest and with the consent of the community. Only when citizens have control over the laws and policies of their society are they truly masters of their own lives and free. As Joshua Cohen has said:

> A [self-consciously free] person wants more than the availability of alternatives within the system of laws and institutions that they view as a set of constraints imposed by others on their own actions. Rather, they want to be able to regard those institutional constraints as themselves conforming to their own judgments of what is right...The free person wants to affirm the framework of rules itself; they want to 'have their own will as a rule' (quoted in Christiano, 1996, p. 21).

Secondly, there is the legal-civil equality that the rights view of the rule of law advocates. Democracy could not offer a political system of equality without including equal standing before the law in respect of civic obligations and of individual and communal protection. Though many have chosen to isolate political equality as the fundamental feature of democracy, the legal-civil equality of the rule of law is part of the same fabric. If, as autonomous responsible citizens, everyone has the right to decide what the law should be (or at least who the lawmakers should be), they must also have the right to enjoy the protection and benefits of the law. It is a hollow democracy that allows multi-party elections, but denies a universal application of human rights.

The representative system devised for large modern states, commonly known as liberal democracy, provides a cluster of rights to secure political equality:

1. An equal right to debate legislation, whether proposed or enacted.
2. An equal right to a free choice of representatives to be lawmakers and an equality of votes between electors.
3. An equal right to stand for election.
4. An equal right to seek to influence government and change law through the democratic process.
5. An equal right to a full and open accountability from elected representatives.

To secure legal-civil equality, liberal democracy provides a further cluster of rights:

1. An equal right to open and clear publicity concerning law and changes made to it.
2. An equal right of access to the legal process, irrespective of status or area of residence and without having to endure excessive delays or costs.
3. An equal right to just adjudication of law by an independent judiciary and bureaucracy, giving no preference based on ethnicity, gender, class, age or religion.
4. An equal right to take anyone to a court of law and to demand that they are subject to the law, whatever their position or power.
5. An equal right to a full and open accountability from all those in the judiciary, bureaucracy and security forces as to how and if they enforce the law.

A democratic state requires not just an electoral system that treats all citizens as equals, but also a legal system that treats all citizens equally. As O'Donnell argues:

> Democracy is not only a (polyarchical) political regime, but also a particular mode of relationship between state and citizens, and among citizens themselves, under a kind of rule of law that, in addition to political citizenship, upholds civil citizenship and a full network of accountability (O'Donnell, 1999, p. 321).

A democracy's legal system will uphold both the political rights and the civil rights of the whole population, and it will create systems of responsibility and accountability for state agents and private citizens (O'Donnell, 1999, p. 318). The rule of law is the measure of equality and the guarantor of it. A legal system that treats everyone as equal ensures that domination by the powerful is excluded.

This democratic theory is of course rarely realised in full in those countries widely regarded as having democratic systems. In practice there is often only an approximate equality as to how law is determined, how it is framed, how it is applied by the courts and how it is enforced by the police.

Although democratic theory requires that law should be determined by the community, presidential decrees are common in 'delegative democracy' where the president, once elected, regards himself (sic) as entitled to govern as he sees fit, with little regard for the legislature (O'Donnell, 1996). Those who advocate 'cosmopolitan' democracy do so in the face of what they see as the inadequate decisions of state legislatures (Held, 1995). Since the International Tribunal at Nuremberg it has been proclaimed that when international rules that protect basic humanitarian values are in conflict with state laws, the former must have precedence. And heads of western states now speak of international law and standards with scant reference to representation by and consultation with an individual political community. Their 'international justice' talks of imposing democratic values on elected governments, although they may have broken no laws of their own country, have violated no external treaty, nor pose any threat to other countries. Bombing campaigns and sanctions have been (and will be) used to bring them to do what is right. The fear is that when representative governments cannot be trusted, those with force will undertake the responsibility for global leadership and uphold global justice and rights protection (Chandler, 2000).

Law in a democracy will reject any legislation that is either discriminatory, violates basic rights, involves arbitrary application or that excuses certain groups and institutions from its provisions. Yet although democratic law should prevent the abuse of the weak by the strong, it is frequently found that law in democratic countries is very selective as regards what anti-social behaviour it addresses. It is striking how frequently what is proscribed relates to conduct primarily found amongst categories defined by wealth or gender. It criminalises anti-social conduct commonly committed by the majority poor, such as hunting in Africa which becomes 'poaching' and omits certain abuses carried out primarily by the minority rich. Again in the case of prostitution it is the female provider and not the male user that is criminalised.

Democracy will also want to avoid discrimination in the application and interpretation of law in the courts and by bureaucrats using their powers of adjudication and discretion. However, in practice criminal law in democracies is noted for the discriminatory character of its court sentencing. With a sideways glance at the prison system of the USA, Jean-Paul Brodeur comments that it is becoming doubtful whether the equity associated with the rights view of the rule of law can continue to be equated with the enforcement of state criminal law that has a disproportionate number of racial minorities incarcerated (1999, p. 82).

Law is meant, according to democrats, to preserve and maximise individual freedom. A legal system, however, that is powerful enough to restrain the most powerful necessitates a state monopoly of violence. By violence is meant the use of physical, harmful force with the aim of intimidating, enforcing dominance or killing others. This is a formidable power and those who enforce it have a grave responsibility not to misuse the instruments of coercion or to abuse the powers of discretion granted them. The principle of the rule of law is meant to restrain law enforcement from behaviour that is partial, arbitrary or unnecessarily violent, whilst democratic principles seek to ensure that law enforcement is fully accountable to its citizens as regards who does it and how. In practice it is very hard to keep powerful law keepers like the police and para-military units in check. The power to arrest and charge lawbreakers is a temptation to frame, harass and extort. The power to carry arms and other means of coercion easily translates into the power to intimidate, extort, or even kill. This is especially so under conditions where the law enforcers' lives are at risk and where the evidence required to secure a successful prosecution is not readily obtainable. In the light of worldwide reports of human rights abuses and corruption by the law enforcement agencies, the controls for regulating law enforcement are evidently universally inadequate. Where pay and conditions are poor and supervision is minimal, this is even more likely to be so. The age-old questions are, how can the law enforcers be prevented from being lawless and who will enforce the law when they are lawless?

Whatever the divergence between the theory and practice, there is a fundamental mutual dependency between democracy and law. Democracy and the law mutually reinforce one another. If popular control weakens then the law weakens and vice versa. For instance, if popular control over the executive weakens (e.g. through an ineffective legislature) then there may be an increase in presidential decrees and the law becomes personalised and potentially oppressive. If it is the legislature that frees itself from popular control, then there may be legislation that is based on factional interest or self-interest. If control of the judiciary by the people and the legislature weakens, then the judiciary may be susceptible to executive influence or intimidation, bribery by powerful interests or personal partisanship. The result is an inevitable loss of consistency in the application of justice. If people lose control over electoral law and procedures and appointees of the incumbent government determine it, then unrepresentative or false election results are likely.

Likewise, if the rule of law weakens, then there are serious implications for democracy. Once law enforcement is undermined by reduced capacity, or courts fail to impose legal sanctions because of bribery or inept prosecution, then some may be encouraged to ignore the laws passed by the majority. If the judicial process is corrupted or ineffective, then some may take the law into their own hand and mete out their own brand of punishment on those deemed guilty. If those elected to office are seen to be above the law, then some may be discouraged from participation in formal politics. Moreover, if the security forces or members of the government act outside the law, then some in government may be tempted to prevent its disclosure. If law is applied partially, then those discriminated against may demonstrate intolerance to all members of the favoured group or vice versa. If groups are illegally kept from participating in elections or from winning them through corruption, then they may turn to violence to gain their political aims.

As this book traces the failure of the rule of law, we can expect, therefore, to observe an impact on the new African democracies which is likely to be an obstacle to their consolidation. And because of the mutual relationship of law and democracy, unconsolidated democracies will in turn allow the continuance of law enforcers taking the law into their own hands. If this degenerative spiral is to be stopped, the relationship needs to be understood in detail, so that the points where intervention is most likely to break the cycle can be identified.

2 The Construction of Attitudes Towards the Law

Democratisation in Africa has brought genuine changes, particularly in the formal institutions of central government and in political rights. Since 1990 there has been in large measure a return to regular elections for political office, the right to organise and join political parties and freedom to express opinions contrary to the government. Political equality has (to varying degrees) been restored. There may not be an equality in direct decision making in Africa, any more than there is elsewhere in the world, but there is an equality of votes between electors for decision makers, an equal right to stand for election to political office (with certain exceptions where parents are deemed to be of foreign origin) and an equal right to make one's voice heard (unless it denigrates the president, undermines national security or overly threatens the electoral success of the ruling party). Within a representative system, equality of opportunity, if not actual capability, has entered the political arena. The constitutional right is there, even if there are significant structural barriers that impede the poor, women and certain minorities. The changes have also removed most discriminatory and racist laws from the statute book. In addition they have opened up a degree of space for the media and human rights groups to expose illegality and corruption by the government. Though the governments may be essentially elitist, the reforms largely institutional and neither the elections nor the processes of government totally free of corruption, the transformation is enough, certainly in the eyes of democratic minimalists, to mark the arrival of liberal democracy.

There are two areas, however, where democratisation has been slower to bring change. First, it has been unable to dislodge those shared understandings that militate against democracy, such as authoritarianism. Secondly, it has failed to make serious inroads in the area of legal rights. Both have serious implications for the rule of law, since widely held beliefs and values shape the practice of the rule of law, whilst legal rights define the content and parameters of the rule of law.

The particular issue of the rule of law that this book focuses on concerns those who seek to enforce rules that are embodied in state law. How do they act? Even if their objective is lawful, are the means that they use lawful? How do the means they employ impact on state institutions? That a large gap can emerge between the legitimate end of upholding the law and the illegitimate means used to do so is, of course, a problem that precedes the modern state and democratisation. Abbink traces how longstanding methods of mediation to resolve transgressions of cultural norms amongst the Suri of southwest Ethiopia were transformed by the arrival of modern semi-automatic weapons in the late 1970s. The young men who gained access to these took to violent revenge, rather than the traditional negotiation, to tackle cattle raiding and the like within the group and with other local ethnic groups. Violent revenge may have been an easier and quicker way of settling disputes and providing security, but the killing of women, children and elders went beyond the accepted cultural and ritual bonds. The violence defied reconciliation and left the community floundering as to how to handle this new disorder created by those who sought to uphold the communal rules (Abbink, 2000). Is it possible that under democratic regimes also, law enforcers have stepped out of line from the social norms embodied in state law and, if so, have they left the new democracies floundering in the same way as the Suri? This is the topic that will be examined in the ensuing chapters.

The Prevalence of Authoritarianism and Disciplinarianism

Shared Values

Social groups commonly share a set of ideas and values that can be used to think about the wider worlds of politics, work, leisure, crime, punishment and ultimately, liberty and individuality. They are lived as well as held, for the values determine action by members of the group and how they respond to the actions of others. They are also expressed in collective representations, which in turn influence people's subjective dispositions towards others. Mereleman captures an important element of their function when he speaks of 'the collective vision of liberty' (Mereleman, 1991).

This is not to say that a single cultural view prevails in every single country or that it is fixed. The cultural arenas in Africa's heterogeneous states are typically ones of conflict rather than consensus. This conflict includes attitudes and responses to the political system, government responsibility and personal entitlements and duties. Kamrava takes such hotly contested and fragmented political cultures to be the *defining* feature of the Third World (Kamrava, 1993). Similarly Chazan asserts that, 'A constant tug of war exists between competing institutions and orientations, between alternative explications of consciousness and meaning' (Chazan, in Diamond, 1994, p. 60).

How prevalent, therefore, are democratic values or norms that uphold the rule of law? It is true that most of the ruling class in Africa currently publicly subscribe to democracy and the rule of law, but there is reason to doubt the sincerity of many. It will not be forgotten that most of the nationalist leaders of the 1960s likewise embraced democracy, but proceeded (whether in government or opposition) to show, in most cases, that their commitment was only transitory. And today the actions of leaders often contradict their speeches to the international community. Political culture, however, is not just what the ruling class articulates. Despite all the resources at their disposal to disseminate their ideology and suppress alternatives, the ruling elite has never been able to achieve hegemony (Baker, 2000, pp. 108-10). What Mbembe calls African society's 'historical capacity for indiscipline' ultimately undermines and defeats them all (quoted in Young, 1994, p. 279). This has no doubt been in part due to the absence of adequate political institutions that could integrate ideas and accommodate differences. As Schatzberg observes, a wider perspective is necessary that considers not just the formal and the dominant, but the informal and the dominated:

> We must examine the diverse means by which people voice political ideas indirectly. In other words African political thought must be redefined to include the works of novelists, dramatists, poets, musicians, journalists, theologians, philosophers, social scientists, proverbs, fables and oral literature (Schatzberg, 1993, p. 445).

This array of ideas that exist apart from those held by the elite can arise in two ways. On the one hand, they may be the product of standard socialisation in a sub-group. On the other hand, they may be the product of the conflict and frustration that occurs when, despite sharing many of the values of society as a whole, a group is blocked in its efforts to achieve those values.

Generalisations about cultural values in a country, therefore, must be expressed with caution. For the purposes of this book it will suffice to show that the values of democracy and the rule of law have not permeated very far into the conduct and conversation of township bars, village mosques, hospital wards, shop doorways, school playgrounds, army barracks and police stations. In particular, though it cannot be quantified, there is evidence that the values of authoritarianism and what might be called 'disciplinarianism', persist amongst many and shape their attitude to handling what is perceived as lawlessness.[1] In this context, authoritarianism is taken to mean a style of oversight that demands unquestioning obedience and submissiveness, and is itself exercised with minimal restraint and with minimal or no input from those supervised. By disciplinarianism is meant a style of behaviour that enforces rules through harsh punishment, particularly corporal punishment. Their combined presence in society and, in particular, amongst those that seek to enforce law, helps in part to explain some of the features that are recorded in the subsequent chapters. It may be that this is a sub-culture of law enforcers and their institutions, but it is likely to also have a wider distribution. Inkeles has spoken of the authoritarian personality syndrome in societies that is the inverse of democratic values. He describes it as composed of faith in powerful leaders, hatred of outsiders and deviants, a sense of powerlessness and ineffectiveness, extreme cynicism, suspicion and distrust of others and dogmatism (Inkeles, 1961, pp. 195-8). The next two sections will examine the degree to which authoritarian and disciplinarian attitudes are found, first in law enforcers and second, in society in general.

Authoritarian and Disciplinarian Attitudes amongst Law Enforcers

On 24 July, 2001, in Nairobi, police removed from a bus seven men suspected of being on their way to conduct a bank raid, made them lie down on the ground and riddled them with bullets in full public view. Police later defended their actions by claiming the men had been shot by the police in self-defence after they themselves were shot at.[2] They also responded to widespread criticism in the press by claiming that they were regularly targeted by criminals and by accusing magistrates of routinely letting criminals off after accepting bribes. What do these actions and attitudes tell us about the police? Are they 'one offs' or are they symptomatic of wider shared attitudes amongst the police force? Reviewing the work of Peter Katzenstein on the police and military in post-war Japan, Tanner makes the general observation that:

Cultural norms of internal security and law are both a dependent and an independent variable and exist in the middle range of flexibility. They change, but not easily, and only as a result of bitter political contestation and historical contingency. Once fought out, affirmed, and/or modified through practice, norms become institutionalized historically until they become social facts that make powerful claims upon behavior. Nevertheless... norms shape but do not determine policies and outcomes in societies and institutions (Tanner, 2000, p. 112).

As law enforcers leave an authoritarian era and enter a democratic one, therefore, there may well be change, but it is unlikely that it will be as fast as other elements of society. There is an authoritarian inertia that impedes the transformation of values. As Pinheiro notes of Brazil in the early 1990s, when it came to the impeachment of the President for corruption, the government, political society, the judiciary and civil society all adhered to the rules of the democratic game. Yet at the very same time:

government agents directly participated in gross human rights violations... These contrasting events show that the government has not succeeded in changing many of the arbitrary practices of its institutions or in imposing the restrictions expected of the state's monopoly of legal violence (Pinheiro, 1997, p. 261).

Both authoritarian and disciplinarian norms commonly shape the behaviour of those formal and informal agencies in Africa that seek to enforce law. The norms may be brought with them, if policing attracts a disproportionate number of those with authoritarian personalities. Unfortunately the evidence from Africa is lacking, but most policing studies on policemen in the West (e.g. Reiner, 1985) argue that the norms arise in large part from their response to their organisation, their operational circumstances and their required functions. They have developed a patterned set of understandings that help them to cope with the pressures and dangers they confront. This sub-culture is one that is much more tolerant of, and even endorses, violence, because of its utility. Indeed it may be those within their ranks who refuse to use violence that are regarded as inadequate. Since the circumstances in which African law enforcers operate have changed little with democratisation, it is not surprising that the sub-culture of those who enforce the law has shown only marginal change. Of the many factors that have shaped and reinforced the shared values of African law enforcers, four persistent ones stand out.

The first is the context of danger. It is the nature of military and para-military organisations facing the threat of sudden attack, to be hierarchical and disciplined to the point where obedience is unquestioned and disobedience is severely punished. This is to ensure that those who face physical unpredictable risk and who hold weapons, exercise that power only under the command of their leaders and that when put under the pressure of conflict, remain a coherent and effective force. In such male dominated organisations, isolated from society in general and their own locality in particular, and devoted to the use of instruments of coercion, 'militarism', 'the pervasiveness of symbols, values and discourses validating military power', inevitably becomes the prevailing philosophy and authoritarianism and disciplinarianism thrives (Luckham, 1998, p. 15). Further, the internal solidarity that provides support in danger can also work so as to provide silence when abuses are committed.

The second factor that has shaped the values of African law enforcers is the presence of insecure government. When political control has come under intense challenge, political leaders have frequently looked to those concerned with law enforcement and internal security to act to preserve their position. Whether under the control of colonial authorities, military autocrats and state leaders fighting to preserve their power in bloody civil wars, or even local warlords and commercial companies, those given the instruments of coercion have first and foremost been required to concentrate on preserving order and suppressing unrest. Only secondarily have they been agents of the law concerned with crime prevention. In other words, the distinction between them and forces concerned with external security have been less than distinct. Armies have engaged in policing and police forces have frequently been of a para-military nature, that is, armed and coercive. In the past para-military policing has meant the gendarmerie of the French Colonies or, in the British colonies, the British West African Frontier Force and King's African Rifles. Today it includes gendarmeries, special mobile units and presidential guards. The significance of the latter is not just that they have military capabilities, but that they are accountable to the regime as opposed to the state:

> Private groups connected to the regime usually owe their primary allegiance to non-elected officers who pursue policies benefiting only a narrow section of the population. These forces are often parallel to the existing armed forces and report directly to the President's office. This crucial difference between state and regime becomes most evident when these 'parallel' militaries defend the regime against the national military, attack regime opponents or when they draw resources away from the country's armed services (Howe, 2000, p. 23).

The law enforcement role of state agencies, therefore, has traditionally been not so much policing, as maintaining the authority of their masters, with little concern for human rights or due legal process. Special powers and declarations of emergency could always legitimise setting aside the law if it was thought necessary, or *de facto* immunity from prosecution could always be established. Says Hills:

> In Africa impartiality was (and remains) a novel concept – intelligence systems invariably became personalized and politicians expected to bend the rules for appointments and prosecutions. State security became defined in terms of regime security and was expressed in terms of the dominant type of political competition; state organizations such as the police become significant weapons. The police were inevitably entangled in the reorientation of political authority because they had to enforce law and order (and maintain their own interests) just as intimidation became an important political weapon (2000, p. 35).

A history of insecure government, whether that government is the state, warlords or commercial interests, combined with serious threats, is a breeding ground for authorities to attempt to legitimise their rule through coercion. At the same time, it is an opportunity for weapon holders under their control to indulge in extrajudicial killings, summary punishment, torture and any other form of lawlessness. As representatives of those lacking in legitimacy, they are unable to turn power into authority, where the use of weapons is less necessary. Instead their role only attracts greater resistance.

The third factor that has shaped the values of African law enforcers is poverty. In extremely poor economic conditions, to hold instruments of coercion offers opportunities of looting, intimidation and extortion that are hard to resist. The availability of resources for those involved in internal security, however, may not just be the result of small or declining national income. Hills argues that state police forces in Africa have been consistently underpaid and under-resourced, not just because of the weakness of the economies, but for political reasons. She sees it as the deliberate choice of the political leadership to ensure that the police could not become a threat to the regime in terms of investigating regime officials suspected of violating the law. In her words, 'Deliberate under-resourcing is a key factor in African policing' (2000, p. 45). Whatever the truth, anyone who has confronted illegal roadblocks by police, local vigilantes or militias of regional strongmen, knows that these private enterprise schemes successfully supplement very poor wages. Observing the rule of law doesn't always pay.

The fourth factor influencing the conduct of those who hold weapons so as to enforce law, is the setting of a weak state. A weak state, whether colonial or independent, means that there is only minimal oversight of who holds weapons and how they use them, be that state or non-state agents. The weak oversight is not just in terms of what is done, but who does it. Many of the police and armed forces personnel are former combatants in guerrilla or rogue armies. They have been incorporated into the new forces as part of the peace settlements, for instance, of Mozambique, South Africa, Sierra Leone and Uganda. Similarly, officers who engaged in human rights abuses under former authoritarian regimes have had to be retained. Whatever training these personnel of the current security forces may have received, it is evident that it was and is in the interests of the state's preservation of peace not to look too carefully at their conduct with a view to ejecting them. The situation, therefore, is that many of those who are asked to enforce the law lawfully today, were yesterday acting lawlessly. In addition, many perpetrators of abuses in high office before democratisation, are given immunity from prosecution during the transitions. As Tanner asks, 'how does a new democratic state establish popular norms of the rule of law if many of its hated criminals can escape punishment because of the power they once held?' (Tanner, 2000, p. 118).

Today, over much of Africa, there is little knowledge concerning the conduct of security forces or non-state groups that are confronting disorder on the ground. Policing is only partially policed. Those suppressing lawlessness can be a law unto themselves with little fear of restraint, disclosure or prosecution.

These four factors have shaped the norms of internal security over a very long period. One looks in vain in recent history for pivotal events where those norms have had to yield under challenge. Outside of Africa, confrontation with street protesters has made internal security forces face their own violence and repression and hold back from shooting or applying brutal force to maintain the regime, as in the Philippines, Indonesia, Yugoslavia, Eastern Europe and Russia. There, they stood back rather than use violence against their own people. Not that Africa has lacked social protest. From an annual rate of about 20 incidents a year during the 1980s, the number of political protests in Sub-Saharan Africa rose to 86 major protest events in 1991 (Bratton, 1997, pp. 70-1). In the last months of 1989 and throughout 1990, people took to the streets of 15 capital cities in Sub-Saharan Africa – Benin, Zimbabwe, Gabon, Comoros, Cameroon, Kenya,

Niger, Cote d'Ivoire, Central African Republic, Congo-Brazzaville, Sierra Leone, Zaire, Zambia, Togo and Burkina Faso. But faced with pro-democracy protesters then, or later in Nigeria and Zimbabwe, state internal security forces have not buckled. At the command of their masters they have fired on and beaten the protesters. The norms that have controlled their conduct for so long have held. Their fear that restrained tactics would lead to social collapse prevailed. The dominant outlook remains that anything or anyone that challenges authority and will not submit is an enemy and deserving of severe punishment.

The principle new element influencing the outlook and conduct of the law enforcers is political pressure to deal with crime. In this new context the internal security agents are expected to serve the public, rather than just their political masters. Yet this has to be done at a time when crime, and how it is handled, is much more freely reported than before. Not only is there pressure from the public for 'results', but also from the politicians, who see combating crime as an important factor in maintaining internal support and investor confidence in the ruling party. Policing is thus under considerable external pressure to 'deliver'. To achieve the success now expected of them and that they themselves desire, internal security agents may well choose to ignore the donor-subsidised human rights training and 'bend the rules'.

Authoritarian and Disciplinarian Attitudes among the Wider Community

The degree to which authoritarian and disciplinarian attitudes are found in law enforcers has been discussed, but what of the general populations? Are we to assume that authoritarianism and disciplinarianism resides only in the minds and conduct of law enforcement agencies? Is it solely the product of their organisation and function? Do those who enforce law really operate as an atypical enclave? What are the norms that society holds as regards the treatment of lawbreakers by law enforcers? What levels of violence and coercion and 'law bending' will they permit as acceptable conduct? How do they define unacceptable treatment of lawbreakers? Robert Fisk, in his study on Israel and the Palestinians, records the political scientist Uri Avneri's analysis as to why everyone he knew was convinced that the Israeli Defence Force was the most humane in the world:

> It would be nice to believe that people who have undergone suffering have been purified by suffering. But it is the opposite, it makes them worse. It corrupts. There is something in suffering that creates a kind of egoism... When such monstrous things have happened to your people you feel nothing can be compared to it. You get a moral power of attorney, a permit to do anything you want – because nothing can compare with what happened to us (Fisk, 1990, p. 394).

Have the atrocities experienced by those who lived through the terror of Amin or the atrocities of RENAMO affected them in the same way? On the other hand some societies are said to have shown a deep-rooted hostility to all manifestations of authoritarianism and disregard for the law. Chazan speaks of Ghanaians in the 1980s as having 'a deeply ingrained indigenous culture of consultation, autonomy, participation, and supervision of authority... [which] has enabled them to combat the uncertainties of state domination and the tyranny of its leaders (Chazan, in Diamond et al., 1988, p. 120). Or is there a co-habitation of authoritarian attitudes to crime with liberal attitudes to political rule? Coulon once said of Senegalese political culture: 'It is a combination of rather authoritarian values and beliefs, compensated for by a propensity for debate, political gameplaying, and a conception of power that depends more on the interdependence of actors than on organized violence' (Coulon, in Diamond et al., 1988, p. 159).

Many speak of widespread support for authoritarian and disciplinarian responses to crime and disorder within the context of a contemporary and comparatively recent 'culture of violence' (Hamber, 1999). By the latter they mean an endorsement and acceptance of violence. With violent crime so endemic, the argument goes, violence has come to be met typically with violence. From this perspective, lawless, and at times violent, law enforcement is a legitimate response and corresponds with social patterns. It is a symptom of violence in general.

Others seek to root authoritarian and disciplinarian responses in traditional African notions of justice. The President of the South African vigilante group, Mapogo, argues:

> This man has three children and is working. He does crime in his life and according to the [western] law, he should be thrown in jail for hundred years. Who is going to feed his children and wife?... The children of this man will grow and become criminals, because no one is feeding them. An African man will take that man and tell him to sjambok [flog with a hide whip] him so that he will get rid of this criminal behaviour and go work for his children. What I am saying is that the African way to stop crime is best (Presidential address, August 1999, quoted in Harris, 2001).

The Northern Province chairperson of the Congress of Traditional Leaders supports this interpretation of traditional African attitudes to law breakers: 'fundamental [human] rights are good but they cannot be applied, raw as such, to a given society. We are a different society... [Congress] has been calling for corporal punishment to be retained' (Harris, 2001).

Certainly there is across Africa a widespread readiness to condone the use of harsh investigative methods and retributive punishment, including corporal and capital punishment, and to do so in a summary fashion (Muthoga, 1997, p. 1). As regards harsh investigation, it was found that only 53 percent of South Africans 'disagreed' or 'strongly disagreed' that the police should be allowed to use force to extract information from criminal suspects (Pigou, Greenstein and Valji, 1998). And as regards judicial capital and corporal punishment, the vast majority of African countries use it, with apparent widespread popular support.

The limited penetration of a human rights culture is also seen in domestic violence against women, which frequently has higher prevalence rates in Africa than the West (Jacobs and Suleman, 1999). Surveys conducted in sub-Saharan Africa report 46 percent of Ugandan women, 60 percent of Tanzanian women, and 42 percent of Zambian women, being verbally or physically abused by their husbands (Wood and Jewkes, 1997). In a Nigerian survey, 81 percent of married women reported being verbally or physically abused by their husbands (Odunjinrin, 1993). And in a detailed study of clients of a health clinic in the Mitchells Plain, Cape Town, 49 percent reported being physically or sexually abused, 10 percent in the previous month (Jacobs and Suleman, 1999). 49 women were actually killed in Kenya by their spouses in 1998 according to the Kenya Human Rights Commission, where the Coalition on Violence Against Women argues that 'people have become desensitised to it...beating your wife has become an accepted part of our society'.[3] The same condonation, or at least toleration, of violence against women, is noted in a study in Ghana, where 50 percent of women and 43 percent of men said a man was justified in beating his wife if she used a family planning method without his expressed consent.[4] This is, says Ruth, the patriarchy where masculinity demands warrior-hero qualities of toughness and force and where laddish behaviour is applauded as machismo (Ruth, 1980, pp. 46-7). Such values allow men to distance themselves from, and excuse ill-treatment to, women.

The same resort to violence to enforce authority and discipline is seen in the treatment of children. Though the use of corporal punishment in schools has recently been banned in a few countries, it is still widespread in schools and homes. One Kenyan lawyer who specialises in children reported that in schools:

> Many of the cane-users are violence-prone and tend to misuse the cane... The Education Act restricts the use of the cane a lot more than it did in my days as a student. In my days as a student there was no limitation whatsoever. You got beaten for doing bad things, you got beaten for coming late, you got beaten for wearing a torn shirt, you got beaten for anything. The only way you got spoken to was through a whip... And we haven't got away from that, although we have written into the Education Act the regulations on how to use the cane (Muthoga, 1997, p. 3).

Likewise adult social deviants, such as criminals or adulterers, are commonly beaten by families and communities. This common use of violence may appear illiberal to western minds, though of course it is by no means absent from western culture, but it has to be seen in its African context.

Authoritarian and disciplinarian attitudes amongst the community have, in particular, been shaped by three factors: fear of social collapse; the absence of the state; and a predatory state. Fear of social collapse or destabilisation is a powerful impulse. Cattle raiders, rapists, armed bandits and attacks by rival clans represent something more than criminal actions to many victims. Such actions constitute threats to the very social structure of a society where cattle are the main source of wealth and status, and where a virgin daughter is crucial to a family receiving bride wealth, let alone to maintaining family honour. With such devastating consequences in mind, the death penalty carried out by the aggrieved might seem to the community concerned anything but 'lawless' and certainly the contrary idea, that the perpetrators have human and civil rights, might be met with incredulity.

For communities isolated from the state, survival may include values that would be rejected in a liberal democracy. Take for instance the Kanyok of the Congo:

> For the Kanyok short-term and selfish utility is more important than abstract justice or fairness. They value community more highly than individual rights, and their fear of internal and external disorder overshadows their concern for official misconduct. They concede great power to a leader because they believe his or her innate stature is superior to that of the subjects. The Kanyok accept minimal limits on government so long as rulers appear generous in redistributing the spoils of the political system. And finally they have

unrealistically high expectations of the positive rights government should deliver (Yoder, 1998, p. 506).

The local agents of security and justice in such communities are seen as acting as purifiers of society, restorers of order, avengers of wrong. If national law forbids this, then it will be seen as an obstacle rather than as an effective guarantor of social control. Their judgment may be summary, if by that is meant there is no use of formal courts and the presentation of forensic evidence. But it does not necessarily mean the lack of witnesses or established guilt that satisfy the standards of the community. What others call authoritarian and disciplinarian could be seen as no more than the preservation of the community.

The second factor shaping authoritarian and disciplinarian attitudes amongst the community has been the absence of the state. Some of what might be termed by outsiders as 'lawless' responses to crime may often be a reflection of the lack of state provision, when non-state justice may be (or at least appear to be in the eyes of the perpetrators) the only available remedy. By the 1980s, Sandbrook records:

> In practice, many [African] governments were so lacking in authority, resources, and expertise that they have been unable even to control a burgeoning black market, smuggling and simmering insurrections, let alone design and implement complex economic policies, maintain essential services or engage in strategic planning (Sandbrook, 1993, p. 59).

This has not just been the case in remote rural areas, but also in sections of the cities. Even by the last twenty years of colonial rule it became increasingly apparent that the rule of law had collapsed in many African townships. For instance in Nairobi, Kenya:

> It would be accurate to state that the police had no effective presence in African locations from 1947 to 1953. In the intervening years, gangs effectively controlled these locations. It would have been suicidal for anyone to report the presence and activities of these gangs to the police, whose everyday presence was almost nonexistent (Maloba, 1993, p. 41).

In one sense the situation actually worsened with independence, as Hills explains:

> The first ten years of independence saw a sweeping transformation of authority patterns at the local level, most marked in the replacement of the all purpose authority of the chief with a multiplicity of government agents whose work was not directly co-ordinated with that of the chiefs. The new patterns of authority highlighted the lack of effective groupings capable of protecting individuals or acting as a check on interpersonal violence. In a real sense, the state had become more remote in rural areas, leaving individuals to deal with a distant police force, an alien judicial system, and chiefs whose powers had been dramatically weakened (Hills, 2000, p. 31).

State policing has always been an urban affair from colonial times onward. Conversely, most of the population of Africa has never seen much in the way of the state provision of policing. The detection and punishment of crime remains largely where it has always been – in their own hands, or more particularly, in the hands of local authoritarian and disciplinarian powers.

The third factor shaping authoritarian and disciplinarian attitudes amongst the community has been a predatory state. Neither colonialism, independence nor democratisation have yet brought to the villages and the townships of Africa a state that can guarantee protection of life and property, or the arrest, successful prosecution and appropriate sentencing of lawbreakers. Indeed sometimes it is not the absence of the state, but its presence, that encourages people to continue with their own policing and criminal justice. An inefficient, partial, biased, corrupt, ineffective state and one that is sometimes exploitative, criminal and violent itself, is no incentive to handover control. Thus whether by its weakness or by its harshness, whether by its absence or by its presence, the state has not secured a monopoly of the use of violence or of its own law over local rules.

How influential are societal norms on the law enforcers? With law enforcers being part of society they inevitably reflect the wider values, for all that they live in relative isolation and function at considerable distances from administrators. In the West there is talk of the normative gap between law enforcers and the public, especially in terms of authoritarianism and disciplinarianism. But elsewhere this gap is much smaller. There is evidence that despite having won electoral rights, citizens use their newfound influence to promote a continuance in abuses of civil rights and the rule of law in the name of law and order. Referring to Latin America, Rodley writes, 'Public anxiety about "law and order" is reaching psychotic proportions in many countries' (in Mendez et al., 1999, p. 34). In the same continent it has been observed that many in the upper and middle classes openly support norms of police brutality against poor and marginalised groups, who are commonly portrayed by the police and media as criminal groups. In such a climate the police can conduct lawless violence with impunity, especially against those who have the least effective access to the justice system (Mendez et al., 1999). Similar widespread tolerance for police norms of brutality is also evident in Africa (Brewer, 1994) and only recently are they beginning to be challenged by the media and human rights groups (e.g. Seleti, 2000).

The Practice of Authoritarianism and Disciplinarianism

Factors that have shaped authoritarian and disciplinarian attitudes among law enforcers and the wider community have been considered. The following section briefly surveys the outworking of these attitudes over time. Tracing law enforcement, certainly over the last 150 years, reveals persistent trends and the embedding of those values.

Pre-colonial Law Enforcement

No reliable account of law enforcement before the arrival of European colonisation in Africa can be given, since there are few records. It could be assumed that many of the powerful traditional rulers maintained bodies of men whose roles could be likened to those of the police. On the other hand, it may have been that there was only a minimal need for coercive policing during this period since the legitimacy of lineage societies was largely based on ideological coercion, rather than physical coercion. Only if the ruler's despotism was based on class relations would primarily physical coercion be required to maintain the relationship and extract the surplus product through wage. If, when tribute was paid to the lineage ruler, it was out of deference to the senior member of the lineage, to the representative of the ancestors, to the divine personage, then it would be largely unquestioned and normal, particularly in a society that had not yet embraced the concept of the individual. In this situation the use of physical coercion to extract wealth and enforce the ruler's will would be directed towards neighbouring tribes, rather than the ruler's own subjects (Sangmpam, 1994, pp. 98-100).

Colonial Law Enforcement

Whether or not the pre-colonial authorities enjoyed hegemony borne of ideological persuasion, the European overlords, both commercial and state, clearly lacked legitimacy. They were alien and invading forces of oppression and had no alternative but to resort to physical coercion. 'Military supremacy was indispensable to the achievement of hegemony. Few if any African communities would have accepted submission to European rule unless European military power was a part of the calculus of choice' (Young, in Rothchild and Chazan, 1988, p. 41). The Europeans came with the latest military hardware of Gatlin machine guns (first used in Africa in 1874) and the Maxim machine gun (deployed from 1889), which gave them firepower beyond anything the Africans could match. Just as importantly, they equipped themselves with 'a legal arsenal of arbitrary regulations to carry out [their] responsibilities: diverse master-and-servant ordinances, specified periods of obligatory labor service at state defined tasks, plenary powers to local administrators to impose penalties for disobedience' (Young, in Rothchild and Chazan, 1988, p. 47). Thus, for instance, charges of 'vagrancy', 'prostitution' and 'beer brewing' were used to criminalise Africans and to repatriate them to 'native' areas. Should people rebel against these impositions, then the forces of coercion, largely staffed with recruited Africans, could compel obedience.

In the early phases of European domination, commercial interests acted with little supervision. They were not slow to resort to force to achieve their ends. To secure labourers in his new private domain of the Congo (acquired 1885), King Leopold of Belgium used mercenary troops. Later, in 1888, he organised them into the Force Publique, which grew over the following years to 19,000 men – black rank and file and white officers. It combined the roles of counterinsurgency, occupying army and company labour police force. To secure the necessary rubber tappers and porters for Leopold's enterprise to be so profitable, people were dragged from their huts, beaten, chained together and forced to carry loads. Elsewhere quotas of rubber to be tapped from the wild vines were allocated to villages in exchange for a minimal payment. The quotas were so high that they necessitated virtually full time labour by the men in the forest. The Force Publique supplied the firepower to the rubber gathering companies under contract, although companies also had their own militias. Villages that refused to submit to the rubber regime had their entire population shot by the Force Publique or company troops and their hands cut off as 'evidence' to the officers that the job had been done. Between 1880 and 1920 the population of the Congo is estimated to have dropped by half, that is by about 10 million, due to slaughter and the starvation and disease associated with burned villages, displacement and forced labour (Hochschild, 1998).

The British South Africa Company was another commercial enterprise that was not averse to using coercion to increase profit. At the time of the Shona Rising of 1896, in what is now Zimbabwe, the company's BSAP (British South Africa Police; a para-military organisation formed in 1889) were entering villages to collect the hut taxes, lashing people and demanding goats and cattle be slaughtered for them. It was said that the Shona objected as much to the method of collecting the hut tax as the hut tax itself. One headman was recorded as saying that it was the police who:

> ravished their daughters, and insulted their young men, who tweaked the beards of their chieftains and made lewd jokes with the elder women of the Great House, who abused the law they were expected to uphold, who respected none but the native Commissioners and officers of police, who collected taxes at the point of their assegais, and ground the people in tyranny and oppression (quoted in Schmidt, 1992, p. 37).

Patrolling on horse and mule, the BSAP enforced the company's law and if need be were prepared to fight as a military body, being organised into two small cavalry regiments.

When colonisation by the European powers became formalised, little changed. With such limited human and financial resources to control the large territories, the resort to coercive forces to impose their rule was inevitable, until such a time as the populations became 'quiescent.' When that had been achieved, public order in British Africa was the responsibility of civilian police forces who were separated from the military. These were small in number. In Kenya in 1947-49 there was just one police officer to every 1,000 inhabitants; in Nigeria in 1930 there were only 85 police officers for a population of 20 million; and in Nyasaland no more than 500 police officers all told (Hargreaves, 1988, p. 11). The numbers were kept small since, even where the colonial rulers had little presence on the ground, as in most of rural Africa, coercion was imposed on the populations by local rulers. These acted on behalf of the colonial powers in recruiting labour, gathering taxes and handing over to them certain criminal cases that troubled the colonial rule. Mamdani aptly calls this delegation of rule and legal authority to local power holders, 'decentralised despotism' (Mamdani, 1996). The colonial state, therefore, was bifurcated; there were two forms of power under a common domination. In urban areas Europeans used direct rule, together with a white racialism that excluded Africans from civil rights; in the rural areas they turned to indirect rule. The latter entailed installing tribal leaders, reconstituted as state appointees or fabricated in the case of stateless societies, as the authorities. They followed, therefore, the African tradition (one of many) of the monarchical chiefs of the conquest states. The chief fused in a single person many roles: judicial, legislative, executive, administrative and coercive. It was they who defined (or invented) and enforced customary law to regulate non-market relations in land, familial and community affairs. Seeing that the whole system was sustained through their sanctioned use of coercion, it was as authoritarian and disciplinarian as direct rule. Hargreaves describes the policing as being carried out by:

> native Administration forces (who often adopted crude pre-colonial methods of law enforcement) or by small units of uniformed Court Messengers. There were indeed frequent complaints about the ways in which such forces collected taxes, recruited labour, or enforced colonial law, but these were usually alleged unsupervised acts of extortion, partisanship or vindictiveness rather than centrally-directed tyranny (Hargreaves, 1988, p. 11).

In Mozambique, such were the coercive and often lawless practices of the agents of the colonial state that there was large-scale migration to the neighbouring British colonies of Southern Rhodesia and Nyasaland. For instance, between 1900-1920, 300,000 Makua fled (Newitt, 1981, p. 119). The reasons given to British officials by the migrants for their flight were: excessive poll tax; rigorous collection; enforced labour on plantations for tax defaulters; payment for work in the virtually valueless Portuguese paper currency; arrest and detention of women when the man was not found; and the violation of women by police at their houses (Alpers, 1984).

It was the growing nationalist challenge, whether political or armed, that showed the degree to which the colonial state would use force to maintain its hegemony and repress dissent. The way the British authorities responded to the Mau Mau rebellion in Kenya provides a clear example. Having declared a state of emergency in 1952, British and African (the King's African Rifles) troops were called in and the police numbers greatly expanded. Thus whereas in Nyeri district before the emergency there were just two police stations and 35 men; by 1954 there were 28 police stations and 500 men (Maloba, 1993, p. 88). Having targeted the Kikuyu, Embu and Meru as the 'rebellious tribes', the administration sought to round them up and screen them, particularly in Nairobi, and to interrogate and deport

Mau Mau suspects to reception camps and the Reserve. 30,000 alone were removed from Nairobi in 'Operation Anvil' in April 1954. Restrictions were imposed on their movements with the introduction of passbooks; 'villigization' was pursued, with over one million Kikuyu settled by early 1955; and development projects were withdrawn from 'bad areas'. More seriously, troops, both professional and in particular the Home Guard of Kikuyu 'loyalists,'[5] proceeded with increasing illegal brutality to contain the unrest. They showed little regard for the law as they tortured to secure information, executed suspects, and looted and extorted goods. Under the rule that in protected and special areas forces could shoot those who failed to stop when ordered to do so, thousands were killed:

> The armed forces viewed themselves as agents of law and order pitted against murderous and sadistic rebels and felt no constraint whatsoever in their brutal suppression of the revolt. Ironically, however, the forces of law and order did not believe in the rule of law (Maloba, 1993, p. 91).

Canon Bostock, archdeacon of central Kenya, observed that, 'there are far too many instances of cold-blooded murder by members of the Security Forces, and of beating...' Similarly, the Moderator of the Church of Scotland in East Africa complained to the Governor of 'instances of brutality which, under the cloak of justice, law and order, the forces of the government have indulged in to an inordinate degree' (quoted in Maloba, 1993, p. 92). Significantly, few troops were ever prosecuted and the amnesty offered to the rebels in 1955 was careful to include the Home Guards as well. By the end of the violent offensive in 1956, it was said that more than 11,000 Mau Mau had been killed and 1,000 captured wounded. No figures were released as regards Mau Mau 'shot while attempting to escape' or who perished at the hands of the Home Guards.

The colonial responses to challenges to their legitimacy were authoritarian and disciplinarian, but so were the less extreme measures of everyday government. Despite important variations, every European power in Africa maintained authoritarian governments that had little space for popular participation. Not only was participation removed from the people at the level of their daily experience, but also an alien state structure was superimposed over the local levels. Like the local level, this too had largely unelected officials making decisions that profoundly affected daily life. Yet in this case, the officials could not even claim a measure of legitimacy born of cultural and linguistic familiarity. The small fraction of colonial power that was open to election by a few Africans was little more than tokenism. Before 1945 very few elections were held in any African colony at the territorial level and those that did occur involved a franchise restricted almost entirely to European residents (Collier, 1982, pp. 34-5). From this foundation of wide unrestrained power, their half-century rule was characterised by state repression and the ever-present threat of violence. Crowder summarises the colonial state as one that:

> was conceived in violence rather than in negotiation...it was maintained by the free use of it...It must be remembered too that the colonial rulers set the example of dealing with ...opponents by jailing or exiling them, as not a few of those who eventually inherited power knew from personal experience (Crowder, 1987, pp. 11-13).

This use of coercion by internal security forces of the colonial state and their collaborating local rulers to sustain an autonomous state was the model provided by the colonial period. Proponents of repression to maintain control over threatening social forces did not have to overcome a significant liberal heritage. By and large the colonial approach was imitated by the new post-colonial regimes in their own approach to security.

Post-Independence Law Enforcement

In a short time following decolonisation, almost all the independent states abandoned formal democracy for some form of authoritarian regime. Commonly the change began with moves to one-party rule and, typically, one-man rule. Authoritarian rulers saw the early experiment with democracy as an inadequate solution for establishing national unity across the deep ethnic divides. Apart from the fact that they were corrupted by fraud and abuse, the elections became what Collier termed, a 'focus for unbridgeable political rivalries' (quoted by Diamond, in Diamond et al., 1988, p. 4). Mistakenly they imagined that firm personal rule could keep the nation together and secure their own legitimacy. Surely Mazrui is right when he observes of the African state that, 'it is sometimes excessively authoritarian in order to disguise the fact that it is inadequately authoritative' (quoted by Chazan, in Diamond et al., 1988, p. 120). For many in the military as well, civilian politics was too volatile and divisive for their liking and the politicians, including heads of state, were not deemed fit to have access to the resources of the state, or the right to exclude them. There erupted, therefore, a spate of military coups. By the early 1970s virtually all of Sub-Saharan Africa had either military or one party regimes. With that came the severe repression and elimination of political opposition through the use of the army and police. 'Personal rule' prevailed, where authority is ascribed to the person rather than the office holder and where links are not with the 'public' but with patrons, associates, clients and supporters. In 1989, of some 46 Sub-Saharan Africa states, there were 29 single party states and 11 military dictatorships. The authoritarian rule of colonial times lived on.

The new authoritarianism of the independent nations did not quash all serious challenges to their legal authority. The autocrats faced twin challenges; from rebels and from criminals. The one was a challenge to the legitimacy of their authority over part or all the territory, the other a challenge to the effectiveness of their authority to enforce conformity.

Few would deny that defective boundary demarcation during the colonial period, which was not rectified at independence, left young states with a fragile and contested inheritance. There was the potential for civil war in just about every African state. Sadly this potential was realised in many cases. African countries have had to face serious internal security problems because certain populations within them have not accepted that they are part of that country. Insurgency and civil war has occurred for much of the independent existence of Angola, Burundi, Chad, Congo-Brazzaville, Congo (DRC), Ethiopia (since the fall of Haile Selassie), Mozambique, Rwanda, Senegal, Somalia, Sudan and Uganda. And it has featured over a number of years in the Central African Republic, Comoros, Equatorial Guinea, Guinea-Bissau, Liberia, Mali, Mauritania, Niger, Nigeria and Sierra Leone. The option of securing national unity across the fracture lines of ethnicity, religion and language through economic prosperity has not been open to the impoverished states. Consequently, to safeguard their nations' very existence, state leaders have resorted to coercive internal security. Ironically they have found that colonial emergency provisions and paramilitary police could serve their interests as well as their former masters'. Similarly, the security forces were all too willing to commit abuses in their quest for success against the rebels and bandits.

With the police distracted by security affairs, concentrated in wealthier urban areas, understaffed, under-resourced and under-skilled, criminal activity prospered. Frustrated by the difficulty in securing witnesses and forensic evidence that would stand up in court, police resorted to confessions made under duress or even to handing out summary punishment. But the problems went beyond training and resources. Those who held weapons and had information on security provision (or the lack of it) were in a unique position to exploit their advantage during times when pay was low and irregular. Of the Nigerian Police Force, Hills comments:

> Their performance record in the mid-60s was much the same as in the mid-80s, when the federal police minister acknowledged that they had recovered less than 14 percent of the $900 million worth of property reported stolen in the preceding six months. Police collusion with criminals was common, as were official appeals to officers to change their attitude toward the public and become more honest (Hills, 2000, p. 36).

Law Enforcement in the New Democracies

Bringing in political rights in the 1990s was relatively easy, but what have so far been much slower to change are legal rights. When it comes to legal/civil equality the situation in the new African democracies is problematic. Equality before law, as expressed in the new constitutions, is not fully translated into equality of access to the law, legal protection, or equality of treatment by the legal system. Popular control over who are the lawmakers and, in part, over the laws they make, may have been regained, but not popular control over how, or if, the laws are enforced. Too often laws are systematically flouted and ignored by the agents of the state, whilst law enforcement over others can be partial, inconsistent and even non-existent over large areas.

The period after independence, when military or civilian autocrats held power and showed scant concern for the process of law or to human rights, lasted 30 years. It established a tradition that the new democratic constitutions and legal and democratic institutions have not been able to alter overnight. Though heads of state have been willing for the most part to curtail their own ordering of lawless violence for political ends, many of the agents of the pre-democratic state security services remain in office and some inevitably continue their old practices. In societies where there is still widespread ignorance about the new rights, only limited contact with the centre and little exposure to the media or civil rights groups, abuse is not likely to draw much attention. Nor is there convincing evidence that governments are fully in control of their scattered security forces. At best, there are admissions of corruption, weak systems of accountability, inadequate training and flawed investigations. As for actual prosecutions of individuals, and thorough overhauls of the command structure and training, there have been minimal achievements.

Ironically, the abuses of the law by those who would crack down on lawbreakers are often in the name of defending another democratic value, namely freedom. The prevalence and apparent growth of criminality and insurgency over the last 15 years has prompted both agents of the state and citizens to resort to arbitrary violence and lawless behaviour, especially where lawful systems of law enforcement are not succeeding. The informal legal systems operated at times by both may, nevertheless, be sanctioned by the community and officially or unofficially by the state. As mentioned above, there is evidence that in the new democracies citizens are frequently willing to tolerate abuses of civil rights and the rule of law in the name of law and order. It is a blind eye that allows law enforcement to act with lawless violence, especially against the powerless. It appears that the return to democratic constitutionalism in Africa has not (yet) eradicated authoritarian and disciplinarian values and practices. Indeed, to many, the rule of law is seen as more of an obstacle to maintaining social order than as an effective guarantee of it.

In many ways these are the problems associated with what has been called a 'backwards democratisation', that is, where the process is one of electoral competition for office *preceding* the firm establishment of the 'modern' state with its commitment to the rule of law, its civic institutions that offered independent viewpoints and its horizontal accountability to other members of the elite (Rose and Shin, 2001). This order is in stark contrast to the first wave of democracy that saw a prolonged process of building the modern state, to be *followed* with the progressive widening of the franchise until a universal one was installed. Three features characterised that process. First, rules that were binding and fairly administered were established before democratic institutions such as elections were organised. Second, rulers were accustomed to horizontal accountability to fellow elites such as the judiciary and the owners of property and capital, before the vertical accountability to the mass of the electorate was involved. Third, power bases independent of the state that opposed or proposed state policy already existed before freedom of association and speech were granted as a constitutional right. Where, however, universal political rights are introduced before that rule of law has been engrained and where society is deeply divided not only in terms of class but of race, then the contradiction of so called illiberal democracies arises – the government holds elections, but it does not consistently follow the rule of law. The development of institutions and procedures that effectively enforce the rule of law is proceeding only slowly. Equality is reduced to (limited) political rights and freedom of choice for the individual.

This chapter has focused on attitudes towards law enforcement in Africa and on the difficulty of imposing democratic institutions based on one set of values on communities and law enforcement agencies that may share very different values. Given this lack of harmony one can anticipate persistent problems in ensuring the law is enforced lawfully. The following chapters trace the details in six different countries, covering the activities of a range of law enforcers from national armies and police forces to semi-official and informal vigilantes. They examine what happens to democracy when the army, police, state militias and local people take the law into their own hands.

Notes

1. The Liberal Democracy Index compiled by the Human Sciences Research Council, Pretoria, 2000-2001, following extensive surveys, comprises one point for each of six principles: freedom of speech, inviolability of constitution, accountability, party pluralism, information control and freedom of association. The score average for South Africa was 2.73, for Lesotho 3.41, for Namibia 2.97, for Zambia 3.45. In the rural areas of North Western province, South Africa it was down to 2.10 and in Ovambo, Namibia it was 2.21 (Rule, 2001).
2. *The Nation*, 26 July, 2001. There have been 1,119 people executed by the police in Kenya in the previous six years.
3. *The Nation*, 30 July, 2001.
4. *Time*, 10 May, 1999.
5. www.afrol.com/Categories/Women/wom003-violence-unfpa.
6. At first a private initiative of the Roman Catholic Missions, but co-opted into the official security forces in 1953).

PART II
THE ARMY TAKES THE LAW INTO ITS OWN HANDS

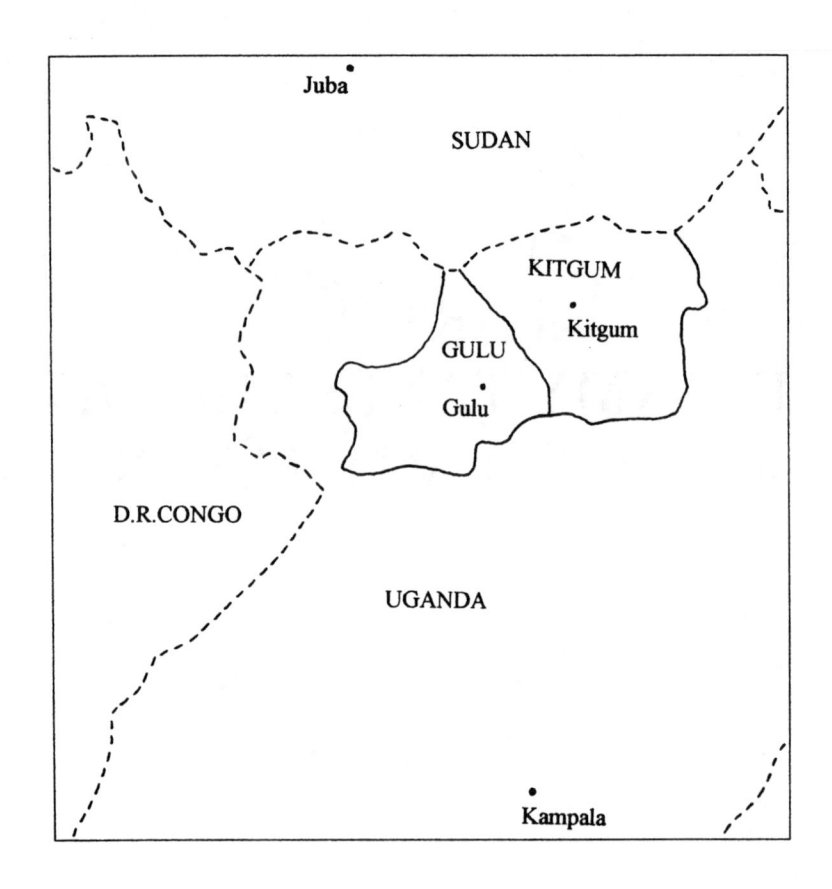

Figure 3.1 Northern Uganda

3 The Ugandan Peoples Defence Force and the Northern Rebellion

The Origin and Nature of the Insurgency

What later became known as The Lord's Resistance Army (LRA) began as one of several armed rebel groups in Northern Uganda that arose after the defeat of the Uganda National Liberation Army (UNLA) in January 1986 by Museveni's National Resistance Army (NRA). Many of the Acholi soldiers in UNLA, who made up almost two thirds of the army, fled to their northern homeland in Gulu and Kitgum provinces, fearing retaliation because of the association of Acholi fighters with the abuses of the regimes of Amin, Obote, and the Okellos, who were themselves Acholi. The return to peasant life proved too hard for many who had had a taste of the high life. Some resorted to pillaging, others joined the successor of UNLA, the Uganda People's Democratic Army (UPDA) which was set up in May 1986, or one of the other groups dedicated to the overthrow of Museveni. Their resolve was strengthened when the NRA battalions who were stationed in the region from March 1986 began, as feared, retaliatory acts of looting, burning of homesteads, rape (of men and women), torture and extrajudicial killings. Their fears were exacerbated by radio broadcasts that called the Acholi 'primitive' and 'murderers', the internment of many in politicisation camps and the violent methods used in the search for weapons (Behrend, 1999c, p. 25, 190; Doom and Vlassenroot, 1999, pp. 14-15; Behrend, 1998a, p. 108). In addition, the cattle raids of the Karamojong in 1986, which removed over 200,000 head of cattle, virtually ending the livestock farming of the Acholi, was thought to have had the tacit support of the NRA (Oxfam, 2000b).[1] Not surprisingly, the Acholi interpretation of these events was that the new government had decided to destroy Acholi culture, if not kill all male Acholi.[2]

The newly formed groups not only fought the NRA but one another. Their followers regularly changed their allegiance, but one quickly came to prominence. It was known as the Holy Spirit Mobile Forces (HSMF or sometimes, the Holy Spirit Movement). Formed by a young spirit medium from Gulu, Alice Auma, it was both a military organisation and a regional cult. Alice claimed to be a medium of, amongst others, a spirit of an Italian Christian, who was titled Lakwena (the Acholi for messenger). From this came her popular name of Alice Lakwena. The 'Holy Spirit' in the title of the group is thus a reference to the good spirit of Lakwena, not to the Third Person of the Trinity in the Christian Godhead.[3] Recruiting especially in Kitgum from the remnants of the UNLA and from sections of the UPDA, she offered warfare that was far less conventional than the UPDA. She promised one that was led by good spirits – they provided the code of conduct for soldiers, the battle tactics, the intelligence reports on the enemy, the supernatural protection (on condition of obedience) and the healing of the sick and injured. It was to be a war against the use of evil spirits (witchcraft), against the past and present impurity of her fighters, against the threat of southern oppression and ultimately a war to hasten in a new era of security and racial harmony. For thousands of Acholi who were demoralised by military defeat, cursed by the spirits of those they had killed, and fearful of revenge by an anti-Acholi NRA, this was redemption. Initially it did have some military successes and some 7-10,000 moved in an arc through the eastern territories towards Kampala, with other non-Acholi groups rallying to the march. However, after repeated battle losses, it was decisively defeated and scattered by NRA troops near Jinja in November 1987 (Behrend, 1999c, pp. 78-98).[4]

Though Alice's father sought to lead the remnants of the HSMF, it was Lakwena's reputed cousin, Joseph Kony, who assumed leadership of the northern rebellion with an armed group which he had formed in early 1987. His movement, confusingly called at this stage the Holy Spirit Movement, had adopted many of the HSMF positions both on spirit leadership and protection, and on its insistence on moral discipline. Kony was also a medium for the spirit Lakwena and others and shared with Alice the mission to destroy the evil forces in the world and, in particular, to destroy all those who wanted to fight in Uganda (Behrend, 1999c, p. 179).

Where he differed from the HSMF was in his preferred use of small, mobile, armed groups which he recruited largely from the Gulu district. He frequently clashed with the UPDA and integrated captives into his own movement, but when most of the UPDA signed a peace agreement with the NRA in May 1988, the rump joined his movement. The UPDA commanders only further emphasised conventional guerrilla tactics so that spirit-led tactics declined, although religious ritual and discourse still played a dominant part in their organisation (Behrend, 1999c, pp. 178, 182-9).[5] It was from this time in particular that Kony's newly named Uganda Peoples Democratic Christian Army (or Lord's Army), began increasingly to use terror and violence against the local civilian population to force them into support.[6] It frequently kidnapped school children, students and young men and women to act as porters and, following the rescinding of the prohibition against fornication and adultery, as sex slaves. Egregious incidents were the attack on the Lacor Hospital and the Sacred Heart School, Gulu, in Easter 1988, when 120 were kidnapped, including many schoolgirls and the abduction of 139 girls from St Mary's College, Aboke, 9 October, 1996, of whom 30 are still in captivity (Behrend, 1999c, p. 180).[7]

From 1991 the NRA stepped up its counter-insurgency operations in the north and in addition organised local militias, but not without fearful consequences:

> Kony's soldiers took terrible revenge on the populace, which seemed to have taken sides against them and, in their eyes, committed treason. They kidnapped more than 50 men, women and children and maimed them by cutting off their noses, ears, and hands or by boring a hole through their lips and padlocking their mouths, mutilating their bodies to mark them as traitors. Others were cut to pieces with *pangas* (Behrend, 1999c, p. 189).

To avoid the NRA, Kony's movement, now called the Lord's Resistance Army or LRA, began operating from bases in southern Sudan. There, following the collapse of peace talks with the Ugandan Government, the Sudanese provided military and logistical support for joint operations against their own rebels, the SPLA (Behrend, 1999c, p. 193).[8] The LRA continued their attacks on residents in Gulu and Kitgum, killing hundreds, possibly thousands. They have also maintained their practice of torture, rape and maiming (cutting off noses, lips and ears and breaking legs with hammers), attacking schools and clinics, burning and looting homes and stores, and abducting thousands.[9] Those abducted have endured beatings, torture, rape and executions and have been used as porters, front line fighters or sex slaves. In 1999 the US Bureau of Democracy, Human Rights and Labour reported that the LRA continued to:

> Attack civilian targets, as well as some refugee camps. After a year of few major attacks, the LRA began a series of assaults on civilian targets in late December [1999]. Attacks by the LRA during the year caused about 30 deaths and the destruction of homes and property. The LRA abducted about 250 civilians, some of whom later were released. No new incidents of mutilation were reported. The LRA continued to abduct children and, at clandestine bases, terrorized them into virtual slavery as guards, concubines, and soldiers. In addition to being beaten, raped, and forced to march until exhausted, abducted children were forced to participate in the killing of other children who attempted to escape (US Department of State, 2000).

A year later things had changed little:

> LRA attacks increased during the year [2000], and the LRA was responsible for the killing of approximately 175 civilians, including children...The LRA abducted approximately 700 persons, including young girls abducted as sex and labour slaves...[it] engaged in looting and destruction of private property...In particular [it] tortured children by beating them, forcing them to witness atrocities, forcing them to march until they collapsed, and denying them adequate food, water, or shelter (US Department of State, 2001).

They ambush vehicles and attack cyclists and walkers on the roads or they raid the villages, taking everything from the houses before burning them, killing adults and abducting children. There are reports of captives returning telling of children as young as six hacking fellow children to death who tried to escape.[10] Faced with the possibility of this at any time, more than 450,000 have been displaced by the northern conflict since 1986. They live in camps or at night simply move into the bush or into the centre of the towns.

> At the end of the day, after the [army] patrols have returned, hundreds of families walk into Kitgum from nearby villages, even from the town's suburbs, carrying blankets and small bundles of clothing. School children carry their uniforms and books for the next day's schooling. They take refuge in the grounds of the Mission and Government Hospitals, where they bed down on the covered walkways (Oxfam, 2000a).

Though there are no more than 1-2,000 fighters in the LRA, 60 percent of whom are children, the 12,000 Government troops stationed in the area have been unable to eradicate them, due, it is said, to the insurgents' ability to take refuge across the Sudanese border, where they have received modern assault weapons, anti-personnel mines and even anti-aircraft weapons.

There have been few expressions by the LRA of political goals. It is usually assumed, however, that since most of the insurgents are Acholi, they are seeking to free the Acholi people from a government dominated by other ethnic groups from the South and West and who discriminate against them because of their association with the military abuses of the former regimes. There was an occasion, too, in 1998, when a letter was received, purporting to be from the LRA, which called for an Acholi nation to be carved out of northern Uganda.[11] However, neither reform nor secession truly characterises their aims. Rather, they appear to have adopted three roles. First, one of hired terrorist organisation, paid for by the Sudanese Government. As such they fight the SPLA and defend the southern Sudanese town of Juba from its attacks. In addition they seek to undermine support for Uganda's President Museveni and to dispose him to abandon his policy of support for the SPLA rebels fighting the Sudanese Government.[12] Secondly, they have undertaken a role as a warlord/criminal organisation that uses violence to acquire power and seize food and women that would otherwise be beyond their means. War, as Keen observes, can serve 'as a smokescreen for the emergence of a wartime political economy' from which combatants may be benefiting (2000, p. 27). Thirdly, they pursue an anti-system role that vents its rage by destruction and brutality of a system that has excluded them:

> Kony-type upheavals do not aim at a radical change of the system; they want to destroy it. Not because they want to replace it with something 'higher', by a new way of living, but out of anger and frustration, because their lives do not fit into any system any more...Their rebellion is political inasmuch as it is a result of the world political and economical system in place. It is, for those engaged, non-political inasmuch as they no longer believe in politics. For the majority of the rank and file, it is a survival strategy, a way to obtain things which are out of reach by all normal means: consummatory rewards as ideological drive. For those in charge, the brokers, it is a tool to acquire access to power, status and some wealth: rebellion as a career (Doom and Vlassenroot, 1999, pp. 35-6).

In July 2001, former LRA captives report that the 2000 amnesty by the Ugandan Government had been rejected by Kony and that he had lost confidence in the Carter Center peace negotiations.[13] However, partially cut off from his units in northern Uganda by tighter border control and Sudanese pressure, those units have been left without supplies. They resorted once more, therefore, in late 2001, to ambushing aid convoys and attacking IDP camps in search of supplies, which they removed using abducted adolescents.

The Response of the State Security Forces

The overall strategy of the Ugandan Government towards the LRA has primarily been one of meeting violence with violence. 'We will kill, kill these people' shouted Museveni at a public meeting in 1996 after the death of 200 people in a month. In future, he said, he was no longer prepared to engage in peace negotiations with Kony but would seek a military solution.[14] Later the same month, Salim Saleh, then Commander of the northern forces, opined, 'The LRA will go on killing until they are killed'.[15] It is true there have been periodic peace negotiations, such as those held in 1994, but the sincerity of them seems in doubt (Doom and Vlassenroot, 1999, p. 24). More consistent has been the Government's two-fold response that it is impossible to negotiate with a group that has no demands and that the Government is not prepared to offer any amnesty to 'terrorists and criminals'. It also has to be added, however, that the military policy against the LRA is not pursued with much vigour. The units seem to avoid head-on confrontation with the LRA for much of the time and numbers were considerably reduced when the war in the DRC (the Democratic Republic of Congo) began.

That there are real political, economic and social problems in Acholiland that, at least in part, fuel the rebellion is acknowledged by Museveni himself.[16] The use, therefore, of up to 12,000 Ugandan troops (now known as Ugandan Peoples Defence Force or UPDF) stationed in and around Gulu, cannot be the complete solution. It has all the inherent risks associated with unloosing the military for internal policing:

> Military forces do not automatically deal with ...internal opposition with due regard to human rights principles, democracy and the rule of law...Even when a state has acquired new [democratic] procedures...there is no guarantee that the armed forces will conform to the democratic ethos (Wilkinson, 1996, p. 1).

The genuine and yet uncertain danger in which UPDF troops are placed by guerrilla activities should be recognised. This is specially so for the local militias, known as the Local Defence Units, that are in the front line, (Behrend, 1999c, p. 189). As should the likelihood that soldiers will be exasperated by the restraints of law, inevitably leading to *some* of them acting lawlessly. Frustration, anger and fear breed spontaneous and undisciplined responses. An army's training and objective are to kill external forces, not to apprehend internal lawbreakers and secure their conviction before a court of law. Though the army has not committed abuses to the same degree of barbarity as the LRA, excessive use of force has been prominent in their counter insurgency operations. Both suspected rebels and civilian supporters have been subject to house searches without warrants, arbitrary arrests, detentions incommunicado, beatings, rape, extrajudicial executions and the burning of homesteads (Amnesty International, 1999b; US Department of State, 1999, 2000, 2001). Hence the attacks and counter-attacks show no sign of abating. The cycle of violence is familiar: state security forces that over-react to security crises provoke violent reaction by discontented people, which in turn causes retaliatory violence by state security forces.

Ascertaining how high in the command structure decisions go as regards ground troop conduct is difficult. What is clear, however, is that whether at the direction of army commanders and, ultimately, the Head of State as the Minister of Defence and Commander in Chief, or despite them, UPDF troops commonly ignore the Ugandan Constitution and laws and the international conventions on human rights. In their determination to track down and eliminate the rebels and to deter support for them, legal requirements are brushed aside and they take the law into their own hands. The evidence to this effect is presented below.

Extrajudicial Killings

Rebels are not only killed in armed clashes. Members of the UPDF and the police have committed extrajudicial killings, or at least have used such coercion in their operations as to cause the death of both suspected rebels and innocent civilians. For example, in August 1999 UPDF soldiers executed two rebel suspects in Lira and in January 2000 killed two rebels wounded in an unsuccessful attack on the Paloga trading centre, Gulu (US Department of State, 2000, 2001). Amnesty International claims that it has documented 'scores of killings of unarmed civilians, including children' by Government forces 1996-99 (Amnesty International, 1999a).

Irregular Arrests and Detention

The Ugandan Constitution carefully prescribes conditions for arrests and detention, but the requirements are frequently ignored. Thus detainees suspected of rebel acts, or of collusion with the rebels, have until recently been illegally held in barracks. Some, contrary to the law, are held in unregistered places of remand, are not charged within 48 hours of arrest, and are not always told of the reasons for their detention. Frequently, when rebel suspects are charged, it is with 'treason', since under this charge the suspect can be detained for up to 360 days without bail. 226 suspects, mostly from the rebel areas of Uganda, were accused of treason at the end of 2000, although this did represent a drop in numbers from previous years. Prisoners are also held for excessive periods. In November 1999 more than 400 prisoners held on charges of treason without trial since at least 1997 staged a protest at Luzira prison in Kampala and were subsequently released (US Department of State, 2001).

Torture

Despite torture, beatings and degrading treatment being outlawed by the Ugandan Constitution, it appears that security forces commonly beat suspected rebels and innocent civilians and sometimes subject them to torture to force confessions and the disclosure of leading information. There are also reports that UPDF mobile forces beat civilians regularly, rape women and children and that deaths have occurred in detention (Amnesty International, 1999b).[17] In 1998 an incident was reported where 18 UPDF soldiers were arrested in the Gulu district for beating 21 civilians (US Department of State, 1999). The arrests, however, did not stop the abuses continuing and the following year it was said that 'UPDF forces in the north on occasion beat and abused civilians, although there were significantly fewer reports of such abuse during the year' (US Department of State, 2000). In a court case concerning a woman who was allegedly stripped naked and sexually abused by soldiers at the army barracks in Gulu in 1999, it was revealed that civilian women are regularly 'punished' by having their heads forcibly shaven with blunt razors.

Behrend, who visited the area in 1991, recalls that by 'behaving more violently towards the local inhabitants than the UPDCA soldiers' [the LRA was briefly called the Uganda Peoples' Democratic Christian Army] the NRA ensured that, 'at least in some areas, Kony's troops could count on the silence and toleration, if not support, of the people.' Further, the severe treatment of those suspected of sympathizing or collaborating with the UPDCA only roused 'sympathy for the UPDCA and led a number of young men to join the rebels' (Behrend, 1999c, p. 188).

Displacement

Ugandan law does not cover displacement as such, but international humanitarian law asserts it is only permissible when the security of civilians is endangered or military reasons are imperative. It also obliges authorities to keep displacement to a minimum, to end it as soon as possible and to provide food shelter water and security. Nevertheless, despite these standards, according to Behrend, the Ugandan Government in 1987-88:

> Forced large segments of the population in Gulu district...to take refuge in camps or in the cities. I was told that many were fleeing not from the rebels but from the NRA who stole livestock and burned houses, supplies and fields. By December 1987 some 30,000 refugees were living in various camps distributed throughout Gulu City. There was not enough to eat, sanitary conditions were inadequate and except in Lacor, medical care had more or less collapsed (Behrend, 1999c, p. 172).

Again, in 1990, and regularly since 1996, the Government has employed 'protected villages', with UPDF units nearby to both defend them (or, as some would say, be defended by them when they are located *within* the camps) and to deny support to the LRA. About 480,000 have been displaced in Gulu and Kitgum (August 2001), that is, some 50 - 80 percent of Gulu's population. The majority are located in 40 local camps. Though some of the villagers have moved voluntarily, there have been innumerable cases where the army's policy has been pursued with the use of threats, the burning of homesteads, and even the indiscriminate shelling of villages which have refused to move (Amnesty International, 1999a). For instance, in February 1999 two new protected villages, Patika A and Patika B, were created near the Sudanese border and villagers in the surrounding area were forced to evacuate their homes and to move to these villages (US Department of State, 2000). Given that initially many protected villages did not have water, electricity, clinics and schools, villagers were at times reluctant to enter them. Hunger and disease were widespread in them. At Palbo camp in February 1997, out of a total of 30,000, there were 1,457 deaths from malaria, 14 from diarrhoea, 490 from 'diarrhoea with blood', 16 from malnutrition, and 48 from upper respiratory tract diseases (Ehrenreich, 1998, fn.9). In many camps there are food and water shortages, sanitation is poor and with people so confined, economic activity is largely at a standstill. As the Bishop of Gulu declared, 'The whole land is dead, there is no life here.'[18] Similarly, the Bishop of Namirembe, on visiting the North, said that he was 'appalled by the poor living conditions among the people... Life in protected camps is pathetic.'[19]

Despite the Government's claims to the contrary, there is evidence that at some camps the villagers are not allowed out even in the daytime to return to their holdings to plant and tend crops. Amnesty International alleges that some of those who have returned to their homes to cultivate or forage have been shot dead by the UPDF. Likewise the Acholi Religious Leaders Peace Initiative has accused the UPDF of beating those who tried to return home or forage for food, raping women and of forcing them back into the camps.[20] With the army's failure to defeat a small insurgent group and the punitive nature of the camps, the Government is widely criticised. They have not even been successful in protecting the occupants from armed attacks and abductions by the LRA. In 1999 and 2000, rebels attacked at least 6 camps killing more than 19 and abducting 44.

In summary, the security system is regularly failing to stay within the law, to respect human rights, to secure evidence that stands up to scrutiny in open court, and to recognise civilian control. If adjustment from authoritarian to democratic ways is difficult in a context of peace, it is much more difficult under insurgent violence and emergency conditions. Yet the failure of the security forces to adopt new procedures and practices exposes the state to charges of 'state brutality' and failure to 'protect its own citizens.'

With massive displacement, the breakdown of Acholi communal life, economic collapse and the disintegration of local government starved of resources, it is little wonder that community leaders in northern Uganda and even the current army commander, Brigadier Katumba Wamala, repeatedly urged the Government to reverse its policy and offer an amnesty and resettlement to the insurgents. Faced with Museveni's preference for a military solution, only a few in Government circles have questioned this. One such was Major General Tinyefuza who in 1996, when Minister of State for Defence, told Parliament that the army had failed to defeat the rebels and that it was time for the top commanders to either negotiate or resign. For his outspokenness he himself was forced to resign.[21] Similarly Museveni's half-brother Salim Saleh, when Defence Adviser in 1998, argued that there could not be a military solution without a comprehensive socio-economic programme to redress the region's marginalisation.[22] The policy of rejecting peace negotiations also ran counter to the views of an increasing number of Acholi. Particularly following Museveni's announcement in May 1996 of his determination to seek a military rather than negotiated solution, a peace movement under the auspices of The Acholi Religious Leaders Peace Initiative gathered momentum among the people, Christian and Muslim leaders, Non-Government Organisations (NGOs) and MPs of the north. It has called for peace talks and criticised the Government's handling of the security situation.[23] Only after 10 years of vainly claiming that the insurgents were defeated or would be very shortly, did the Government finally begin to consider non-military options. The shift in the position came after the LRA abducted eight people from a camp that was supposed to be protected by the UPDF and ambushed a military vehicle on the Gulu-Kampala highway.[24] It was reported that the Government had entered into secret talks with the LRA, although publicly it claimed it would continue its military action while at the same time exploring the possibility of holding talks, provided, 'the evil party repents and gives up its bad ways.'[25] In December 1999, with Kony reported to be critically ill with AIDS, the Ugandan Parliament, despite an unenthusiastic Government, passed the Amnesty Bill, offering all rebels in the country an amnesty if they surrendered and renounced their rebellion.[26]

On the diplomatic front, in December 1999 the Sudanese and Ugandan governments met and pledged to stop supporting each other's rebels. Museveni was initially sceptical and within a month complained: 'we are not satisfied with the implementation.'[27] However, by the middle of 2001 there were reports from defectors from Sudan of cutting off supplies to the LRA so that they were having to loot from civilians and of them being driven out of Juba and forced to locate nearer the border.[28] Further, some 300 abductees had been returned from Sudan with the help of UNICEF. In contrast to Sudan's actions, there are still reports that the SPLA uses UPDF barracks as bases for the forced recruitment of troops from the refugee camps of northern Uganda.

The war, with its abuses by both sides, is far from over. It is true that many southerners give it little thought and that, 'Many Kampala-oriented politicians still consider the conflict as a northern-based intra-Acholi fight with little effect on the rest of the country' (Doom and Vlassenroot, 1999, p. 32). Yet for all its distance from Kampala and the region's relatively low population, northern violence cannot be 'ring-fenced'. As the section below argues, the insurgency as a whole, and the reaction of the security forces in particular, has had a decided effect on the democratic institutions and processes of the whole country.

The Democratic Impact

If the impact of the lawlessness of the UPDF in northern Uganda on the country's democracy is to be measured, the concept of democracy needs to be disaggregated. Democracy is not a single institution, but a cluster of procedures, processes and values. The examination of the effects must cover formal institutions such as political accountability, freedom of information, freedom of the press, legal equality. But they must also relate to more intangible areas, such as democratic values of toleration, negotiation and open debate. These political, social and legal aspects of democracy are explored below.

An Escalation of the Violence

Despite the historical evidence demonstrating the difficulty of eliminating guerrilla type insurgents, democracies, like all other regime types, instinctively react to insurgents with military force. The greater the state's military resources, the more persistent is their commitment to a military solution. Within this response an escalation is almost inevitable. As the state responds to the threat or use of force with greater force, dissidents will resort to greater force. The outcome is an intensification of violence.

It has certainly proved very difficult in Uganda to prevent an escalation of the violence. Each injury or death caused by the LRA or UPDF has lead to retaliation, whilst the determination to enlist intelligence information, or to prevent collaboration, promotes the use of intimidation, coercion, torture and executions by both sides. There was a sense in which the HSMF was restrained from excesses by its moral teachings and discipline. However, its successor movements lacked or loosened the moral checks and, as Behrend notes, 'were caught up in the logic of violence and counter-violence and became increasingly unjust' (Behrend, 1999c, p. 189). Further, in response to declining food production as a result of so many being in camps, since 1998 the LRA has extended its violence to communities previously less affected by the war (Amnesty International, 1999b, pp. 25-6).

In an interview, a primary head teacher revealed: 'Everyone's behaviour has changed, to cope with this hostile environment. The older children think of guns – they see them as a solution...The children from that area [where guns were given out to protect people from Karamojong attacks] definitely see the gun as a solution' (Oxfam, 2000d).[29] In this situation there are always innocent civilians who suffer. For instance, in a clash at Ogole in Kitgum in March 1998, the UPDF killed 30 children abducted by the LRA. In combat situations casualties are inevitable, yet these children were apparently shot from less than 10 metres, though no investigation has taken place and the army still denies that any children were killed (Amnesty International, 1999a). It is hard to conceive of the democratic values of discussion and tolerance being established in a context of perpetual retaliation.

Violence is Becoming the Language of Political Communication

Both the LRA and UPDF read the other side's readiness to use violence in and outside of combat situations as meaning that there is no prospect of a negotiated settlement and that the only way forward is by force. There is a belief that those that speak only in violence can be answered only in violence. In a situation of endemic conflict there is a very real danger of violence becoming the only language of political communication. Thus Museveni can argue, 'You can't have a peace conference with malaria'.[30] Likewise the first deputy premier and Minister of Foreign Affairs, Eriya Kategaya, said in January 2000, 'I am personally not excited about talking to such people whose only business is to loot and kill people. A person like Joseph Kony cannot change, so how do you talk to him?'[31] When soldiers imbibe the mantra that the only language the other side understands is violence, then further unlawful actions are likely. The greater the violence, the better the chance of making one's point.

In this context it is all too easy to dismiss the democratic processes of systematic and open public consultation prior to the formulation of security policy and peace negotiations. There has certainly been ambivalence about the Government's pursuit of a peace agreement with the LRA. In 1994 the Minister for Pacification of the North, Betty Bigombe, negotiated with Kony and reached a ceasefire agreement. But it was scuttled when Museveni made a speech demanding that the LRA lay down its weapons and give themselves up within a week. Next the peace initiative of the Acholi Religious Leaders Peace Initiative was undermined when the Government in 1997 accused seven priests of being 'rebel collaborators'. The Government did launch its own Forum for Peace, but its decision to distribute guns to Acholi communities to defend themselves against Karamojong cattle raiders showed where its preferred solution lay and drove the churches to withdraw from it. The Government did offer in 1998 an amnesty for rebels who gave themselves up (and in May 1999 for Kony himself) and agreed an Amnesty Bill in 2000. Yet Museveni made it quite clear that he was not interested in the Amnesty Law, but had only accepted it because Parliament had forced it on him.[32] It hardly comes as a surprise to hear that the Commissioner in Charge of implementing it has not received sufficient funding to resettle the 357 returnees who have so far renounced the armed rebellion.[33] All this is not indicative of a Government wedded to negotiation, but rather to a policy of force, whether that force be strictly legal or not. In conversation with a church leader in the North in 1998, Museveni made a revealing comment. The church leader said to him, 'Here we practice reconciliation. When you kill my brother, first there is anger. But then, after proper compensation, you must reconcile, and not only the families but also the clans'. Museveni is said to have replied: 'If you kill my son, I must kill yours' adding that perhaps he had taken this Banyankole culture into the presidency (Oxfam, 2000c). Behrend goes further and even suggests that there are sinister forces at work to undermine the peace movement:

> A group of Acholi elders led by Mzee Okeny Tibero sought to end the war through negotiation. Since the war by then had become a lucrative business for many officers and soldiers in the government army, however, these people warned the elders against supporting the peace process. Two elders who continued to press for political negotiations, Mzee Okot Ogoni and Mzee Olanya Lagoni, were murdered early in 1996 (Behrend, 1998a, p. 117).

The question arises as to whether those who have taken the law into their own hands are those who resist a return to the legal arena of legitimate military force and political resolution. For their part, Doom and Vlassenroot suggest that Western interests also ensure that Museveni is less than sincere about wanting the war to cease:

> One factor underpinning Museveni's friendly relationship with the USA resides precisely in his role against the Sudanese regime. Together with other countries – Ethiopia, Eritrea, Egypt – Uganda plays an important role in containing the Sudanese danger, which has become an obsession for the White House. Museveni is hardly in a position to displease Washington at the risk of losing material support. Therefore, he will most certainly back Garang [with whom Doom and Vlassenrot believe he has personal sympathy] into the foreseeable future (Doom and Vlassenroot, 1999, pp. 28-9).

An Acholi leader, MP Norbert Mao, gives the conspiracy theory a local spin, claiming that the war is being deliberately prolonged so as to control the political opposition of the area. In his view it is 'an attempt to dispossess the Acholi people', as a punishment.[34]

The tragedy of the continued violence is that democratic debate leading to consensus or compromise is foreclosed. Though the members of the LRA may have long forgotten the issues that made them turn to rebellion, there are nevertheless underlying issues relating to the area's treatment by the central government that remain unresolved in the eyes of the ordinary citizens of Gulu and Kitgum. The further the army goes in taking the law into its own hands, the less likely are these issues to be addressed.

Government News Management

To ensure the widest possible debate in a democracy, it is important for the media to be independent, accurate and to represent a range of public opinions. In Uganda there is such an independent print media and their publications have demonstrated courageous criticism of the Government. Yet the Government has sought to restrain criticism of the security force's abuses by denying that they have taken place, intimidating the media from disclosing them and generally seeking to discredit the truthfulness of the media.

Regional conflict is never just one of military violence, but a conflict of discourses, with both sides interpreting and justifying their actions (Apter, 1997). The clash of discourses pits the insurgents' attempts to delegitimise the government and legitimate their 'cause', against the government's attempts to delegitimise the insurgents and legitimise themselves (du Toit, 1990, p. 123). Are the insurgents to be seen as the victims, an impoverished minority forced to hit back at the state that neglects and/or oppresses them? Or are they to be seen as perpetrators of violence, callous terrorists who threaten the well-being of every citizen? Concerning the UPDF abuses, the Ugandan Government has assumed the task of denying or justifying them. Certainly they want to counter the argument that the UDPF are not only incompetent and indifferent in their inadequate response, but even terrorists themselves in their use of inordinate violence to quell the conflict. They have sought to portray a Government of reasonable leaders who are in control of the situation and will protect their citizens effectively from this threat while it lasts. Yet though much of the media are under their direct control (e.g. *New Vision* and much of the radio/TV), sympathy for the Government and its security forces can still be quickly lost. A single incident of government troops that failed to defend innocent victims when under attack, or that killed innocent people in the course of eliminating the insurgents, can destroy support anywhere. Two of the most damning actions in the north of Uganda were the abduction by the LRA of 139 girls from St Mary's College, and 29 from the St Charles Lwanga Girls Secondary School, although abductions from so called protected villages may have been equally damaging. In such a situation the people's fear of the insurgents can become anger against, or even fear of, the state. Once citizens have taken the step from anger towards the insurgents, to anger towards the state, it may not be very difficult to persuade some to the next step of disillusionment with democracy and even sympathy for the insurgents.

Beyond putting a 'spin' on the news, there is also evidence that the Ugandan press coverage of the situation in the north has been regularly impeded by the Government. During the security operation in 1991 the NRA cordoned off the north, in what looked like a deliberate attempt to provide a screen behind which it could carry out its activities unobserved. NGOs had to leave and all means of communication were confiscated. Subsequent action against journalists has included detention, arrests and prosecution. There have also been cases of journalists being assaulted by unidentified assailants that may well have been in the pay of the authorities. For example on 29 October 1998, six men attacked and seriously injured an editor on the *Monitor*. He was told, 'this will teach you to keep your big mouth shut.' The assault took place two days after the publication of an article on evidence that the security forces were torturing rebel suspects from another rebel group, the ADF, in secret safe houses around Kampala (Human Rights Watch, 1999, p. 114). Likewise in May 1999 three *Monitor* editors were arrested and charged with sedition and the publication of false news, after publishing the photograph of a naked woman apparently being sexually abused by soldiers. It was claimed that the photograph was taken in an army barracks in Gulu. Despite the fact that both a woman and a soldier were willing to testify in court as being two of the persons in the photograph, the army insisted the photograph was a fake.[35] The responses by the army in and out of court are revealing. Deputy army commander, Brigadier Joram Mugume, issued a statement the day after the publication. In it he accused the *Monitor* of seeking to portray 'the war against Joseph Kony's LRA as having taken a toll on the moral aptitude of the UPDF to an extent that the actions of the rebels are similar to those of the UPDF'. He claimed it was an attempt to depict the army as a force whose discipline 'is in the sewers' and whose leadership 'condones and supports such actions'.

In his view, the UPDF had been the backbone of press freedom in Uganda and had 'exercised great restraint under pressure and given information willingly to journalists. It is greatly disappointed that the *Monitor* can be used to create a negative impression about the institution whose record of discipline is impeccable.'[36] The general policy of the Government appears to be to warn off journalists from reporting on issues that cast the action of the Government in a bad light or that give space for opposition views. The justification for this stratagem is usually in terms of preventing the UPDF from being discredited, morale being undermined, interview space being given to the opinions of terrorists and the exacerbation of ethnic tension. The reality is that lawlessness by the security forces leads to lawlessness by Government officials seeking to cover up the excesses. This is not the route by which to strengthen democratic accountability.

The Mobilisation of Political Opposition

During prolonged political violence, democratic institutions such as the electoral process might be expected to be disrupted or derailed. Registration and voting can be disturbed by both insurgent and army interference and intimidation, whilst access to constituencies in the conflict zone becomes problematic. However, Uganda, like most states in such a situation, has made a concerted effort to prove that it is 'business as usual'. Elections have continued since, when legitimacy is being challenged, it is all the more important to have hard evidence to reinforce the legitimist discourse.

The presidential and parliamentary elections of 1996 were able to proceed largely because the LRA declared a temporary cease-fire over the campaign period. During the campaign the insurgents held many rallies urging people to vote for the opposition presidential candidate Paul Ssemogerere, who was promising to engage in peace negotiations, in contrast to the Government. It was hardly surprising that 90 percent of northern Uganda supported Ssemongerere. Likewise the 2001 Presidential and parliamentary elections proceeded in the North, again with very large support for the opposition. In the Presidential election, the main opposition candidate, Besigye, received more than 75 percent of the vote and, despite strong efforts by the Movement (Museveni's national and inclusive political organisation) and illegal intimidation by the army to dislodge the UPC parliamentary candidates of the north, they failed to do so.[37] Similarly

Museveni's preferred parliamentary candidate for Gulu was comfortably defeated.

The lawless action of the army, therefore, both in its handling of the insurgency and in its partisan support for Movement candidates, has become an issue of political debate and a focus for mobilising opposition. Further, there have been opposition voices in Parliament, led by the Acholi parliamentary group, that have called for serious peace negotiations with the LRA. Their pressure secured the Amnesty Bill 2000. The provincial conflict and the way the Government and army has conducted it has in effect turned the Acholi into an opposition group. It has created the very opposite of what Museveni wanted – the seeds of an ethnic political party based largely on a sense of victimisation. The harnessing of opposition to Museveni and the Movement in the north appears to be in large measure an expression of dissatisfaction over the way the security situation has been handled by the Government and the army.

The Plunder Economy

The disruption to the economy and social life is causing increasing poverty. The number in absolute poverty has risen from 60 percent to 66 percent in the last three years. It is also preventing 300,000 children from attending school. Yet where there is internal instability there invariably arises a war economy from which some gain. Most soldiers, whatever side they fight on (and many of course swap sides according to which offers the best pickings) see fighting, not only as a means of employment, but as a business; a business more profitable than peace.[38] The fighters thus have a vested interest in maintaining and extending the conflict into a wider territory:

> Since current economic conditions...are turning more and more people into 'losers', many see war, especially civil war, as their only possibility of imitating the life made familiar and seemingly desirable by war videos. With the war now having lasted for more than ten years, it has become a system of production and has created a form of life which 'normalizes' and banalizes violence and brutality and blurs the distinction between war and peace (Behrend, 1999c, p. 192).

Though it cannot be proved, UPDF officers do appear to have exploited the situation for their own profit. In the words of the UN Secretary General's Representative on Children in Armed Conflict, 'The war has become a lucrative source of ill-gotten wealth for those who preside over it'.[39] Even the Minister of Defence, Brigadier Katumba Wamala, told Parliament in 1996 that much of the blame for the army's failure to defeat the LRA was due to corrupt commanders.[40]

The prolonged violence, with the associated destruction of the local economy, has brought what Mbembe calls a 'plunder mentality'. Lawless conduct has therefore proved profitable for fighters on both sides, but the terrible consequence is that they have therefore established an interest in keeping the war going.

Social Polarisation and Intolerance

Democracy does not consist solely of formal institutions. It includes societal values such as tolerance, political discourse, acceptance of majority decisions, political participation, consideration of the community's well-being, and support for the rule of law. However, where violence and lawlessness prevail their effect is to promote atomisation, self-interest and brutalisation and quickly undermine tolerance between those of opposing views. People are readily branded as 'enemies' on the basis of their region, ethnicity or religion, irrespective of their true beliefs and practices, whilst political and social rifts emerge between those supporting and those critical of government responses. As Apter says: 'Political violence not only divides people, it polarizes them around affiliations of race, ethnicity, religion, and language, class. It turns boundaries in the mind into terrains and jurisdictions on the ground' (Apter, 1997, p. 1). The army used to refer to Alice Lakwena, not as a human being, but as a 'biological substance' which had to be obliterated;[41] and following the LRA attack that left 13 students dead in April 2001, the press spoke of them as 'pseudo-hominids', 'biological freaks' and 'marauding forms of life'.[42]

Every time the UPDF commits a human rights violation with impunity it further reduces people's trust in the Government and their hope of a lasting peace. A letter in the *Monitor* captures the sense of polarisation that many northerners feel:

> The Acholi are viewed by many [southerners] as killers. For all NRM's 11 years in power there has been that silent but conspicuous 'us and them' attitude in dealing with the Northern question. The predominantly western NRM [Museveni's National Resistance Movement] government and the Acholi still can't talk frankly and honestly with each other, even to simply agree to disagree. Northerners feel that the system treats them unfairly.[43]

The fact that Museveni's new cabinet in 2001 had only nine northerners in it of a total of 66 will have done nothing to dispel these fears. With or without the law the Government seems to be against them. Lawless activity by Government troops can only harden this sense of racial discrimination.

Immunity to Violence

Perhaps one of the worst features of prolonged conflict, where humanitarian rules are not followed, is that people slowly become immune to violence and brutality. Violence becomes banal (Behrend, 1998a, p. 116). Children who have escaped capture by the LRA report that cutting bodies into parts became automatic. One boy of 15 said 'as we went we burned many houses...we came across two hunters and they were killed with clubs and bayonets. This looting and killing continued as we marched. So many people were killed. You had to adapt yourself quickly to that kind of life.'[44] One fears the same would be true of UPDF troops.

People in the conflict area may also become equivocal about the legitimacy of the use of violence, especially if seen to be practised by Government troops. In this respect it should be remembered that there is evidence to suggest that violence is not only more often organised than haphazard, but also that it is more often approved (at least by the immediate society) than disapproved. 'The overwhelming bulk of the most destructive violence consists of organized conduct that is socially permitted, or encouraged, or enjoined as a right or duty. Most violence is not deviant behaviour, not disapproved conduct, but virtuous action in the service of applauded values' (Williams, 1981, p. 27). If this is so, then long-term problems will remain, not only amongst northerners, but ex-soldiers, even if peace is secured quickly. Abuses and lawlessness that seem a short cut to solving rebel activity may have disastrous long-term repercussions on popular attitudes to violence.

Undermining the Criminal Justice System

As disturbing as the UPDF abuses themselves is the apparent impunity with which these abuses are committed. There is a serious failure of criminal and political accountability. Whilst some police and soldiers have been arrested for human rights abuses, few have been brought to court, as weaknesses and overload in the criminal justice system delay trials of soldiers almost indefinitely. In the slander case (mentioned above) against the press over the account of the woman allegedly sexually abused by soldiers in the Gulu army barracks, the prosecution failed. But as yet the soldiers themselves have not been prosecuted. It has not been easy to ensure that the Government and public officials in charge of policy related to the conflict remain subject to the law, with prosecutors hardly knowing where to start and anxious about political interference.

Meanwhile the very abuse of the criminal justice system by the UPDF in continuing 'to arrest and charge persons for treason, especially captured rebel fighters', has overwhelmed the system with greater numbers than it can manage (US Department of State, 2000). The strain is not helped by the fact that rural police stations and sub-courts have been closed on the grounds of being vulnerable to LRA attacks. The frustration is also felt by the police who, according to one report, are not able to carry out effective investigations and have developed a culture of beating as a normal method of inquiry (Amnesty International, 1999a).

The civilian justice system for most people, therefore, either scarcely exists or is not seen to be fair — both serious defects in a democracy built on the rule of law.

Conclusion

No one imagines that handling internal security crises such as guerrilla and terrorist warfare within the constraints of national and international law is easy. The enemy is elusive, dangerous and, in Uganda's case, barbarous. Yet the problem should not just be seen by the Government in the narrow terms of how to secure military victory. Rather, it concerns as well issues of keeping under strict discipline the ground troops so that they do not over-react and ensuring that officers are well-versed in law and legal procedures when it comes to counter-terrorist strategies and processing alleged rebels. This makes the whole operation much more problematic, but failure here will have implications for the political development of the north and of the country as a whole. The tragedy of the UPDF's actions in the north is not just that their military strategy has failed, but that the lawless way that they have conducted themselves at times has had a serious detrimental effect on important aspects of democracy. Lawless law enforcement comes with a heavy price.

Notes

1. The cattle population in Kitgum district alone fell from 156,000 in 1986 to 3,239 in 1998.
2. See also Pirouet, L. (1994), 'Human Rights issues in Museveni's Uganda', in H. Hansen and M. Twaddle (eds), *Changing Uganda*, Currey, London.
3. The confusion, together with the group's adoption and adaptation of certain Christian rituals and commands, presumably explains why so many speak erroneously of the Movement as a 'fundamentalist Christian group.'
4. Alice Lakwena lives now in the Dadaab refugee camp, Kenya. Talking to reporters in June 2001 she insisted that she had not lost her vision: 'I am a prophet who is inspired to bring good to the world by alleviating the suffering of my people.' She is convinced that her army failed only because 'the boys became indisciplined... they were disobeying the spirit. They were looting and indulging in sex' (reported in *The Nation*, Nairobi, 2 July, 2001).
5. One girl, abducted in 1994 for two years, recalled that 'You have to obey the Spirit's command. For example the Spirit may say "you must not kill any chicken for the next three weeks. Then after three weeks, when you kill a chicken, then you can start killing people"...During 1992, when you had been captive one week, they tied a necklace round your neck. They said that the Spirit dwells in the necklace.' A young boy, taken in 1995 said, 'From Sudan, when we were to return into Uganda, Kony holds a big ceremony, Spirit Appraisal. The Spirit tells us what will happen. If it says 5 of the rebels will die, then 5 will die. The Spirit says "Go and kill a lady from a particular place, a centre or village". If you do it your path will be safe. If you believe in the Spirit it works. If you don't believe, then it won't work' (Oxfam, 2000e).
6. The UPDA local units plundered and terrorized the populace to secure food from the beginning of the movement's formation (Behrend, 1999c, pp. 25, 56).
7. See also Els de Temmerman, *Aboke Girls: Children Abducted in Northern Uganda*, Fountain Publishers, Kampala, 2001.
8. President Bashir admitted in August, 2001: 'we used to support the LRA. We used to provide them with logistics, ammunition and everything. That was a response to support Uganda used to give to SPLA' (*New Vision*, 21 August, 2001).
9. Of some 14,000 children abducted since 1987, up to 5,144 remain missing as of January 2001 according to the Gulu Support the Children Organisation. UNICEF gives the figures as 9,818 children and 18,399 adults abducted between 1990 and September 2001.
10. *New Vision*, 13 June, 2001.
11. *Africa Research Bulletin*, 35, 7, 1998, p. 13195.
12. One time LRA official spokesman, David Matsanga, said they were 'A fifth column of the Sudanese army' *Africa Research Bulletin*, 36, 4, 1999, p. 13523.
13. *New Vision*, 23 March, 2001.
14. *Economist*, 23 March, 1996.
15. *Mail & Guardian*, 23 August, 1996.

78 *Taking the Law into Their Own Hands*

16 In July 2001 Museveni admitted that whilst the level of absolute poverty had reduced from 56 per cent to 35 per cent in most of the country in the last three years, in northern Uganda the figure had risen from 60 per cent to 66 per cent (*The Monitor*, 30 July, 2001).
17 Soldiers and civilians are accused of widespread raping of women and children in Gulu protected camps by Human Rights Focus, Gulu (reported in *The Monitor*, 10 May, 2001).
18 *Africa Research Bulletin*, 36, 1, 1999, p. 13416.
19 *New Vision*, 23 March, 2001.
20 IRIN website, 25 July, 2001.
21 *Africa Research Bulletin*, 35, 6, 1998, p. 13158.
22 *Africa Research Bulletin*, 1998, p. 12964.
23 For example, an Acholi women's pressure group within the Uganda Women's Network or UWONET; a multi-denominational church leaders group; even USAID in its report, *The Anguish of Northern Uganda*. They have tried to organise humanitarian aid and the publication of reports on the war victims.
24 *Africa Research Bulletin*, 35, 5, 1998, p. 13124.
25 But see *Africa Research Bulletin*, 36, 5, 1999, p. 13557.
26 In June 2001 the LC5 Gulu Chairman made contact with the LRA leadership (with the support of NGOs like Gulu Support the Children Organisation and World Vision) and claimed that the LRA wanted to persist with the informal ceasefire. The UPDF, however, poured scorn on the talks. In a statement they opposed the demand of the LRA not to attack them during the talks and claimed that the LRA was planning fresh attacks (*New Vision*, 18 June, 2001).
27 *Africa Research Bulletin*, 37, 2, 2000, p. 13860.
28 *New Vision*, 30 May, 2001.
29 In contrast, George Omona, Project Coordinator, Gulu Support the Children Organisation, reported that he was told by one ex child soldier to tell the international community 'I have been in this thing, I have fought so many battles with the SPLA, I have fought with the Uganda Government, neither the Government of Uganda nor the LRA can solve this problem militarily. So the only message is dialogue' (reported on www.antislavery.org, accessed 19 June, 2001)
30 *Economist*, 23 March, 1996.
31 *Africa Research Bulletin*, 37, 1, 2000, p. 13846.
32 The Minister of Internal Affairs said in April 2001 that they had a list of Kony rebel collaborators and were planning to crack down on them, although the Minister of State for the North had said in March that the Government was engaged in direct efforts to link with the rebel leaders.
33 As of July 2001. He expects 50,000 rebels to return once the implementation exercise begins. The Commission needs $176.5 million yearly to run. (*The East African*, 23 July, 2001).
34 *Africa Research Bulletin*, 35, 10, 1998, p. 13303.
35 CPJ web site, www.cpj.org, accessed 11 January, 2000.
36 Quoted in the *Monitor*, 12 May, 1999.
37 See accounts of UPDF harassment of campaigners for incumbent MP, Ronald Okumu in *The Monitor*, 29 May, 2001; and of Museveni's partisan campaigning in Lira to unseat Cecilia Ogwal MP in *New Vision*, 25 June, 2001. According to *New Vision*, 29 June, 2001, 30 people were beaten up in Gulu city during a curfew aimed at stopping 'unnecessary and excessive election victory celebrations.'

38 *New Vision* reported on 20 March, 2001 that over 1000 UPDF veterans in Kitgum district had been mobilised and registered to wage war against the Government.
39 *East African*, 28 May, 2001.
40 *Africa Research Bulletin*, 35, 6, 1998, p. 13158.
41 Commander Kajabago Karushoke, quoted in *The Nation*, 2 July, 2001.
42 *The East African*, 9 April, 2001.
43 *The Monitor*, 8 April, 1997.
44 Quoted in Human Rights Watch, (1997), *Scars of Death*, New York, p. 14.

Figure 4.1   Casamance, Senegal

4 The Senegalese Army and the Casamance Secessionists

The Origin and Nature of the Insurgency

Casamance is the region in southern Senegal that lies south of The Gambia River and the state of The Gambia. Many of the 900,000 people of this region have never felt part of the independent, largely Muslim and Wolof dominated, Senegalese state.[1] They are not only physically detached from the main body of the nation, but are culturally distinct, being themselves predominantly Diola and Catholic/animist in religion. This means that they have close links with those in The Gambia and Guinea-Bissau and explains the presence of Casamançais in both the war of independence and the civil war in Guinea Bissau. The area has not been so deprived of Government assistance in recent years as in the earlier days of independence. It is, nevertheless, only loosely integrated into the political economy of Senegal and just one bridge across The Gambia River links Dakar to the main town of Casamance, Ziguinchor. Not surprisingly, Diola still say, when going to Dakar, that they are 'going to Senegal' (Linares, 1992, p. 212). Certainly the perception of the Diola is that they are both ignored by the central Government and colonised by the 'nordistes' (northerners). Since the land tenure reform of 1972 there has been large scale immigration into the area by northerners, who have received preferential treatment in the redistribution of land. The Democratic League/Labour Party Movement claims that between '1980-81, about 2,000 parcels of land were expropriated or allocated exclusively to non-indigenes in...districts of Ziguinchor' (quoted in Dykman, 2000, p. 10). The result was that local people were driven to the outskirts of the city where there was no electricity, running water or health clinics. 'This has created in the Casamance population a real feeling of being dominated by strangers who occupy all the posts in the administration, in education and private enterprise (Trincaz, quoted in Linares, 1992, p. 222). Sekou Diatta, head of the Evangelic Fraternity of Senegal claims:

> The local population in Casamance is bitter that northerners have taken all the plots in Ziguinchor, the provincial capital and pushed them to the forests and robbed them of their trade in fish and prawns thus creating perpetual unemployment. Woodcutters from the north hew down their forests...During the mango season [you can see] the rotting fruits for want of a market. Northerners come with their lorries to buy them cheaply so as to sell them dearly in Dakar. This creates a lot of bitterness among the helpless unemployed people.[2]

Though the Government introduced a decentralisation programme giving greater autonomy to the regions, this has done little to defuse the discontent in Casamance, for in the regional elections of 1996 'there was widespread fraud and procedural irregularities, gerrymandering, illegal fundraising, and voter list manipulations' (US Department of State, 2000). The ruling party, then the Socialist Party (PS), secured control of all the regional councils.

The movement that leads the fight for secession is the Mouvement des forces démocratiques de la Casamance (MFDC). It was set up following a pro-Casamance independence demonstration in Ziguinchor, in December 1982 (Darbon, 1984).[3] Initially they only organised demonstrations, but the Government deemed that the movement was a threat and determined to break it by force. In a violent demonstration in 1983 hundreds of demonstrators were imprisoned with sentences ranging from two to fifteen years. Yet eight years of this tactic produced no political response, but only severe military and judicial suppression. Seeing itself not only as the victim of political manoeuvring that incorporated the region into Senegal, but as the victim of state violence, The Movement adopted a policy in 1990 of armed rebellion. With covert support from neighbouring Guinea Bissau,[4] it set up an armed wing known as Atika ('Warrior').

The Senegalese Government's response to secessionism has always been that of insisting on state territorial integrity, namely that they have an inalienable and absolute right to the exclusive ownership of the land (Diaw and Diouf, 1998, p. 272). President Diouf spoke of the 'permanent and historical fact' that Casamance was an integral part of Senegal, hence the Government could not 'allow an inch of the national territory to slip out of its authority.' He was adamant that 'the situation does not require a national conference, but a mobilisation of the nation around the head of state, to help the national army fulfil its mission of defending the territorial integrity and national unity.'[5] His Government's 1998 policy paper on the Casamance conflict offered no compromise solutions, but only a refutation of the claims of the secessionists, the affirmation that Casamance had always been an integral part of Senegal and the insistence that to question national sovereignty was disallowed by the Constitution. Likewise, the current president, Abdoulaye Wade, argues, somewhat ingenuously:

> I am not thinking along the lines of independence for Casamance for the simple reason that Casamance does not want independence. The constitutional referendum I presented to the people on 7 January [2001] was for a united and indivisible Senegalese republic, and 76 percent of the people of Casamance region voted and 75 percent voted yes to the constitution... I am talking to the pro-independence leaders of Casamance and the curious thing is that none of them has talked to me about independence... There was nothing in [the programme we have signed] about independence.[6]

Apart from short cease-fires in 1991, 1993, 1995 and 1999, and the peace agreement of 2001, the MFDC has maintained (at least in elements of the Front sud of the organisation) armed conflict with the Government forces to the present day. There are frequent small arms attacks, ambushes and clashes with the military and soldiers that have been taken prisoner have been executed. They are also responsible for attacks on civilians to obtain supplies. Fuel, livestock, produce and cash are commonly seized from villagers, or demanded on pain of beating, the burning of their homes or even death. In addition, they have attacked those villages thought to have supported the security forces, executing alleged Government collaborators (such as leading figures in the ruling party), abducting women and destroying food supplies (US Department of State, 2001). Premeditated attacks on villagers, particularly on the non-Diola population, have included one in 1997 on a youth centre in Djibanar that left 10 young people dead, including two girls of six and eight (Amnesty International, 1998, pp. 5, 45), one in 1999 when seven fishermen in the village of Saloulou were killed, and one on the village of Singuere that left six dead. Their widespread and indiscriminate use of land mines, used in an effort to terrorise both the Government security forces and the civilian population, has killed many. RADDHO (Recontre africaine pour la defense des droits de l'homme), a Dakar based human rights organisation, estimates that between 1997 and 1998 land mines killed and injured some 500 civilians in the Casamance (US Department of State, 2000). They continued to lay mines in 1999 and 2000 to protect themselves and their economic assets such as cannabis fields and to prevent farmers' access to their fields. There were 195 victims of anti-personnel mines registered in 1998 and 59 in 1999.[7]

A split occurred in the Movement following the cease-fire in 1992. The Front nord (northern front), renounced the armed struggle, whilst the Front sud (southern front) continued. The Front sud itself split over a ceasefire negotiated by its Secretary-General, Father Diamacoune Senghor, in 1999. In talks with former President Diouf, he agreed to disarm and to drop the demand for independence on condition that the Government provided greater socio-economic development of Casamance. In addition, according to some, it was agreed that the Movement would be recognised as a political party.

Many of the MFDC's military wing, however, were not prepared for anything less than full-scale independence and continued to fight throughout the negotiations and after the election of the new Senegalese President, Abdoulaye Wade, in March 2000. They gave little credence to the new president's assertion that one of his main priorities in office was a 'global package' for Casamance, entailing pacification, the removal of land mines, the sinking of bore holes for irrigation, the re-establishment of rice growing, fishing and tourism, and locating the second presidential residence there.[8] During 2001 the MFDC underwent an internal struggle between those wanting to reach a settlement and those wanting to continue with the armed struggle. The latter won the day. Diamacoune was replaced as Secretary General and given the largely ceremonial post of President. Meanwhile the rebels escalated the fighting. They mined roads, attacked and robbed villages, looted shops and began to attack civilian road convoys.[9]

It is thought that in the course of the 19-year war something like 3,000 people have been seriously wounded or killed.[10] Many villagers have fled to the towns or across the Guinea-Bissau and Gambian borders to escape the threats and intimidation of the rebels. 5,000 Casamançais refugees were registered in The Gambia in June 2001. A further 38,000 people have been internally displaced.[11]

The Response of the State Security Forces

The overall strategy of the Senegalese Government towards the rebels, as in Uganda, has primarily been to use armed force. This has the two-fold purpose of defending the territorial integrity of Senegal and of deliberately keeping the civilian population of Casamance in a state of terror to repay and undermine support for the rebels. In the course of the conflict the region has been increasingly militarised. A military governor was appointed 1990-91 and approximately 5-6,000 Senegalese security forces, of a total army strength of 17,000, have been employed on a more or less continuous basis throughout the trouble in the two administrative regions of Casamance, Ziguinchor and Kolda. They comprise the army, the paramilitary gendarmerie (particularly the Gendarmes' Intervention Legion, the LGI) and the police (particularly the Mobile Intervention Group, the GMI). The army has made large-scale arrests in an attempt to destroy the MFDC's chain of command and has also conducted very large sweeps with ground troops and air attacks of the rebel held areas, particularly along the Guinea-Bissau border, aimed at flushing out the secessionists and capturing their bases. These took place in 1992, in 1994 when they were aided by French reconnaissance aircraft, in 1996 and 1997 when they had support from the forces of the Guinea-Bissau. They have also taken place since President Wade's peace accords of March 2001, with a concerted assault on rebel bases near the border with The Gambia being launched in June, destroying a number of villages and causing more than 2,000 to flee into The Gambia for safety.[12] Yet, as in Uganda, military force has proved an inadequate response to a region with real political, economic and social disadvantages. Similarly, it has run into the same problems that are always associated with unloosing an army not trained to apprehend internal lawbreakers and secure their conviction before a court of law. The real threat to life in which troops are placed by ambushes and mines inevitably makes soldiers prone to disregard the restraints of law. Even the gendarmerie and police, who are used to internal policing, are prone to use excessive force when under political pressure to curb prolonged insurgency. Securing evidence that will stand up in court from a public that is either cowed or supportive of the rebels has largely proved to be beyond their resources and will.

Attacks and retaliations form a continuous cycle and neither side has been willing or able to halt their combatants' human rights abuses. Concerning the army's conduct, they have been accused of arrests without trial, summary executions and torture. Though human rights organisations have offered the Government detailed evidence about these, the practices appear to have continued and even increased over recent years. This reluctance to curb abuses is despite the fact that in 1997 the Government enacted a law to strengthen the National Committee on Human Rights. This Committee, which includes members from the Government and civic organisations, including human rights groups, failed to investigate a single case of abuse during 1999 (US Department of State, 2000). Amnesty International takes the view that in the light of the generally good record of the Senegalese security forces for discipline and clear command structure elsewhere, it is difficult to dismiss evidence of the security personnel taking the law into their own hands as simply unrepresentative action by renegade individuals. They argue that the abuses are so regular and widespread that they must be seen as part of Government policy in its prosecution of the war and therefore 'the responsibility of the highest authorities of the State' (Amnesty International, 1998, p. 42). On the other hand, it is reported that the army is poorly equipped, that salaries are sometimes paid late and that the soldiers are demoralised in a war they cannot win as long as the MFDC bases lie outside the country. In fact there are reports that at times they have refused to fight during recent MFDC attacks (Evans, 2000, pp. 656-7). Whatever the case, the security forces commonly ignore Senegal's Constitution and Penal Code and the international conventions on human rights. In their pursuit of eliminating the MFDC and undermining its support base, legal requirements are neglected, as the evidence presented below demonstrates. Much of this evidence is concealed from the public, which explains the extraordinary levels of support for the army as an institution that have been found across the country. For instance in a 1999 Senegal Values Survey, more confidence was expressed in the armed forces than any other single national institution. 59.3 percent said their confidence in the army was 'very strong' and 32.1 percent said they had 'some confidence'. Only 1.6 percent said they had 'no confidence'. Even among those who identified themselves as supporters of the then opposition parties, 49.1 percent had 'very strong confidence' (Vengroff and Magala, 2001, pp. 148-9).

Extrajudicial Killings

Over the past 19 years there have been dozens of cases of rebels dying in detention or simply disappearing without trace. The likelihood is that many of these have died as a result of extrajudicial killings committed by the security forces, or at least as a result of the use of excessive force in their detention. Witnesses report how soldiers burst into homes and kill people on the spot. For example, according to local press reports, on 1 April, 1999 Government security forces looking for rebels, stormed a house in the town of Thionck Essyl and shot dead a young man who was fleeing from the house. Apparently neither the man nor his family had any connection with the MFDC (US Department of State, 2000). There are several other reports of persons shot or their throats slit, at roadblocks (Amnesty International, 1998, pp. 36-7). The motive often appears to be in reprisal for MFDC arbitrary killings of soldiers. RADDHO claimed that on 3 June 1999, in response to a rocket launch attack by MFDC rebels, Government security forces undertook a 'clean-up operation', during which several persons suspected of rebel activity were killed and many arrested, whose whereabouts have never been revealed (US Department of State, 2000).

The disappearance, following arrest by the security forces, of known or suspected rebels is a common feature. According to RADDHO's 1999 report, 10 arrested during the course of 1999 remained unaccounted for at the end of the year. They included two civilians arrested in September and December 1998 respectively; three of fifteen suspected rebels rounded up in April 1999; seven civilians who disappeared in June 1999 after a military clean-up operation; a young man, taken from his house in Ziguinchor in July 1999; and another abducted by soldiers in August 1999 (US Department of State, 2000). The discovery of two mass graves at Niaguis and Niambalang Bridge may well be connected with these disappearances. Corroborating this accusation is the testimony secured from Senegalese soldiers under the guarantee of confidentiality. One said:

> The army executes people. People who have no identity card are regularly arrested and executed; several people have been buried at Nyassia, Niambalang and Lindiane. As soon as someone is arrested, they are taken to the camp; suspects are questioned by the lieutenant-captain; they are pushed around, tortured, told to dig a hole and executed. Torture by pouring molten plastic over people is commonplace (Amnesty International, 1998, pp. 41-2).

An investigative team to the Casamance area from RADDHO in October 2000 concluded that there was a net improvement in the behaviour of the army in the area, and the populations were no longer reporting torture and extra judicial executions. Nevertheless the practice continued of arresting 'people suspected of offences' and handing them over to the justice authorities.[13]

Irregular Arrests and Detention

The Senegalese Constitution, Penal Code and International Law carefully prescribe conditions for arrests and detention, but the requirements are frequently ignored. Warrants issued by judges are required for arrests, although police may hold without charge a suspect for 48 hours and for 96 hours in the case of crimes against State security. During the initial 48 hours of detention the accused has no access to family or a lawyer. If the prosecutor decides to forward the case to an investigating judge, then the suspects are provisionally charged and detained (bail is rarely used). The accused may be held in custody for six months. But the investigating magistrate can extend it for an additional six-months. In practice the authorities may detain a prisoner for long periods of time while they investigate and build a case against a suspect. They also routinely hold prisoners in custody unless and until a court demands their release. Despite the six-month limitation on detention, the time between the charging phase and trial averages two years.

Many problems also arise from the fact that the army assumes police roles in Casamance and makes most of the arrests:

> [They] immediately use torture against the people they have arrested, using lists of suspects drawn up by the gendarmerie on the basis of anonymous denunciations. These acts of torture are not used to obtain confessions to be included in any judicial statement. The army has no mandate to conduct investigations. Its remit is merely to arrest suspects and hand them over to the gendarmes, who are the only ones empowered in their capacity as *officers de police judiciaire*, to conduct interrogations. This means that torture is being used by soldiers as revenge for loss of life or in order to terrify civilians who fall into their hands (Amnesty International, 1998, p. 24).

Most of the hundreds arrested have not been arrested during fighting or whilst in possession of arms, but in their homes or workplaces and on the basis of anonymous accusations, which are by definition unverifiable and possibly malicious. They may even be rounded up as suspected rebels on the basis of their Diola names. There are also cases of hostage taking. One man reported:

> The soldiers had gone to my home to arrest me. Since I was not there, they took two of my children to the camp. 'Your father is a rebel' the soldiers told them. 'He has helped to feed the rebels and given them shelter.' Although threatened with death if they didn't confess, my children said their father had never been a rebel...Unable to get anything out of them, the soldiers let them go (Amnesty International, 1998, p. 15).

The International Covenant on Civil and Political Rights requires that any person detained be informed of the charges brought against them and be brought before a judge as soon as possible or be released. Nevertheless many of those arrested have been in prison for long periods without trial and have endured violence at the hands of the gendarmes. Where charges are preferred, prisoners do not usually get the opportunity of reading, or having read to them, the judicial statement of their interrogation and their forced 'confession', before being required to sign it. The charge is normally one of 'threatening State security and the integrity of the nation' or 'participating in a rebel group.' The general lack of charges and trials indicates that prisoners are held primarily for political reasons, to serve as a bargaining chip in the Government's talks with the MFDC. Thus, when the State wanted to facilitate dialogue in 1999, it released 167 suspected MFDC members who had been detained without trial, some for several years. There were about 60 suspected MFDC rebels left in prisons without trial at the end of 1999. Revealingly, some prisoners were told on being released, 'the future depends upon you. If you stay peacefully in your village, more prisoners will be released...The Senegalese government has made a gesture; now it is up to you to make one' (Amnesty International, 1998, p. 20). In other words, those arrested were hostages, not suspected lawbreakers. This policy is also apparent in the authorities treatment of the MFDC leadership. Father Diamacoune Senghor was held in detention from April to December 1991 and was under house arrest for most of the period from April 1995 to July 1999 without ever appearing before a magistrate or having charges brought against him. Likewise, four members of the MFDC's national bureau were also arrested in 1995 and held under house arrest until April 1997, when they were released to travel to France to engage with the Movement's external wing prior to the peace talks.

Torture

Despite torture, beatings and degrading treatment being outlawed by The Senegalese Penal Code and by the UN Convention against Torture and other Cruel, Inhuman and Degrading Treatment of Punishment (ratified by Senegal in 1986), they are practiced widely and with impunity by the military, gendarmerie and police. There is extensive testimony that the security forces systematically use torture, usually beating, on those suspected of being rebels or of assisting them, including the elderly, women and young people. Another frequent method is the 'monkey walk' which consists of making detainees walk in line, bent over, with one hand between their legs holding the hand of the detainee behind them, while they are beaten on the back. Some instances seem to be gratuitous violence; other to be acts of revenge for the death of soldiers in rebel attacks. They are also intended both to extract confessions and leading information, and to have a deterrent effect on those who would support the MFDC, particularly when carried out before the victim's families. There are eyewitness reports of beatings with rifles, batons and whips; the use of electric shocks; the burning of bodies with melting plastic or cigarettes; hanging prisoners upside down; forcing the ingestion of harmful products; and maiming.

A former prisoner recalled:

> They [soldiers] began to beat us for no reason. They slapped us with both hands, kicked us and hit us with their rifle butts. Then they took us to an office where they flogged us with whips. They smoked cigarettes and stubbed them out on our bodies. They tore hair from our beards and moustaches; they cut my hair and forced me to eat it (Amnesty International, 1998, p. 22).

One 73-year-old suspect reported that when he was taken to the gendarmerie brigade:

> From eight o'clock in the morning until midday, I was tied up with my hands and feet bound behind my back and I was interrogated and beaten while in this position. They accused me of being an informer for the rebels...They poured solvent on my genitals...I suffered from [its] burns for more than 20 hours (Amnesty International, 1998, p. 30).

The lawless conduct of the security forces detailed above, speaks of a security system that is largely unused to acting within a democratic framework.

The Democratic Impact

The Casamance insurgency as a whole and the at times lawless reaction of the Senegalese army in particular has not only affected the people of Casamance, but has had a detrimental impact on the procedures, processes and values that constitute democracy in the country. The varied effects on the political, social and legal aspects of democracy are explored below. It has already been recorded that, despite the conduct of the armed forces, there are extraordinarily high levels of confidence across the country in the armed forces as an institution. This may well be due to ignorance of what actually is happening in Casamance, but it does mean that many of the effects of the abuses reported above are going to have a muted impact outside of the region.

An Escalation of the Violence

Where the security forces are an instrument of coercion and extortion in their own country, they will provoke opposition to the rule of the state. This is even more so if its coercion is beyond the limits of legality. Each injury or death that is the result of injustice and inhumanity leads to retaliation, which in turn provokes further abuses by the security forces to revenge the losses. Despite occasional cease-fires, tit for tat attacks by both sides in the Casamance hostilities have been more or less continuous. As the region has been militarised, insurgents have launched assaults on civilians and economic targets and on the army. Meanwhile the army has retaliated with its own violence, legal and illegal. Deaths have run into hundreds each year; not just of fighters on both sides, but of civilians caught in the crossfire. Yet in the logic of rebellion this only encourages further assaults rather than less. Thus members of the internal political wing of the MFDC, at a meeting in June 2001 to discuss future policy, spoke of the need to maintain the struggle. To do otherwise, they claimed, would mean a 'disservice to our dead comrades in the struggle to liberate Casamance from bondage'.[14]

The principal hope in breaking this cycle of violence must be that at least elements of the Government and MFDC now see the futility of persisting in it. They have yet to persuade their own forces and probably lack the necessary discipline over them to enforce it.

Violence is Becoming the Language of Political Communication

When violence is used so extensively and with so little regard for human rights and the law, the parties to the conflict readily assume that negotiation is futile. They become so locked into a commitment to violence that they become deaf to alternatives or at least cynical about peace negotiations.

The account of the peace negotiations is one of prolonged failure. Peace talks and an agreed cease-fire in May 1991 led to the removal of the military governor and the release of 400 detainees. However the peace broke down in December 1991, following the killing of a PS (Socialist Party) deputy and a local village chief, although the MFDC denied responsibility. The Government began a new initiative in January 1992, setting up a Peace Commission with representatives from the Government and the MFDC. Yet following the killing of a police officer in July and violent clashes in August in Ziguinchor, the Government authorised a large army operation. Negotiations finally broke down in October 1992, following MFDC attacks on civilians and soldiers. The army retaliated with another major security operation in December 1992. Despite serious armed clashes in March 1993, the Government said in the April that it was willing to observe a truce and by July of that year the two parties signed a ceasefire. Although the rebels were frustrated by the slow progress of the talks and of the promised economic initiatives, the peace more or less held until four French tourists went missing. The MFDC denied involvement in any abduction, but the army, assuming their guilt, began a major operation against the rebels and the MFDC resumed its attacks. A further attempt at peace was begun in September 1995 when the Government set up the Commission Nationale pour la Paix en Casamance (CNP) to act as a mediator between themselves and the MFDC. It began talks with the MFDC leadership, but renewed attacks in October by rebels led to another army offensive. With the CNP's help, a meeting was held between Diamacoune and the Government in December 1995. Diamacoune issued an appeal to the MFDC to lay down arms and called for exploratory talks to begin, to be followed by peace negotiations in a neutral country. The Government responded by releasing members of the MFDC's political bureau and 50 other detainees. With a truce in place, formal peace talks began, but they rapidly stalled over the Government's refusal to allow MFDC representatives to go to France to meet with external supporters. Relations further soured in July 1996 after three soldiers were killed and the MFDC had issued a warning to the army not to enter territory that it controlled. Talks began again in August 1996 between Diamacoune and Diouf's private chief of staff. Yet following armed clashes between the army and the rebel forces in March, July and August, the army launched yet another major offensive during September to October and in January 1998 worked alongside the Guinea-Bissau army in a border operation. Diamacoune indicated in January 1998 that the MFDC would give up its demands for independence in return for economic and social development. However, by March serious clashes had occurred between the MFDC and army and the army launched a new operation, shelling rebel positions and villages in August 1998. Then, following talks between President Diouf and Father Diamacoune Senghor, a peace deal did seem to be reached in December 1999. The Government promised a five year economic development plan for the region that would include mine clearance, the reinforcement of border security, assistance to displaced people, the reconstruction of bridges, the regional hospital and airport, and the recognition of the Movement as a party. In return, Father Diamacoune Senghor offered disarmament and to drop, at least for the time being, demands for independence.[15] A conference of MFDC was held in June in The Gambia, which reiterated their commitment to peace and negotiations.

Hence, although there were repeated peace talks, they invariably failed following fresh outbreaks of violence involving armed forces of both sides. It is arguable whether these incidents reflect bad luck, elements of the armed forces not under adequate political control or deliberate sabotage of the negotiations by the armed forces of one side or the other. Whatever the appearance of these repeated Government 'peace initiatives', the reality is that the Government has in the past relied on a military solution, that is, military success by any means. Thus there have been the large army operations in 1992, 1994, 1996, 1997, 2001 and 2002; the willingness to tolerate arbitrary arrests and the torturing of prisoners; and the use of detainees as negotiating pawns. All the indications have been that the Government, or at least the army, has been intent on a military solution notwithstanding the rhetoric. Such policies have a momentum of their own that condones the violation of human rights. Illicit violence that fails is seen as requiring not so much the cessation of violence, as its intensification.

During the later stages of Diouf's presidency, however, and into Wade's presidency, there emerged an increasingly vocal peace movement calling for negotiations. In one display of support in August 2000, women's organisations staged a march in Ziguinchor demanding an end to the insecurity and for the return of displaced persons.[16] Later in the year, 4,000 schoolchildren marched for peace in Ziguinchor, prior to talks between the Government and the MFDC, leaving a statement calling for peace at the home of MFDC leader Diamacoune Senghor and the area governor's residence.[17] Then in July 2001, farmers associations undertook a 60 km walk for peace through areas where there had recently been fighting.[18]

President Wade began his Casamance policy slowly. RADDHO referred to his policy as 'delaying tactics, the strategy of keeping negotiations confidential and the total absence of transparency', due either to 'the absence of a clear perspective for peace in Casamance or simply an extreme caution that paralyses the action of the President of the Republic.'[19] But in time Wade seemed to inject some urgency into a peaceful resolution of the conflict and met Diamacoune. He reached two accords with him, signed in March 2001. Elements of the deal included: surrender and destruction of MFDC weapons; encampment of MFDC forces; return of military to barracks; release of all political and rebel detainees; exchange of prisoners in due course; end by both sides of arbitrary arrests, abductions, torture, extrajudicial killings; free movement of people and goods and end of highway robberies; return of refugees and internally displaced persons; mine clearance; commencement of economic and social development programmes; and implementation of road construction projects.

Though 16 MFDC members were released in March, doubts still persist over the commitment of the army. A sustained military campaign that has at times exceeded legal restraint has a momentum of its own. Persistent failure at negotiation confirms the need to use force, whilst the possibility of judicial inquiries into army abuses following a settlement greatly reduces its attraction. Peace talks scheduled for May were postponed after a week long attack on rebel bases that left more than 100 dead and more than 200 displaced. Meanwhile Guinea Bissau troops burnt villages populated by Casamance refugees in search of MFDC members, driving them back to Senegal. The Senegalese army, for its part, is still obviously suspicious. When a senior army officer, prior to a major new operation against the rebels on the Gambian border in June 2001, was asked if he thought there could be a military solution to the conflict he said, 'If 20 years of diplomacy cannot end the conflict, a military option is only logical'.[20]

There are also doubts about whether the agreement will have full MFDC backing, since no prior MFDC congress was held of the internal, military and external wings; some of the key political and military leaders were absent from the negotiations; and no agreement was reached about the status of Casamance. In other words, Diamacoune, faced with a divided MFDC, decided to go it alone in the hope of bouncing the entire Movement into following him so as to secure the economic benefits of peace, even without the formal political settlement. But at the Movement's forum in summer 2001 he paid the price by loosing his role as secretary general, being given the largely ceremonial post of President. Nor was there any agreement at the conference since, faced with an army that clearly believed in a military solution by any means, the hardline faction felt that force must be met with force.[21]

Government News Management

In the conflict of discourses in the insurgency, the Government, as much as the MFDC, energetically interprets and justifies the actions of its army and demonises the 'enemy' for their atrocities. Every incident of alleged lawlessness by Senegalese troops is therefore hotly disputed by spokespersons of both sides. The army and Government either denies it, or says the rebels committed it, whilst the MFDC denounces the army and portrays itself as a victimised minority which is justified in hitting back at the state. Both are intent on delegitimising the other and legitimising themselves. For example, the MFDC spokesperson in The Gambia, Alexandre Djiba, said in October 2000 that, 'most of the fighting in

Casamance has been provoked by the Senegalese army and security forces who are terrorising the population in Casamance.' Of the attack on Ziguinchor in September he said; 'We all know that the attackers were wearing the uniform of the Senegalese army. The MFDC has never distributed such uniforms to its fighters. As a matter of fact, Atika, our army, does not own such specific outfit of a regular army.'[22]

A conflicting interpretation of the lack of peace negotiations has characterised both sides as well. The Government put it out in the Senegalese daily, *Sud*, in October 2000, that the minister for the Armed Forces had made direct secret contacts with the MFDC, that is, that the Government was doing its best, but that the intransigence was to be found among the rebels. Yet the MFDC publicly denied there had been any and accused the army of propaganda and of trying to manipulate groups within the rebel movement. In other words, it wanted to cast the Government as the one prolonging the war.[23] And who has been responsible for the highway attacks during and after the March 2001 peace settlement that have threatened to undermine it? The MFDC dissident group, say the Government; common bandits, says Diamacoune. And of course there are always two sides to casualty rates. Few communiqués come from the Senegalese army about the number of lives lost, but overall they have admitted to no more than 100 dead over the entire duration of the conflict. On the other hand they claimed at least 300 rebels killed in the 1996 offensive alone.

Democracy should be a system that allows difference of opinion and criticism to be honestly debated prior to a settlement or compromise being reached. It requires that facts, not propaganda, be widely broadcast through an independent media. In Senegal before 1990, according to Lambert, the Casamançais nationalist position was concealed from public view:

> It was disseminated by word of mouth and through banned publications... With the outbreak of violence, discussions over why the Casamance should be independent moved out of the informal, at times clandestine, conversations and into the public arena. The violence drew national attention to Abbe Diamacoune Senghor and gave him the opportunity to present the MFDC's reading of the history of Casamance (1998, p. 588).

In Senegal there is, like Uganda, a broad spectrum of opinion available in the print media and five privately owned radio stations including political views often critical of the Government, although this does not apply to the Government controlled newspapers (e.g. *Le Soleil*) and television broadcasting. Though the Constitution provides for freedom of speech and of the press, there are laws that prohibit the expression of views that 'discredit' the State, incite the population to disorder, or disseminate 'false news.' As the law stands, the burden of proof rests with the accused in a defamation suit. 'This places the media in a quagmire, because building their case amounts to disclosing their sources. Journalists are convicted if they decline to provide the necessary documentation.'[24]

Denial is a common resort. Although cases of extrajudicial killings, 'disappearances' and other abuses of human rights by the security forces have been reported by human rights organisations over many years, the Government, 'continue to deny the truth of this information and have constructed a wall of impunity behind which those responsible can hide' (Amnesty International, 1998, p. 7). It has rarely responded to detailed accusations, or has dismissed the accusations as lies and fantasies not worthy of investigation. The Senegalese Minister of the Armed Forces told Parliament that one of Amnesty International's reports was 'an incredible story written by a Casamance secessionist officially identified by the Senegalese Government' (Amnesty International, 1998, p. 47). Similarly the Minister of Justice spoke of Amnesty International's 'fantastic communications and accusations, which rest on no evidence that can be produced' (Amnesty International, 1998, p. 47). The White Paper of October 1996 even went so far as to assert that security forces never arrested people unless they were in possession of arms or were known rebels. It claimed the Government had received no formal complaints from the relatives of 'pseudo-victims'; choosing to overlook the obvious fact that most would have feared reprisals.[25] In the same vein the Minister of the Armed Forces said that the army could not conduct inquiries into events it knew nothing about. He maintained that there had been no cases of extrajudicial killings and that disappearances were simply cases of people leaving home for personal reasons. In fact there *are* documented cases of people being brave enough to risk reprisals by lodging formal complaints, but no inquiry has ever been launched as a result (Amnesty International, 1998, p. 49). At the local level, too, there is a refusal to take action. Thus when a farmer accused the security forces of torturing him when in detention in September 1997 and took a medical report to his Prefect and his local mayor, he was simply told to go to the hospital for treatment (Amnesty International, 1998, p. 28). The closest the authorities have come to admitting that mistakes have been made by its security forces is when they have pleaded with complainants that they should view the incidents as an inevitable feature of war and that they should be forgotten since it was 'time to turn the page.'

If not in denial, the state has frequently resorted to severely restricting the news flow beyond a general outline of events (Dykman, 2000, p. 13). Fearing that the crisis might spread to other marginalised areas and raise the issue of national boundaries, information has been restricted to a trickle:

> The absence of real and objective information from the state-owned media has entailed some degree of indifference on the part of the Senegalese public opinion. Only the deaths of some of the soldiers in the southern region confer, from time to time, some reality to the crisis (Diaw and Diouf, 1998, p. 281).

Even when some 3,000 troops were sent to Guinea Bissau during their civil war, the television and radio news hardly mentioned the subject, the newspapers concentrated on an electricity strike and the Government refused to tell parliament how many casualties there had been.

Beyond denial and restriction of information, the Government has pursued a policy of intimidation of those who would criticise the security forces in Casamance or the Government's handling of the troubles. Wade's Government decided in August 2000 to sue a Dakar daily, *Le Matin*, for publishing false information likely to damage army and public morale, as well as state security. *Le Matin* had published an article alleging that heavily armed MFDC guerrillas were moving about freely in Ziguinchor. The National Security Council ordered an investigation into the validity of *Le Matin's* report, although charges were subsequently dropped. Presumably the episode was meant to be a salutary warning. Nevertheless in December 2000 the Wade Government issued a warning that anyone suspected of 'breaching or complicity in breaching national unity, particularly through the dissemination, propaganda or amplification of separatist views' (that is, of disseminating communications from the MFDC) would be regarded as attempting to sabotage the peace negotiations and would be prosecuted. On the same day the publisher and editor of *Le Populaire* were interrogated by the central intelligence after publishing a review of the Casamance conflict, and were charged with 'disseminating false news and undermining public security.' These charges, too, were subsequently dropped.[26]

If the Government actions to suppress news look anti-democratic, encouragement can be taken from the response of the independent press. They were unbowed: 'My goodness! It is serious and we're already trembling,' the weekly *Le Temoin* taunted. It noted that not nine months had passed before the so-called 'Government of change' was ordering journalists 'to give accurate information, meaning information they would receive obsequiously from the official commission in charge of negotiations, or... to shut up if they do not want to go to prison.' Commenting on the deterioration of these relations, *Nouvel Horizon* wonders: 'Are the authorities more nationalistic than the journalists? Is their desire for peace more than that of the press?'[27] Yet for all their maintenance of independence, the national press has rarely gone beyond presenting some of the previously neglected regional issues, with their main emphasis being on security in Casamance rather than development. While the Government have got something to hide, the situation is unlikely to change.

The Disruption of Party Politics

The Senegalese Government has been as anxious as the Ugandan Government to assure national and international publics of their democratic credentials. Every effort has therefore been made to allow elections to proceed, even in the troubled region of Casamance. In fact President Diouf actually began his Presidential election campaign in 1993 in Casamance, despite MFDC warnings that it would oppose such activity (Da Costa, 1993, p. 60).

The determination to proceed with elections has faced much greater challenges in Senegal than in Uganda. Violent assaults by both sides have characterised the election campaigns of recent years. As the rebels have used violence to prevent participation and to thus delegitimise the elections, so the army have used pre-emptive strikes to prevent the MFDC terrorism. 30 voters were killed by rebels on the day of the Presidential and Parliamentary elections of 1993, whilst during the National Assembly elections of 1998 there were dozens of fatalities. In the latter campaign, the MFDC attacked the airport, fired shells at a village to intimidate voters and generally succeeded in minimising turnout. 'MFDC fighters terrorized people to make them boycott the elections, because they challenged their legitimacy. Afterwards they also took punitive action ...against prominent personalities who had voted' (Paye and Diop, 1998, p. 339), especially senior figures in the ruling Socialist Party. One, for instance, was killed a week after receiving President Diouf (Amnesty International, 1998, p. 43). In two other incidents, a vehicle conveying election results hit a rebel mine killing 2 soldiers and rebels killed 6 when they attacked a funeral ceremony in Ziguinchor on polling day. For their part the army killed 30 rebels in an attack on rebel bases during the 1998 polling week to stop them carrying out disruption to the polls.[28] In the 2000 Presidential election there were several attacks and four deaths (two civilians, one soldier and a gendarme) in Casamance. In addition rebels cut off the electricity supplies to Ziguinchor and ransacked shops there.

The consequence of this insurgency and counter-insurgency violence has been to depress participation. Although in the May 1998 elections voter turnout averaged 47 percent in most parts of the country, it was only between 35 and 40 percent in southern Casamance, according to the Minister of the Interior.[29]

What has not happened, despite the long history of army lawlessness, is the aggregation of opposition support that has occurred in Uganda. This is in part because political parties based on ethnic loyalties are banned. But even the established national political parties, with few exceptions, have had little to offer the voters of Casamance specifically. The concern of the ruling Parti démoctratique sénégalais (PDS), when it was the major opposition party in the 1990s, was always to maintain its place of influence within the Government, whether in or outside formal coalition. As a result it seemed unwilling to raise the Casamançais' complaints about army abuses and economic neglect. It had no involvement in Casamance even when one of the party's local deputies was appointed as chairman of the PS Government sponsored Peace Management Committee. It was the small opposition parties outside the Presidential Majority, and Niasse, who led the criticism of the Government over their policy towards Casamance, through statements to the press calling for dialogue and national consultation.

Things may, however, be about to change. What was apparent in the 2000 Presidential election was the region's strong support for FAL (Le Front pour l'Alternance), the Wade/Niasse led coalition that, *inter alia*, criticised Diouf's handling of the Casamance question. It also enjoyed in the person of Niasse, someone endorsed by Cardinal Thiandoum, the leading figure in the Catholic church in Senegal; a fact of importance to Casamance's Catholics (Evans, 2000, p. 658). It was striking how, in the subsequent parliamentary election campaign in 2001, Ziguinchor received campaign visits from almost all the parties, each claiming to have the solution to the crisis. By this time Niasse had been dismissed as prime minister, but it did not appear to reduce his popularity. In the May 2001 parliamentary elections, when the opposition secured only 30 seats overall, Niasse's Alliance of Progressive Forces (AFP) took 11 of them.

In Uganda army violence has been seen as an issue mobilising political opposition. In Senegal the two main parties are too closely identified with government policy and the army to venture making it central to their agenda. Thus army conduct in Casamance not only contributes to the disruption of party politics and the obscuring of socio-economic issues under security concerns, but it also intimidates politicians from voicing concern.

The Plunder Economy

The long running insecurity is a tragedy for most people living in the conflict zone. The war has led to the closure of schools comprising 1,500 classrooms and disrupted the education of 22,000 pupils between 1990 and 1997.[30] Further, up to 80 per cent of the arable land in the areas of Ziguinchor, Sedhiou, Oussouy, and Bignona are unusable due to land mines (RADDHO, quoted in US Department of State, 2000).

Yet for some, particularly elements of the combatants, traders and certain government officials, the war has been an opportunity to realise economic gain. The prolonged violence in Casamance, with the associated destruction of the local economy, has promoted a 'plunder mentality' amongst MFDC fighters cut off by the army from supply lines (e.g. ransacking shops)[31] and amongst army personnel bearing the brunt of separatist attacks. The rebels have driven villagers out of their villages and seized their property and livestock for themselves. Meanwhile the army is accused of extorting goods, plundering the local population and settling scores.

The overall lawlessness has opened the door for other illicit activity. 'In this framework criminal activity becomes an overt element of economic life in drugs or weapons dealing, smuggling, mercenary services, and so on' (Paye and Diop, 1998, p. 342). Seeking funding, the MFDC has turned to the growing and smuggling of cannabis as one means of support. The armed gangs from across the Guinea-Bissau border, who looted and stole cattle in the Kolda region in the summer of 2000, were not identified. They could have been bandits, MFDC elements, or rogue soldiers from Guinea Bissau. Whatever the case, they caused both large-scale displacement and provoked the formation of community self-protection groups that closed the border crossings (Evans, 2000, pp. 652-3).

Over the course of the years of unrest there has been a growing criminalisation of the conflict. Combatants have exploited a war economy in a lawless situation and others have joined them to exploit the situation for their own profit.

Social Polarisation and Intolerance

Violent conflict in Africa all too easily takes on an ethnic dimension as the various sides are identified with certain ethnic groups. It is then a short step to the use of violence against civilians for no other reason than their ethnic identity. The Senegalese security forces tend to assume that any Diola automatically sympathises with the MFDC:

> It would seem that most of the people imprisoned have been arrested because they were members of the Diola ethnic group and, for that reason alone, considered to be potential rebels. Some peasants have been reproached simply for being Diola and, when they have refused to confess their membership of the MFDC, the security forces have claimed that the Diola are secretive people who never tell the truth. Others have been accused of being from Guinea-Bissau, a country considered by some soldiers to be responsible for starting the conflict (Amnesty International, 1998, p. 16).

Perhaps in response to a felt sense of racial discrimination, the MFDC have themselves pursued racial harassment. Amnesty International reports: 'Members of the Manjak, Mandingo, Balante and Mancagne ethnic groups have often been the targets of attacks by the MFDC, which feels that these non-Diola populations are not involving themselves in the struggle for the independence of Casamance' (Amnesty International, 1998, p. 12). The manner in which rebel and army troops have handled the conflict has also brought a religious dimension to the intolerance. Sadio Fatty, a marabout (Muslim holy man) in Marasoum told a reporter that because the MFDC had failed in their objective, they were pursuing a policy of eliminating Muslim religious heads in Casamance. 'Have you ever heard of a priest or father maimed and killed by the rebels?' He called on the entire Muslim community to pray for the downfall of the rebels.[32]

Inevitably the social polarisation taking place in Casamance has spread beyond the war zone. Some have claimed that there has been an increase in racism in Dakar, with the Casamançais commonly referred to as lazy, backward or 'Niak' (forest people). This has been fuelled by the Government's attempt to delegitimise the MFDC by playing the ethnicity card (Lambert, 1998, p. 587). They have portrayed the insurgents as a Diola ethnic organisation and as such have questioned the Diola's Senegalese credentials. The danger of this backfiring and convincing Diola that they have no part in the nation are obvious. Apter has already sounded the warning:

Where dignity, through no fault of their own, is hard to come by, civility virtually non-existent, respect a travesty, and above all where democracy falls short of its defined responsibilities, political violence becomes a common and frequent recourse. It is a truism that where people despair of improving solutions, they become more inclined to tear down the institutional framework itself (Apter, 1997, p. 26).

Undermining the Criminal Justice System

Where the judiciary lack security of tenure as in Senegal, they are always susceptible to external influence (Freedom House, 2001). Not only has the impartiality of the judiciary in handling insurgent suspects been questioned, but also there appears to be political pressure to avoid investigation and possible punishment for troops taking the law into their own hands. Some of the abuse is obscured in the separate military court system that exists for members of the security forces. Yet even in the civilian courts matters are not dealt with adequately. The Constitution provides for an independent judiciary, but in practice:

> The Minister of Justice and subordinate authorities have extensive authority to influence judicial procedures by keeping the accused in pre-trial detention... Magistrates are vulnerable to outside pressures due to low pay, poor working conditions, and family and political ties (US Department of State, 2000).

Certainly the judicial system has suffered from disinclination to investigate suspected abuses. Hence when a prisoner appears before magistrates bearing visible signs of ill treatment, or when lawyers report cases to the local public prosecutor, they are rarely investigated (Amnesty International, 1998, p. 49). This reluctance to undertake investigations or prosecute members of the military, gendarmerie, or police for human rights abuses is despite stronger legal provisions against torture put in place in 1997. 'Those cases that are pursued often take years before final judgment is reached' (US Department of State, 2000). The political class and military are seen to be above the law, and a significant group of citizens do not have access to seek redress for injustices.

Conclusion

As long as the abuses by the Senegalese army in Casamance continue with impunity, the accountability of the Government is discredited, its representation of minorities is unsustainable and its control of the armed forces is mocked. Either it knows about the abuses but has insufficient control of the army to stop them; or it knows and has ordered them; or it does not know what is happening. None of these scenarios does any credit to a democratic regime which at the very least should protect all its citizens and have full civilian control of its army.

The past dependence of the Senegalese Government on military force in Casamance could be seen as part of a wider pattern of regime dependency, where disputes with neighbouring Mauritania and Guinea Bissau have been resolved by resorting to military force. However, the military have been content to close ranks around the civilian and military leadership. If either of the parties has exploited the situation it has been the Government. In the view of Paye and Diop they have cleverly brandished:

> The spectre of a military coup d'etat to win over various players in the Senegalese political game. The latter were convinced that any protracted protest that rattled the Diouf regime would not lead to their own accession to power but would open the gateway to a military alternative (1998, p. 341).

There is evidence that President Wade, who was himself a political prisoner, may pursue a policy in Casamance that is far less reliant on a military solution. Yet it does not necessarily follow that he will be able to instil a respect for human rights into the army when they are confronted with the MFDC in the forests of Casamance. However, if he fails, a major pillar in institutionalising democracy will be absent: law enforcement that abides by the law.

Notes

1. More than 94 percent of the country's population are Muslim and 40 percent are Wolof. Diola account for 5 percent of the population, but they span both The Gambia and Guinea-Bissau borders.
2. Interview with Panafrican News Agency, 2 April, 2001.
3. It was first created by Casamance nationalists in 1947 and joined the BDS led by President Senghor in 1948, but after that nothing was heard of it until 1982 when it published a pamphlet advocating secession.
4. This was disclosed by General Mane after he was sacked January 1998. According to him several high ranking officers in the army, with the connivance of the then President

Vierira, engaged in the trafficking, in part because they felt a blood debt for the Casamançais help during Guinea Bissau's liberation war. See Mbaye Fall, 'Nostalgia for Ancient Empires and the Casamance Rebellion', posted on web site of Panafrican news Agency, 30 October, 2000.

5. Quoted in *Africa Research Bulletin,* 34, 11, 1997, p. 12905.
6. In an interview with AllAfrica News agency posted on allAfrica web site, 6 February, 2001.
7. *Landmine Monitor Report 2000,* quoted in www.afrol.com, 7 September, 2001.
8. *Africa Research Bulletin,* 37, 3, 2000, p. 13892.
9. *IRIN,* 10 September and 8 October, 2001; *Panafrican News,* 15 November, 2001.
10. Dykman claims a figure of between 1,200 and 3,000 (2000, p. 2). Handicap International claims that more than 400 were killed or maimed by landmines alone 1997-2000 – *Africa Research Bulletin,* 37, 7, 2000, p. 14058.
11. Panafrican News Agency, 22 March, 2001.
12. Advocacy Network for Africa, available at www.africapolicy.org, accessed 22 November, 2001.
13. UN Integrated Regional Information Network, IRIN web site, accessed 19 October, 2000.
14. Interview with *The Independent*, Banjul, 11 June, 2001.
15. *Africa Research Bulletin,* 36, 5, 1999, p. 13554.
16. IRIN, 31 October, 2000.
17. IRIN, 13 December, 2000.
18. Panafrican News Agency, 11 July, 2001.
19. IRIN, 19 October, 2000.
20. Quoted in *The Independent,* Banjul, 29 June, 2001.
21. IRIN, 8 June, 2001.
22. *Daily Observer*, Banjul, 9 October, 2000.
23. *Daily Observer,* Banjul, 9 October, 2000.
24. Campaign for the Protection of Journalists (CPJ), www.cpj.org, accessed 12 April, 2000.
25. The UN Convention against Torture prescribes the launching of an impartial investigation whenever there are reasonable grounds to believe an act of torture has been committed and whether or not there has been a formal complaint.
26. IRIN, 22 August, 2000; CPJ, www.cpj.org, accessed 22 November, 2001.
27. Panafrican News Agency, 8 December, 2000.
28. *Mail & Guardian,* 26 May, 1998.
29. Quoted in *Mail & Guardian,* 26 May, 1998.
30. According to the Catholic charity, Caritas-Ziguinchor, quoted in Panafrican News Agency report, 30 October, 2000.
31. *The Independent*, Banjul, 15 June, 2001 and *Africa Research Bulletin,* 37, 2, 2000, p. 13878; IRIN, 8 October, 2001.
32. *The Independent*, Banjul, 29 June, 2001.

PART III
THE POLICE AND STATE MILITIA TAKE THE LAW INTO THEIR OWN HANDS

5 The Mozambican National Police and Crime

The Legacy of the Civil War

Establishing public policing in post-conflict societies, such as Mozambique, has a number of special difficulties. The police were understandably under-resourced compared with the military during the conflict years. During the civil war state policing simply ceased to exist over large areas of the country and, where it did continue, the introduction into the criminal justice system of flogging between 1983-89, only encouraged the police to act in an authoritarian manner. They imagined that they had a licence to act with brutality against enemies of the state and to use torture to secure information that would preserve state security. In the process, of course, they not only undermined their own legitimacy, but that of the Frelimo regime as well (Amnesty International, 1998b).[1]

Their paramilitary nature during the conflict meant that they were not well equipped for civilian duties after it ceased. They were neither familiar with the concept of being accountable to the public rather than to the state, nor with the procedures of evidence-based investigations as opposed to confession-based methods. With this historical legacy they had to face working in a very different social context after 1993. It was one where there was a surfeit of weapons left over from the conflict, where many social constraints on crime had broken down and where relaxed international border controls allowed a sudden growth in organised crime (Scharf, 2001).

As regards the public, not only did it have very high expectations of the state that it would quickly restore security and order, but at the same time it had a wariness of the police born of years of police brutality, which even the state controlled media's silence had failed to stop being widely known. Further, the fact that the police had fought alongside the military on the Frelimo side reduced their credibility in areas of RENAMO support.

As the civil war came to a close, therefore, the need for improved civil policing in Mozambique was a national priority. The Mozambique

Government was under no illusions that the public expected rapid improvements in public policing within a very short period of time. Failure to do so would mean losing its legitimacy and risk the emergence of informal and unaccountable policing alternatives to fight crime and maintain order.

An obvious place to start to improve security was to remove some of the weapons. In the aftermath of the civil war, the UN Secretary-General cited the following difficulties facing Mozambique:

> The protracted hostilities in Mozambique have disrupted infrastructure to a great degree, contributed to the existence of armed banditry and created conditions for lawlessness in some parts of the countryside. Between May and September 1993 alone, the number of reported crimes in Mozambique included 167 homicides, 726 armed robberies and hundreds of cases of physical assault, rape, etc. . . . A number of additional factors should also be taken into account. There is no efficient arms control system in place, and estimates put the total number of assorted types of weapons in 'non-official' hands at approximately one million (Woods, 2000*).*

The work of UNIMOZ (the UN Mission to Mozambique), with its CIVPOL (UN Police Force) that was meant to monitor the new Police of the Republic of Mozambique (the PRM), had only a minimal effect. The Government dragged its feet as regards giving CIVPOL access to the Rapid Reaction Police and to police training centres, whilst the PRM proved reluctant to take disciplinary measures against police offenders. It was a case, as in so many democratic transitions, of limited reform allowing authoritarian inertia. As a result, in the years that followed, the conduct of the PRM seemed little different from the previous force, not helped of course by the continuing low rates of pay.

The problem facing the Government, however, was not just one of the quality of policing. A whole culture of lawlessness had been created. Hanlon expresses it eloquently:

> The war has created two problems relating to corruption and ethics. In an environment of generalised mayhem, destabilization has numbed the senses. Corruption seems less serious to some people. This is reinforced by the amnesty under which RENAMO guerrillas, who have massacred people and committed unspeakable atrocities, can go free and are given land and help to start anew. Secondly, a decade of destabilization has made the military an extremely powerful force in the country. The lack of prosecutions of corrupt army officers supports the widespread belief that the government is afraid to probe too deeply into military corruption for fear of provoking a coup. That

deepens the moral ambiguity. If the two biggest sources of corruption – foreign donors and the army – are untouchable for justified fears of retaliation, why should smaller-scale corruption be singled out for contempt? (Hanlon, 1991, p. 235).

Crime in Mozambique

In the post-conflict period Mozambique's cities were caught up in a crime wave, which the police seemed unable to control. Such was the extent of rising crime, especially in the capital, Maputo, where several expatriates were killed in late 1996, that donor countries (such as Switzerland, Germany and Spain) threatened to freeze their aid unless the Government showed a firmer commitment in the fight against crime.

Several factors may have contributed to the increased crime rate. First there was economic liberalisation. This had increased the amount of consumer goods in shops but had done nothing to increase the public's purchasing power. Second, thousands of migrant workers from East and West Germany had lost their jobs following unification and returned to Mozambique. Third, the 93,000 demobilised soldiers quickly ran out of demob pay and the only skill they had to secure a living was the use of the army gun most had kept.[2] Fourth, the remaining armed forces were increasingly impoverished and undisciplined. Fifth, arms caches that had not been declared to UNIMOZ at the end of the war began supplying criminals. Finally, social constraints had been breaking down following the 15 years of civil war. The result of all these factors was that violent crime soared and public confidence in the police, which was already low, was virtually destroyed. Along with their ineffectiveness, most Mozambicans also considered the police force highly corrupt. Many, therefore, took the law into their own hands, with violent consequences.

Urban crime, especially in Maputo, rose steeply in the 1990s. Police records for 1996 show that there were 2,370 recorded crimes against property, of which 658 were robbery (135 of these were armed). Travelling on some main roads outside cities at night became particularly dangerous. Armed robbery and carjacking appears to be primarily motivated by economic need. Vines interviewed in 1995 one such 'highwayman', Alfredo. He was nineteen and explained why he got involved in crime:

> There is no work for me. I have few skills except using a gun and it's easy money. The occasional action makes money. I used to be Frelimo, then joined RENAMO, then joined Frelimo. I have played war for both. Now I work for

myself and my group. As long as we move around, we get few problems. We can pay for information about police activity. Prices have gone up since those South Africans got involved. Our secret is to be careful. We try not to kill people, but accidents can happen during confusion (Vines, 1998).

In another interview, a young man involved in armed crime told Vines that he had paid his way out of jail in 1995 and had turned to crime as one of the few ways to make ends meet. Joao, who is 31, explained:

What is there for people like me to do? A gun gives me a job! My family struggle on the land and they can't feed me. I need to help them. The police use guns all the time to make money. So can I! Everything around here is about money. Eh, without it you have nothing. So I make money with a gun (Vines, 1998).

With so many arms caches left over from the war, there is no shortage of available weapons and ammunition for such young men to purchase.

The Response of the National Police

The forces responsible for internal security under the Ministry of Interior are the Criminal Investigation Police (PIC), the Mozambican National Police (PRM), and the para-military Rapid Reaction Police (PIR). Many of them came from the army or the former police force (and some from RENAMO), all of which had histories of serious violations of human rights ranging from deaths of detainees to attempted assassination and mass killings of protestors.[3] In 1999 the PRM consisted of 18,500 personnel, as against a projected need of 40,000, with no more than 200 stations and posts across the country.

Aware of the large quantity of illegal weapons circulating in Mozambique and the growing banditry, police patrols along the main roads were stepped up from 1995. If reports are to be believed, they have had considerable success. In the first three months of 1995 alone, 30 armed gangs were apprehended and 69 arms caches uncovered. Between November 1995 and November 1996, 50 arms caches were discovered and 214 armed gangs were apprehended. In September 1997 the Mozambican police announced that since 1995 they had uncovered and destroyed 11,734 firearms of different calibres (Vines, 1998). To tackle banditry specifically, however, special police units were formed. One such unit, known as the 'Lightning Battalion', was deployed in June 1995 along the

Maputo-South Africa main road, after armed men killed a South African tourist. Four gangs, consisting of sixteen criminals, that were operating along the road were arrested in the following weeks. One reason for establishing a special unit was that regular police units were reticent to make arrests, probably because a significant proportion of armed banditry is carried out by current or former soldiers, often known to serving policemen. One FADM (Mozambican Defence Force) soldier revealed to Vines that, 'We make money by selling guns from the arsenals. Some of our people also engage in banditry to get extras. It's a way to survive. I don't agree with it; its a continuation of bad habits from FAM [the former Mozambican army]' (Vines, 1998).

Despite their apparent success in seizing weapons and arresting armed gangs, popular confidence in the police is low because of their inefficiency, suspected complicity with criminals and their human rights abuses. Policemen have regularly disregarded the law and constitution, and there are constant complaints from the public of police maltreatment of detainees, especially in Maputo. Since 1995 some 1,000 policemen have been expelled from the force for unethical conduct, including 'using firearms unduly', 'selling and renting guns' and 'homicide'. Even the two most senior officers, the General Commander and the Chief of Staff were not spared. They were both sacked by President Chissano in January 2002.[4] In addition, police are often the main sources of gun-running. According to the Attorney-General, Sinai Nhatitima, many of the guns used by criminals come from the police. 'Guns are stolen or "disappear" from the arsenals and are lent out, rented or sold to be used in criminal activities.' Likewise Artur Canana, the Governor of Manica province, admitted that weapons have been sold out of police stations: 'There is nothing we can do about indiscipline of certain officers, which is making the problem worse' (Vines, 1998).

With human rights training for police officers extending,[5] there has been a slight overall improvement in police conduct. Nevertheless there are still regular occurrences of serious abuses, including extrajudicial killings, the use of arbitrary arrest and detention and the excessive use of force and torture of detainees, as the following examples show. It is a catalogue that is strikingly reminiscent of the abuses of the armed forces of Uganda and Senegal in their response to the lawlessness of the rebel forces.

Extrajudicial Killing

There have been cases every year for at least the last five years where the police have allegedly been responsible for unexplained disappearances of prisoners, of deaths in custody due to brutality and of shooting dead civilians. In 1997 the police allegedly killed the brothers Abel Zefanias dos Anjos and Crescensio Sergio Muchange. Dos Anjos was detained and tortured, but subsequently released after police extorted money from his girlfriend. Later, however, they hunted him down and shot him in Maputo. Muchange, dos Anjos' brother, was accused of theft, beaten and tortured in police custody, and killed. In both cases the police deny wrongdoing, although they have not yet referred either case to the PIC. Amnesty International reports three persons arrested for theft that died of abuse in police custody in 1997. Franque Tchembene was severely beaten and thrown into a pool of water into which bullets were fired by police in Maputo. He died in custody. Intepa Faque was arrested in Nacala-Porto, Nampula Province. He died after a stick was stuck down his throat. Cresencio Muchanga was dragged behind a moving vehicle and subsequently shot by police in Maputo (Amnesty International, 1998b). Also in 1997, police were responsible for the death of Eduardo Machava, for allegedly refusing extortion demands by the police (US Department of State, 1998).

The following year, 1998, an accused thief, Cabral Manica, died as a result of police torture in the far northern province of Cabo Delgado. A police officer was subsequently convicted and sentenced to three months in prison. Again in 1998, a striker was killed after police opened fire on a demonstration. The Government has said that it has investigated, but no report has been released, nor has any action been taken against the officers responsible (US Department of State, 1999). In 1999 only one incident was reported. In March a detainee died in Beira central prison after being seen being beaten by police en route. The authorities claim the man died of an unspecified illness (US Department of State, 2000).

There were several unconfirmed reports of police killings in 2000. In March the police arrested Tomas Paulo Nhacumba and Gildo Joaquim Bata in Maputo for possession of an illegal firearm. The next day they took the accused in handcuffs to their families and demanded $750 for their release. The families were unable to pay and the men were transferred to an unknown facility. They later were found in a hospital mortuary, listed under false names, with bullets wounds to their foreheads. A police inquiry later reported that they had been shot trying to escape (Amnesty

International, 2000b). In May 2000, police at Aube in Nampula province fired upon a peaceful demonstration in support of a jailed RENAMO member, killing six civilians. The Government defended the action as appropriate and lawful. In Marracuene, Maputo province, there were two incidents of police executions in 2000. The first, in June, occurred when police took Emidio Raul Nhancume from his home in Matola. His body was found one month later in Marracuene, having apparently been shot and buried by the police. The following month, Eliseu Geraldo Muainga was seized by police and his body was found two weeks later in Marracuene. The incident has not yet been investigated. In November as many as 41 persons were killed during violence related to RENAMO rallies. The League of Human Rights reported that the police in the northern provinces of Nampula and Cabo Delgado fired on and killed unarmed demonstrators to prevent rallies. They allege that the police commander in Balama, Cabo Delgado province, ordered the police to shoot to kill. In Montepuez, Cabo Delgado province, police shot and killed 17 when RENAMO demonstrators attacked the local jail and Government buildings and took hostages (US Department of State, 2001).

In January 2001 there was even a case of a police officer shooting and killing someone in a suburb of Maputo for failing to obey a police order to remain still (US Department of State, 2002). Such scant regard for human life by those assigned the role of protecting the community can only undermine confidence in the police.

Irregular Arrest and Detention

According to Mozambican law, no one may be detained for more than 48 hours without their case being reviewed by a judge. After another 60 days detention is allowed while the case is investigated by the PIC. In cases of a very serious crime, a person may be detained for up to 84 days without being charged formally and, if a court approves, for a further two periods of 84 days while the police complete the investigation. If the prescribed period for investigation has been completed and no charges have been brought, the detainee must be released. In many cases, however, the police are either unaware of, or indifferent to, these regulations and in addition ignore a detainee's constitutional right to see a lawyer or to contact relatives or friends. Following the clashes between Renamo supporters and the police in Cabo Delgado in November 2000, the police hunted down known Renamo supporters throughout the province, regardless of whether they had been at the scenes of violence or not. The Human Rights and Development

Development Association reported that, 'In Pemba, Chiure, Balama and Mocimboa da Praia, dozens of RENAMO members, or simply citizens were dragged to jail in retaliation for the deaths of the policemen and other civil servants during the RENAMO insurrection of 9 November in Montepuez.'[6] The National Directorate of Prisons reported in 2000 that, of an estimated 6,422 persons in prison, 4,632 had not been charged (US Department of State, 2001). There was even a newspaper report in November 1998 of the discovery of a secret prison in Buzi District, Sofala Province, where police allegedly detained prisoners in underground cisterns. The existence of this illegal prison, however, is denied by local authorities (US Department of State, 2000).

There are also innumerable complaints that police detain people for spurious reasons, such as not carrying identification documents and demand bribes to permit them to continue their journey. In fact, according to the Penal Code, only those caught in the act of committing a crime can be held in detention. Police also at times use traffic checkpoints to harass people and confiscate their possessions at the borders. In addition, as part of an operation to reduce street crime in 2001, police in Maputo detained numerous persons for anything up to 14 days before releasing them (US Department of State, 2002).

Torture

Although the Constitution prohibits all forms of cruel or inhuman treatment, the police regularly practice torture, beatings, death threats and physical and mental abuse. They also use violence and detention to intimidate persons from reporting these abuses. A typical account from 1998 tells of how 13 were arrested at the port of Quissanga in Cabo Delgado, charged with smuggling hashish. They were forced to stand for periods of between 12 hours and three days without food or clean water and threatened with pistols pointed to their heads to extract confessions (Amnesty International, 1998b).

For 1999 and 2000 the League of Human Rights received 78 and 59 complaints respectively of torture, including several instances involving the mistreatment of women, beatings and death threats. It claimed that at least 30 people were tortured or killed by Mozambican police from January to September 2000.[7] When it sent a team of lawyers to inspect prisons in 2001 they reported, *inter alia*, that the police showed, 'absolute disrespect for human dignity' and noted that the practice of beating and torture by the police had led to the hospitalisation of some suspects.[8]

In another case, Macelino Mutolo and Luciano Hom were arrested by the Rapid Intervention Police in January 2000 and taken to police cells, where they were handcuffed to pillars and left all night. The next day they were taken into the bush, whipped and threatened with death if they did not confess to robbing a vehicle. Marcelino was taken to Maputo and forced to withdraw a large sum of money from his bank account to pay the police. The two were finally released after Marcelino Mutolo agreed to obtain a further large sum of money, although instead he filed a complaint against the police (Amnesty International, 2000c). No investigation was known to have been initiated.

The most serious case of police inhumanity in 2000 occurred in November following protests by RENAMO supporters against what they called the 'rigged' presidential elections of December 1999. Though supposed to be peaceful demonstrations, 15 of them took the form of violent assaults against district administration offices and police stations, with the police in several instances using live ammunition, in what they claimed was self-defence. Police detained 457 RENAMO supporters during more than 60 rallies, with reports that police beat and tortured detainees. Three reportedly died of asphyxiation in custody in Beira. In one northern town, Montepuez, clashes between the police and RENAMO demonstrators on 9 November 2000 left 25 people dead, including 7 policemen. The police arrested 162 and, presumably in revenge, placed them in two police cells, each measuring only 7x3 metres. On 18 November an official from the General Command of the Mozambican police ordered the prisoners to be moved to a civilian jail to relieve the overcrowding. The Provincial director of the Criminal Investigation Police, however, ignored the order. Over the next three days 83 prisoners died of asphyxiation. Seven of the original 162 died on 18 November (the police failed to call for autopsies). Belatedly they did then move 112 prisoners out of the cells. Yet on 21 November, the district Police Commander entered the cell waiving a pistol and told the prisoners: 'I'm going to kill all of you, because you came to Montepuez to kill me...Nobody is going to leave here alive.' He then authorised the entry of 42 other detainees into the crowded cell. As a result, a further 76 died that night.[9]

During 2001, human rights groups received complaints of torture, including several instances involving the sexual abuse of women, beating, illegal detention, and death threats. More specifically, it was claimed by the family of Fernando Santos that his death in custody was the result of torture (US Department of State, 2002).

Criminal Complicity

There are almost continuous reports that the police extort money from street vendors, sometimes beating the women and sometimes stealing their merchandise, and that they abuse prostitutes and street children. When a Sunday paper, *Domingo*, in June 1994 asked Maputo port workers how they viewed the relationship between the police and theft at the port, they were told that there were policemen who 'when they leave port in the morning sometimes have more money than the entire month's wages. And they have the nerve to pretend that they don't collaborate with thieves'; or again: 'When the crooks leave, they go in front or behind policemen who clear the way for them' (quoted in Seleti, 2000, p. 363).

Concerning larger scale crime, there are reports (as mentioned earlier) that the police are often the main sources of illegal weapons, either renting out their guns to criminals, being actively involved in the arms trade themselves, or turning a blind eye to the trafficking.[10] Vines gives an account of a Portuguese businessmen with links with senior officials, who smuggled arms and contraband through the port of Nacala (Vines, 1998). Similarly, Bayart claims that certain illegal operators in South Africa have had high-level contacts with politicians and the security forces both inside and outside the country, by which they have brokered business transactions. In particular he mentions Mozambique, claiming that former South African military intelligence operatives had 'influence with Mozambican politicians and officials' by which their trade was facilitated (Bayart et al., 1999, p. 63).

In the same year that Bayart made his general accusations, there occurred a startling case in Mozambique's Supreme Court that appears to bear out his charge and to implicate the police specifically in arms smuggling into South Africa. A South African government official, Robert McBride, appears to have been investigating on behalf of the South African security services (the South African Secret Service, the National Intelligence Agency, and the Independent Commission for the Control of Arms), cross-border arms trafficking, Mozambique police corruption in the licensing of firearms and the use of illegal firearms in violent and political crimes. In March 1999, whilst investigating a gunrunner called 'Mamba' (who had connections with the Mozambican police) he himself was arrested in Mozambique. He was charged with gunrunning and espionage. McBride had gone to Mamba's house to buy illegal weapons with a man called Mbatha (who turned out to be an informer for certain members of the SAPS, keeping them abreast of McBride's investigations, since they were involved with the gun running themselves). But Mamba had already tipped off the Mozambican police of the visit, apparently in revenge after Mbatha had denounced him to South African police as a gun-runner in 1993. Subsequently Mamba confessed to smuggling weapons from Mozambique to South Africa since 1992. His clients included a warlord linked to the Inkatha Freedom Party and Winnie Madikizela-Mandela's secret organisation, Fapla (a political and military organisation founded in 1995 with the aim of overthrowing the South African government). He referred to meetings he had with Madikizela-Mandela and the involvement of two Mozambican generals in the military training of this movement. Money paid to Mamba for the purchase of weapons was given to a Mozambican Director of Police Intelligence Services.[11] Many of the facts of this case are disputed, but it does seem incontrovertible that the Mozambican police were involved to some degree in the gun running.

There is also increasing circumstantial evidence that the police are involved with international drug trafficking. Joseph Hanlon, who has researched the drugs trade believes that 'the value of illegal drugs passing through Mozambique is probably more than all legal foreign trade combined' and is in no doubt that the one tonne of cocaine and heroin that are estimated to be passing through Mozambique each month, could only do so 'with the agreement of the Mozambican police and very senior Mozambican officials.'[12]

In July 1996, Domingos Maita, the Head of the Maputo branch of the PIC, publicly admitted that organised crime had infiltrated the police (although later the Interior Minister said that Maita had meant to say that organised crime was *trying* to infiltrate the police) (Seleti, 2000, p. 362). To Maita it was almost inevitable in a crime-ridden state:

> With state bodies riddled with people forging any and every document, with the crying lack of resources that the police suffers, with miserable wages that are offered, the police run the risk of being commanded by the barons of crime, commanded by outside, through the creation of mafia type conditions, and commanded on the inside by a fifth column that cannot resist the seduction of money (quoted in Seleti 2000, p. 362).

These abuses speak of a police force that has only weak and ineffective mechanisms to ensure accountability to the law and to society. This is a force that is badly trained in respect of human rights and which has no statutory code requiring officers to report abuses. This is a lawlessness that is too often unchallenged since human rights organisations and journalists are largely confined to Maputo and elsewhere the public has no access to an independent complaints commission. It is a lawlessness that undermines much of the progress that Mozambique has made since 1994.

The Democratic Impact

The reports concerning police lawlessness have caused widespread dissatisfaction with both the police themselves and with the Mozambican Government. More than that, they have undermined many of the democratic institutions and processes that have been introduced since the transition in 1994.

A Low Esteem and Respect for the Police

At best the police are widely ridiculed for their ineptness, at worst they are despised and hated as brutal and corrupt. Hanlon was very dismissive of them when he wrote in 1996: 'Corruption extends to an ill-paid police, who must be paid by the victims to investigate a crime and can be paid by a perpetrator to lose the file' (Hanlon, 1996, p. 5). So was Finnegan after he saw a domestic servant of a friend he was visiting report a theft from the garage. The man was trembling lest it be reported to the police, whom he believed would then pick up all the other domestic workers and subject them to robbery and a beating, even though the police knew the gang that had done it and were in their pay (Finnegan, 1992, p. 287). The contempt of the police is apparent in the popular representation of them as fools in popular culture, such as radio plays,[13] and in popular nicknaming strategies. In Nampala in the mid 1990s they called the police *nikawana* (suggesting a penchant for stealing in the Makua language), particularly in the light of the police demands for bribes when arrested persons failed to produce new identity documents (the local registry being unable at the time to supply them). Outraged, the police took to arresting people who used the term, encouraged by the provincial Police Commander, until he himself was reprimanded by higher authorities (Seleti, 2000, p. 359).

In a poll conducted for *Mediafax*, it was revealed that the overwhelming majority thought the then Interior Minister, Manuel Antonio, should be sacked because of his failure to stop the police corruption and inefficiency. The best the Minister could do in reply to the criticism was, in 1995, to answer lamely: 'police are police. I have never seen police who are saints' (quoted in Seleti, 2000, p. 359). Finally, the criticism was such that President Chissano was obliged to sack him in 1996.

Seven years after transition, the police abuse is still so widespread that the Interior Minister, Almerino Manhenje, was forced in May 2001 to call upon the police to make profound changes in their attitudes, so that they would in future inspire the confidence and respect of the public.[14] Their conduct is not only undermining trust in them as an institution, but trust in the principle of the rule of law.

Self Policing

In August 1999 Supreme Court Chief Justice, Mario Mangaze, complained that only 25 percent of citizens had access to the official judicial system. Given, therefore, the absence of a formal judicial system from much of rural Mozambique, and the perception that the police that are available are inept, corrupt and often brutal and pro-Frelimo, it is not surprising that people look to alternative methods to defend themselves and to prosecute and punish alleged offenders. Many have acquired an illegal weapon to defend themselves.[15] Given also that the police are not too particular about abuses against suspects, the many involved in self-policing see little reason why they should not be violent as well. Hence there are reported instances of mob and vigilante killings in both urban and rural areas. 'Violence is increasing and a kind of Wild West justice is emerging. The word "lynch" now exists in Portuguese (linchar) and is used to describe the increasingly common practice of people killing any thief caught in the act' (Hanlon, 1996, p. 5). For instance, a thief caught stealing from a home in Maputo in August 1999 was beaten with the intent to kill by a crowd until the police intervened. In another incident that year, a crowd in a Maputo suburb beat a man to death after he had broken into a home (US Department of State, 2000). Similarly in both Costa de Sol and Matola in the Maputo area, suspected thieves were beaten to death by mobs in 2000 and 2001 (US Department of State, 2001, 2002). Such incidents will continue so long as the state police are perceived to be inadequate and brutal.

More formal militia groups have also arisen, such as the RENAMO armed security guards. At a RENAMO party conference in November 2001 a television cameraman who ignored a prohibition by the party on filming was seriously beaten by the guards and, according to reports, 'one policeman and two unidentified civilians were also beaten up and three others were taken captive.'[16] The sensitivity was because there was a demonstration outside the conference of ex-RENAMO guerrillas, but it shows that the conduct of private security organisations closely reflects that of the public police.

News Management

The Government action makes little attempt to manage the news compared with Uganda. Human rights violations receive extensive coverage in both Government and independent media and from human rights groups, one of which (Human Rights and Development, the DHD) now publishes an annual report on human rights conditions in the country. Nor are there any legal obstacles to the formation of local human rights groups, although they must undergo lengthy and expensive registration procedures. The Government has also attempted to make specific responses to human rights inquiries from Amnesty International, Transparency International, the League of Human Rights, and the DHD, although at times its response has been slow. Further, the Government did not respond formally to the LDH and DHD reports on the 2000 nationwide demonstrations and Montepuez deaths in custody.

As regards the police authorities, however, there is a much greater sensitivity, if not clear anger, to public criticism, especially as it has grown in boldness since 1992. There are many examples of the police themselves using violence and detention to intimidate persons from reporting abuses. The radio playwright, Sweleke, who wrote a satire in 1994 about the police, was told when in detention by a police inspector, 'All you journalists will end up here.' Only a few weeks later, the Nampala Police Commander was quoted as having said, 'If you journalists want war with the police, then let's go ahead. Now I'll arrest all of you' (Seleti, 2000, p. 359). In 1998 the radio journalist, Fernando Quinova, was detained without charge, after reporting on Radio Mozambique that a prisoner, Cabral Manica, had died while in police custody. Quinova escaped from prison, but was rearrested in March 1999 and charged with slandering the police and illegally leaking documents. Neither of these charges actually exists in the Penal Code. After the media publicised his plight, he was quickly freed. The sequel to the story is that in May, the Cabo Delgado provincial court convicted a Police Commander of illegally detaining Quinova, whilst another officer was convicted the following month for the death in custody of Cabral Manica (US Department of State, 2000). Equally serious is the report that, according to the Chairwoman of the League of Human Rights, a police contact warned her of police threats on her life following her appearance in 2000 in a televised debate during which she criticised the PIC.

Of even greater concern than police hostility are the death threats that are made by anonymous but influential figures in the business and political world. That they are not empty is seen in the assassination of the newspaper editor, Cardoso. An investigative team from the Committee to Protect Journalists in July 2001 found widespread fear and self-censorship among journalists. They were reticent to cover any stories that involved the corruption of well placed figures, whether in the police, parliament or business.[17] If the lawless in and outside of the police can prevent their exposure by intimidation, then a vital element of democracy will fail.

The Mobilisation of Political Opposition

When policing entails the arrest of political opposition leaders, then inevitably the police are portrayed as partisan. A dispute in Aube in May 2000 over the payment of tax in the local marketplace shows how short the fuse of violence is among some as regards the police. Because the person arrested was a RENAMO supporter, the incident was seen in political terms. A group of one hundred, led by senior RENAMO figures in the district, responded by attacking the police station with clubs and bush knives, apparently with the intention of seizing weapons. The police, claiming self-defence, opened fire on the attackers, killing at least four (Human Rights Watch, 2001). A new cycle of political violence had begun and was related to the violent assaults of RENAMO protestors in the November and the equally violent retaliation by the police. The violent over-reaction of the police to those violent protests was always going to overshadow the activities of the RENAMO supporters themselves. The clashes led to the detention of 457 RENAMO supporters and in the most confined cells some 85-100 died of asphyxiation. This was in addition to the 17 shot dead by the police when they opened fire on the demonstrators. Given, too, that the trials were completed within just a month of arrest, there arose not just the issue of uncontrolled brutality on the part of the police, but of their use for political ends by the ruling Frelimo party. Inevitably, therefore, RENAMO has sought to make political capital out of the occasion, drawing upon the popular distrust of the police generally and upon the sense of victimisation among RENAMO supporters. Clearly their intention is not just to criticise the police, but also to implicate the Government as those who both condone, or even instigate, the police violence. Lutero Simango, a spokesman for the RENAMO-Electoral Union coalition said: 'Compatriots of ours have died in several prisons in the country because of the torture and ill-treatment inflicted by the police *on the orders of the government*' (emphasis mine). He argued that the deaths were a deliberate tactic 'to silence witnesses who might testify against the police during an investigation into the deaths that occurred during the demonstrations of 9 November'.[18] This is likely to remain an important political issue for some time to come.

The greatest success, however, in galvanising the public into a concerted campaign to see the police reformed, has been the media. Freed from censorship laws and given independence under the new democratic regime, they have seized the opportunity to mount a prolonged and extremely effective campaign criticising police conduct in all its forms. They have also repeatedly called for Government accountability and real change in operational control and prosecution of offenders in the force:

> The media have performed two functions: they have disclosed the society's shortcomings and abuses of democratic provisions, and at the same time have strengthened the democratic process...The media took on a new role as advocate for the new democratic dispensation. Mozambican journalists worked hard to expose corruption and many other abuses that they considered to be inimical to democracy (Seleti, 2000, p. 358).

1995 was a particularly effective year for the press campaign. Throughout the year they focused on exposing the ineffectiveness and corruption of the police and calling for the resignation of the Interior Minister. They were aided by radio and groups like the League of Human Rights who kept up the pressure through broadcasts and letter campaigns. So successful were they that the Minister of the Interior was indeed removed, the prosecution of police officers for torture took place and the Legal Affairs and Human Rights Commission of Parliament was stirred into investigating police corruption itself.

The press investigations into corruption have not been without great personal cost, however, as the murder of Carlos Cardoso, the Editor of the independent Maputo news-sheet, *Metical,* shows. His murder on the streets of Maputo in November 2000 at the hands of professional assassins appears to be linked to two investigations he was pursuing into the Banco Commercial of Mozambique and related political and business corruption. The first concerned an unaccounted $110 million, thought to have been given as loans to Frelimo figures. The second was a $14 million fraud linked with three businessmen who had previously tried to assassinate the investigating attorney for the case. The three had escaped prosecution when vital court papers went missing in the State Attorney's office. The national outcry over his murder demonstrated the depth of feeling that has arisen across the country concerning the press as the champions of freedom and scourge of corruption. Jose Saramago (Portuguese 1998 Nobel laureate for literature) told the *Metical* staff:

> I think what Carlos Cardoso was doing was not looking for 'The Truth' with a capital T, because that sort of truth does not exist. What he was looking for were those little truths. Those truths that are necessary in order to build any project that can bring us all together...Above all, we must not let them convince us that this kind of thing (murder) is accidental, that there is some uncontrolled group which for no particular reason resolved to commit murder.[19]

Seleti argues persuasively that it was this challenge by civil society that has brought about changes in coercive policing methods more than reform from above. 'The popular practices of narrating police brutality in newspapers and media faxes culminated in a groundswell sufficient to pressurize the government to institute a parliamentary commission of enquiry' (Seleti, 2000, p. 351). It has also made the police culture more willing to countenance surrendering accused colleagues for prosecution.

Undermining of the Criminal Justice System

There is evidence that the Government is beginning to take the issue of police lawlessness more seriously. In 1998 the Government allocated more funding for the hiring and training of police, as well as for higher salaries.[20] There is still, however, a considerable degree of police immunity from prosecution. It is true that the Montepuez district police commander, Dahalili Sumail, and 10 other policemen, were arrested for their alleged role in 2000 of the death of 83 people by asphyxiation in a police cell. The arrests followed the suspension from duty of the Cabo Delgado provincial Director of the Criminal Investigation Police and Juma Macequesse, who is accused of disregarding orders to avoid overcrowding in the cells. However, the arrests caused discontent among the rest of the Montepuez police. When Deputy Attorney General Edmundo Alberto visited the station, policemen told him they believed that only 'scapegoats' had been arrested or suspended. They claimed that neither Macequesse nor Sumail had been at their posts when the mass deaths occurred.[21] In June 2001 the public prosecutor dropped the charges against two of the five police officers for insufficient evidence. However, Mithale the police officer on duty and Nhoca, who was in charge of the cell were prosecuted for the cell deaths. The two were found guilty of homicide, sentenced to 17 and 18 years respectively, and were each ordered to pay 20 million meticais ($952) to the family of each person who died. It is to be hoped that it marks a step forward in tackling the lawlessness of the Mozambique police and in establishing confidence in the criminal justice system. At the same time however, other police officers appear to be escaping prosecution. The Government continues to defend the police actions in breaking up nationwide RENAMO demonstrations in 2000 as legal, even though their policy of shooting to kill left at lest 21 dead in Nampula and Balama, Cabo Delgado. The Government's argument is it was an appropriate and lawful response to the threat to life posed by the RENAMO supporters, a claim that was supported by several provincial courts. Other incidents left unattended include the reported torture and deaths in custody of Tomas Paulo Nhacumba and Gildo Joaquim Bata in 2000.

The scale of the problem should not be underestimated. Years of official oppression under colonial and Marxist regimes and during the civil war has bred a tolerance of abuse which, coupled with the widespread ignorance on human rights and legal provision, means that abuses are rarely challenged in the rural areas. Inevitably many victims believe that if they went to the police they would be confronted with demands for bribes or indifference. The comments of the leading writer, Mia Couto, regarding the Cardoso murder, capture the mood of many. He argued that the murder would not be investigated thoroughly as 'many more crimes' would be uncovered. 'Cardoso's murder is part of the wider murder of Mozambique and this is something that cannot be investigated.'[22] Democracy in the sense of experiencing legal equality, is still unknown.

Conclusion

If RENAMO has its way, a discredited security service will lead to a discredited government. Nevertheless, there is always the danger that it might go one stage further, with a discredited government leading to a discredited state and its democratic regime. Frelimo deputy, Teodato Hunguana, one or the members of the Legal and Human Rights Commission of the Mozambican Parliament investigating police corruption, remarked in 1996 that it was obvious to him that human rights violations were not official policy:

> But that is not the point. For when citizens' rights are violated all over the country, then the public inevitably harbour suspicions about the institutions that ought to protect them. If the problem is not solved, the legitimacy of our institutions is weakened (quoted in Seleti, 2000, p. 362).

The same point was made by President Chissano four years later, in the shadow of the death of those asphyxiated in a police cell. Giving his annual state of the nation address to Parliament, he said that the state must act to avoid any repetition of the abuse. He stressed that regardless of the results of the parliamentary commission of inquiry, and of the court cases, 'we have to realise that Mozambicans have died...The state has been tarnished and society has been wounded.' Chissano added that the state's behaviour must be guided by the constitutional principle that 'the state is responsible for illegal acts committed by its agents.'[23] It is this fundamental aspect of the rule of law which many in Mozambique are still waiting to see enforced.

Notes

1. The cycle of violence of course precedes Frelimo. One of the first actions of Frelimo after it opened its armed struggle in 1964 was an attack on a tea company in Milange, which appeared to be a revenge attack for the Portuguese Police brutality. For in 1961 Portuguese police at Milange fired upon a group of workers demonstrating at the company for better pay. 15 were killed. It had been the first serious disturbance in Quelimane district for over 50 years, although there had been brutal suppressions of strikes among dockers and workers at Lourenco Marques and Beira in 1948 and 1956 (Vail and White, 1980, p. 372).
2. 'The number of soldiers from both sides who volunteered for the new army proved to be considerably below expectations. Most of the former military went to their regions of origin with 18 months severance pay, but without any real prospects of economic reintegration, given the protracted economic crisis facing the country. This factor, together with the fact that the technical training provided failed to reach the majority of the soldiers, constitutes probably the single most important on-going threat to the democratic process and stability in the country' (Monteiro, 1999, pp. 31-2).
3. The most notorious being the killing by the police of 600 at a peaceful protest at Mueda in 1960.
4. 555 policemen were expelled from the force between January 1995 and July 1996 for unethical conduct and, between January and October 1997, a further 137 (Vines, 1998). In the first half of 2001 another 156 more cases were reported (Mozambique News Agency, AIM Reports, 213, 6 August, 2001).
5. Begun under the CIVPOL programme of the UNIMOZ mission and continued by human rights groups. A police transformation project as part of an integrated and comprehensive justice system in Mozambique, has been supported by the Spanish, French, Swiss, Dutch and German governments, since the mid-1990s. Originally the whole police force was to be re-trained under the co-ordination of the Government and the UNDP, but the project has been scaled down. The Mozambique project focussed on a selective concentrated change-process: It made an assessment that most of the crime was concentrated in Maputo and some other towns and embarked on the relatively lengthy (3 months) residential retraining of all levels of staff in those priority areas. Within three years they retrained all the staff (some 4,500) at the 18 priority station. The post-training assessment indicated that there was a big morale and commitment boost on the part of the staff and a positive effect on the local communities (Scharf, 2001).
6. Panafrican News Agency, 27 April, 2001.
7. IRIN, 15 September, 2000.
8. Panafrican News Agency, 7 May, 2001.
9. Panafrican News Agency, 3 December, 2000.
10. Reported at Christian Council of Mozambique Conference on, 'The illicit spread of small arms in Mozambique', September, 2001.
11. *Mail & Guardian*, 21 August, 1998.
12. Mozambique News Agency – AIM Reports, 210, 29 June, 2001.
13. See Seleti's account of the arrest of Sweleke's following his radio piece mocking the police, 2000, p. 358.
14. Panafrican news agency, 21 May, 2001.

15 UN claims that close to 1 in 2 or 3 Mozambicans has a gun, mostly illegally; reported the Christian Council of Mozambique Conference on, 'The illicit spread of small arms in Mozambique', September, 2001.
16 Media Institute of Southern Africa, press release, 2 November, 2001.
17 CPJ, www.cpj.org, accessed 5 August, 2001.
18 Panafrican News Agency, 25 November, 2000.
19 Panafrican News Agency, 30 November, 2000.
20 Human rights training is becoming mandatory for all officers, although the LDH discontinued its training programme in 2000, allegedly because of reluctant co-operation from the police (US Department of State, 2001). The US is also providing advanced training courses, run by the FBI to transmit police expertise and techniques for patrolling, interrogation and self-defence (Panafrican News Agency, 10 May, 2001).
21 Panafrican News Agency, 8 December, 2000.
22 *Mail & Guardian*, 23 March, 2001.
23 Panafrican News Agency, 7 December, 2000.

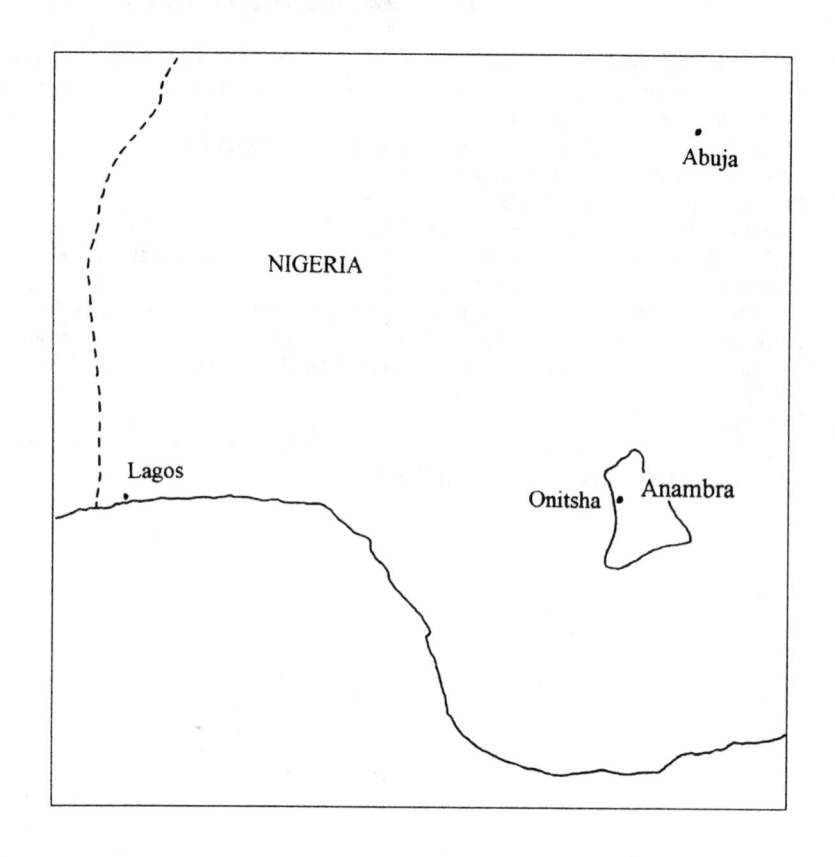

Figure 6.1 Anambra State, Nigeria

6 Anambra State Vigilante Service (Nigeria) and Crime

Crime and Policing in Nigeria

Crime has been getting worse in Nigeria since civilian rule in 1999, or at least this is how it is perceived by the general public. In a nation-wide survey conducted in October 2000, 1,407 respondents were asked, 'has crime abated in your area within the past one year?' 65.8 per cent said crime in their areas had worsened. Of the 33.4 per cent who said the rate of crime had dropped in their areas, most attributed this decline to the emergence of vigilante and anti-crime groups.[1] Perceptions of change may be distorted, but for the inhabitants of the big cities, violent crime is still an ever-present reality. In the period January to July 2001, 400 lost their lives to robbers nationwide. In Lagos alone, between August 2000 and May 2001, a total of 718 robbers were killed and 2,680 suspects were arrested at the scene of armed robberies. In the course of those robberies 273 victims lost their lives and 84 policeman were killed.[2]

Much of the blame for this rise in crime is placed at the door of the 135,000 strong federal Nigeria Police. The press are uniformly critical and frequently call for them to be scrapped. Under the heading, 'Police and Their Myriad Problems', the *Post Express* editorial of 16 May, 2001, spoke of 'one giant sick body', 'highly placed officers mismanage the service' and 'the force is doomed.' Interviewing the public about their views on the police regularly fills many column inches. Journalists sent out by *The News* recorded the views of the people of Lagos as, 'It's better that they are scrapped. I prefer armed robbers attacking us to the atrocities the police commit'; 'It's better they don't exist'; 'All they know is to collect *egunje*'; 'They extort money...They are not human beings.'[3] The *Post Express* recorded similar sentiments. One man interviewed said 'the police has failed in its primary function and should be replaced with any group capable of protecting the weak.'[4] Above all the police are lambasted for their extortion at illegal roadblocks. In some cases it even leads to the police killing those who refuse to pay or who are seen to have large amounts of cash on them.[5]

The negative attitudes to the police are not just the mood of the general public. Even the Anambra state Police Commissioner issued a warning to policemen not to continue to extort money from the public:

> It is a very shameful thing that some of you will stretch your hands to receive money from drivers when your salaries are better than theirs… Stop stretching your devilish hands to take money from drivers… ensure that you serve the people as servants… Imbibe the spirit of the Golden Rule – do to people what you want to be done to you. If you deviate from these rules, God's wrath will await you.[6]

There are also many reported cases of the police colluding with criminals. In one case an Inspector, along with others, robbed a group of businessmen of naira 100 million. In another case a Superintendent of Police ran a car theft syndicate.[7] The Methodist Archbishop of Lagos, alleged that the failure of the police to fight crime was due to the fact that they were 'collaborators and comrades' to the robbers. He appealed to the Lagos State Governor to officially invite members of the Yoruba vigilante group, the OPC (Oodua Peoples Congress) so that they would 'swoop on the hoodlums' and get rid of them[8] (The OPC was not then outlawed). The military have also been implicated in crime. An Assistant Commissioner of Police admitted the likelihood of the military involvement in violent robberies, noting that a wave of armed banditry took place at a market, which adjoined the Ojo Barracks. He believed that soldiers who had served on the ECOMOG Task Force in Sierra Leone could have grown used to instant wealth and were resorting to robbery on their return to their barracks.[9]

Lagos may get most of the headlines, but the problems of growing crime and an ineffective police force are nationwide. Anambra state lies in the South East of Nigeria, in the heart of Igboland. Its market in the main city of Onitsha is reputedly the largest in West Africa, which may account for why it has attracted so much armed robbery. During the year 2000, armed robberies were a regular occurrence. Notorious incidents included the gang of 120 men who attacked a market and left dozens dead and hundreds injured, and the armed bandits who stormed a Lagos-Aba bound bus one night killing over 30 passengers. The robberies had the effect of forcing residents into a self-imposed curfew after 7 pm and of driving many women and children to sleep in churches.

In the words of the Governor's Chief Press Secretary:

> Armed bandits were operating with reckless abandon, unchallenged. Human beings were butchered to death routinely... you dared not in those days walk about with a polythene bag in your hand because armed robbers would think you were carrying cash.[10]

The outbreak of violent crime was frequently associated by the people of Anambra, like the nation as a whole, with the ineffectiveness, if not the collusion, of the Nigeria Police. From the state government's point of view, the police were poorly equipped to deal with the robberies. The Chief Press Secretary to Governor of Anambra State remarked:

> Their number was then grossly inadequate...[they] did not have enough vehicles, communication gadgets, as well as arms and ammunition, unlike the bandits who were not just armed to the teeth with deadly rifles but operated in convoys of luxury jeeps, complete with walkie talkies.[11]

According to the Governor, that early period of his office in the new Nigerian democracy was a traumatic one. 'When they were killing us - these armed robbers; we were shouting and praying and appealing to the Federal Government to come to our rescue. And nothing happened. Nobody came.'[12] Or, in the opinion of one local resident, while these violent crimes lasted, 'the police looked the other way and in fact collaborated fully and saw to the death of people they ought to protect.'[13]

The Response of the Anambra Vigilante Service

Against this background of the ineffectiveness of the police to protect citizens, the Governor of Anambra State, Dr. Mbadinuju, was pressed by Onitsha market traders to choose a radical solution and to invite a vigilante group, the Bakassi Boys from the neighbouring state of Abia. There, following a spate of violent robberies by gangs that operated openly and without challenge, residents of the city of Aba had formed the vigilante group to detect and apprehend suspected armed robbers. Within a space of one year armed robbery had been reduced to a minimum and businesses resumed normal services. As the chief security officer of the state, Mbadinuju agreed to the traders' request and set about creating the Anambra Vigilante Service (AVS) which incorporated the Bakassi Boys.[14] Nigerians have a long history of taking the law into their hands, burning suspected robbers alive when caught. Indeed, vigilante groups called Ndi Nche have operated in every Igbo society for centuries. In addition, Nigeria has had for a number of years special paramilitary anti-crime squads known as Rapid Response Teams operating in every state. Though they have had removed since 1999 the military personnel attached to them, they still constitute an intimidating force. Given this background, it can be argued that the Governor was following a well-trodden tradition. Indeed, he was in harmony with developments elsewhere in Nigeria, as in Lagos there was strong support for the Oodua Peoples Congress (OPC) and similar groups were emerging in the North (the Arewa Peoples Congress) and in the Niger Delta (Ijaw Vanguard and the Egbesu Boys).

The first step was to hold consultations with local governments, traditional rulers, community leaders, town development union officers, labour leaders and the traders. Following their agreement, a bill was passed in the state legislature inaugurating the AVS and stipulating its structure, lines of accountability and duties. It was to do stop-and-search and persons found with incriminating material were to be handed over to the police. In an interview the Governor claimed his motives were straightforward:

> All we want is safety of lives and property... The job of the vigilante is not to kill. Their job is to defend - defend us from being killed. We want people to get these things very clear. We have not imported or raised up any army of killers; no, we have just put up some vigilante organisations to defend the population of Anambra State from being killed by armed robbers. If the armed robbers did not attack us and make us their targets, there would be no vigilante.[15]

The procedure of AVS, popularly called the Bakassi Boys, is clearly defined, according to the Head of Security in Anambra State:

> Bakassi don't just go in and start manhandling people. They bring you out; they interrogate you for some days and they try you just to find out whether you are truly a robber or not. And they also take you to your compound where you live. The people in your compound will be able to confirm whether this man is a thief or not. If they enter into a compound and there is one dissenting opinion that this man is not a criminal after all, he will automatically be set free... They are in full co-operation with government.[16]

There can be no doubt about the dramatic impact of the Bakassi Boys on the crime rate. From the time of their inauguration in July 2000, until January 2001, there were practically no armed robberies anywhere in Anambra State and Anambra claims now to have the lowest robbery rates in Nigeria. A local journalist in Onitsha echoes the feelings of many residents when he says that their achievements are, 'monumental...unlike before when armed robbers attack almost on daily basis, the situation is now normal and we now sleep with all our eyes closed.'[17] For obvious considerations of securing local popular support, the State authorities have been keen to trumpet their success. Hence reviewing the impact of the AVS, the Governor's Chief Press Secretary said in January 2001:

> AVS is a roaring success. Anambra now has by far the least robbery rate of all states in the country. People don't even any more lock their gates, houses or cars. Sometimes there are no incidents of robbery for weeks. Night life is coming back in full swing as people now move from one end of the state to the other at odd hours without the slightest fear of molestation. Even individual policemen are very happy because they are no longer attacked by armed evil men who would dispose them of their guns. Little wonder, the operation of AVS is marked by discipline, honesty, impartiality and thoroughness, rather than arbitrariness. The immense popularity of AVS is truly earned.[18]

The Bakassi Boys clearly see their strongest card in securing support as their role in the reduction of crime rates. Whatever the political problems of private policing, they believe they can point to the virtual eradication of armed robbery. AVS proudly called on journalists at Christmas 2000 to:

> Go to the Main Market [in Onitsha] and see how business is going on this season. Traders from within and outside the country have been transacting their business without fear, unlike what they experienced in the past. We are proud of Bakassi Boys.[19]

Significantly they were also careful to add that the organisation had no problem with the Nigeria Police: 'we work for the same goal of making Anambra State free of criminals.' Asked then why his group seemed to be dreaded by everybody, Okoye, the AVS chairman, replied,

> I think it is the way they have kept themselves and the way they operate. First, we don't take bribe. Once you are caught, you are handed over to the police. Even if you give them ten million Naira, they will not take. It is against their principle to take money from suspects.[20]

Nevertheless, despite all the positive press releases concerning their fairness and co-operation with the police, the overwhelming evidence is that the AVS has used unlawful methods in its pursuit of justice, including extrajudicial killings (typically decapitating suspects and setting them on fire), the use of arbitrary arrest and detention and the excessive use of force and torture of detainees. It is important, however, prior to outlining this evidence, to set the AVS in context. It should be remembered that the national police do not have a good record either when it comes to human rights and legality. In its country report for 2000, the US State Department noted that the Nigerian police:

> regularly beat protesters, criminal suspects, detainees and convicted prisoners...[they] continued to use arbitrary arrest and detention...and to commit extrajudicial killings...By August police in Lagos reported killing 509 armed robbers and injuring 113 during the course of making 3,166 arrests...No legal action was taken against these security officials by years end...Criminal suspects died from unnatural causes while in official custody, usually as the result of neglect and harsh treatment...Police regularly physically mistreated civilians in attempts to extort money from them (Department of State, 2001).

A recent directive handed down to policemen in Lagos was to shoot armed robbers at the scene of robbery.[21] In other words there is a culture in Nigeria of harsh, violent and illegal treatment of criminal suspects and the Bakassi Boys are another reflection of this general attitude.

Extrajudicial Killings

There are many citizen accounts of extrajudicial executions by the Bakassi Boys. For instance, one witness described the death of a robber in front of him as: 'Two of the boys first cut off his two hands, gave him few cuts on his legs, at his back and finally slashed off his head using sharp knives. Blood gushed out and the crowd roared in applause.'[22] Over 130 suspected robbers are said to have been killed by them and many more have fled the state.

One of the most notorious extrajudicial killings was that of 'Prophet' Eddy Okeke. Though members of the Onitsha Market Traders Association failed to secure the Governor's authorisation for the Bakassi Boys to kill Eddy Okeke, for his alleged involvement in robberies and ritual murders in the region, the Bakassi Boys intervened. They seized him on 4 November, 2000, took him away for interrogation and denied his release to the police, on the grounds that he would simply be released. Five days later, the prophet and two of his followers were killed and their bodies publicly burnt before a large celebrating crowd in Onitsha's market square. Similar scenes greeted the 'macheting' to death and burning of a notorious gang leader,

'Derico' in July 2001. Allegedly responsible for a series of bus robberies and raids on police stations for weapons, during which nine policemen had died, he had fled the state. But the Bakassi Boys tracked him down in Abuja and arrested him at a road block.[23]

Criminal Complicity

There are also accusations of the Bakassi Boys' involvement in crime themselves, but disentangling what is the truth and what are attempts by the police to discredit them are difficult. Two days after the killing of Prophet Eddy Okeke there occurred a shoot out with the police at an attempted armed robbery in Onitsha. A gang member was apparently shot dead, who was later identified as a member of the AVS. Moreover, the gang was said to have used a jeep that had been taken by the AVS when they arrested Prophet Eddy Okeke. However, the version of events given by the traders was very different. They claimed that the person killed by the police was not an armed robber, but a victim of 'police brutality', shot during an earlier protest over the arrest of the treasurer Udegbunam in the Eddie Okele case. Similarly the chairman of AVS asserted:

> What actually happened was that the police kidnapped one of our members and killed him later. How it happened was that somebody came to report a case of robbery. In fact, the police is telling lies. Immediately, we sent three of my members. On getting to the scene, they saw the Mercedes Benz car used to block the complainant's car. They decided to examine the car and it was in the process of doing this the police came. They were quite aware that those were AVS men, but they opened fire on them... They ended up abducting one of my men and later killed him. ...And that's what exactly happened. Every other thing that police is saying is a lie. To further corroborate our story, the complainant has come to our camp to tell us that the police were forcing him to tell the whole world that our man they killed was an armed robber. ...But I have to say that it is only very few policemen that are against the AVS. But more than 95 per cent of policemen in Anambra State appreciate what we're doing. But very few of them, who are not clean, who are not happy with the Bakassi Boys are the ones causing this problem.[24]

The weight of the argument in this particular case might have been thought to lie with the AVS, but in November 2001 a similar incident occurred in Onitsha when police shot dead four armed robbers, two of whom were later revealed to be AVS members.[25] The vigilante organisation once more protested that they had only been present because they had been summoned to the scene by the victim. Although this version was accepted by the traders, who subsequently threatened to attack the police for the 'deliberate killings', others will have more serious doubts.

Political Murders

There have also been indications that the AVS has been undertaking either personal vendettas or political murders. The accusations of political meddling have so far centred on the Security Adviser to the Governor. It is alleged that he has used the Bakassi Boys to silence opposition to the current security arrangements. For instance, the minority leader in the State House Assembly was stopped in his car by a dozen Bakassi Boys, 'wielding pump action rifles, axes, hammers and revolvers'. He was ordered out of his car at gunpoint and subsequently arrested. He claims that his arrest was set up by Chuma Nzeribe, security adviser to the Anambra State Governor, who 'wanted me silenced once and for all because we have long disagreed on the security situation in Onitsha.' They stripped him naked, tied his hands and feet and took him to the AVS headquarters. There he was tried before seven men who sat like judges in a court, for opposing the organisation and for having links with the criminal underworld. Apparently the 'judges' adjourned, having disagreed over whether to execute him or release him. At this juncture he was rescued by the police on the orders of the Inspector General.[26] Again, a pamphlet was circulated around the market of Onitsha accusing the chairman of the Onitsha North Local Government Council of harbouring a notorious criminal and declaring him 'wanted' by the Bakassi Boys. The man in question argued that the vigilantes were out to 'settle political and personal scores'.[27]

More recently AVS members are accused of the abduction and murder of Chief Godwin Ezeodumegwu Okonkwo, the chairman of the All People's Party (APP), in Nnewi-South local government area of the state on 18 February, 2001. AVS treasurer, Emmanuel Udegbunam was arrested in connection with this murder, which he strongly denies:

> Nobody for the Vigilance Committee could collect any kobo to kill somebody. We have a common oath against it. The Boys themselves have their own oath. Even among themselves, if any person takes a bribe they kill that person. So I doubt if any AVS member or committee member collected any kobo for anybody.[28]

The nature of the Bakassi Boys' actions is bound to generate strong responses, depending on whether they are seen as allies or enemies. But aside from being a topic on which everyone in Anambra has an opinion, they have also altered the political landscape, as the following section shows.

The Democratic Impact

The Bakassi Boys are only one of many vigilante services that have arisen in the last few years in Nigeria. In the South-west and Lagos the most prominent was the Oodua Peoples Congress (OPC) until its banning and the arrest of its leaders in October 2000. The proscription followed the deaths of some 300 in violent clashes between the Yoruba and Hausa in Lagos, 15-17 October. The fighting had begun following a dispute over the capture and killing of alleged robbers of the Hausa ethnic group by the OPC. Also operating in the South are the Imo State Vigilante service and the Edo State Vigilante service. In the North, the Arewa Peoples Congress (APC) became prominent after the February 2000 religious riots in Kaduna. It was formed by conservative political leaders to be a counter-balance to the OPC. Whilst in the Niger Delta, Ijaw Vanguard and Egbesu Boys are the leading groups.

Though most of these groups have some form of official or semi-official standing in their respective states, they cannot be termed 'responsible' citizen responses, in the sense of always acting with the full approval of and in co-operation with the security authorities. Yet neither are they autonomous citizen responses, that is, groups that act totally independently and often in opposition to the authorities, and who willingly break the law and resort to violence to achieve their goals. They straddle the official, unofficial divide.

A democratic state is at the very least a mutual protection association where the community protects all its members. Many, therefore, from all sectors of society, have endorsed the work that the AVS have done to enhance personal security when public policing in this area is thin or non-existent. The Chairman of Awka South Local Government, Anambra state, Chief Ndubuisi Nwebu, stated the position of the Association of Local Governments of Nigeria as one of 'unflinching support' for the 'able manner' in which the Governor provided for the security of lives and property within the state:

> The best thing that has happened to this state is the operation of the State Vigilante Services. The state governor has done very marvelous thing by providing the state with that security. So the threat by the Federal Government

to ban the State Vigilante services cannot work. This is our state. Somebody who lives in Abuja, Kano, Lagos, cannot from there tell us how we are going to live here or do they want all of us to be killed by armed robbers?[29]

Likewise the Association of Anambra State Development Union, Lagos branch, has said that the AVS is a welcome development to the entire people of Anambra State. Its branch president said it had brought sanity and the protection of lives and property to the people of the state. It was a plus to the development of the entire state and community as a whole.[30]

On the national front, *This Day* offered editorial support for the AVS under the headline, 'Effective And Responsible Law And Order':

> The helplessness of the Federal Government in addressing the rising crime wave across the country brings to the fore, the need for restructuring. A centralised Police Force remote from the communities they police is incapable of providing effective protection to the citizens. Indeed, in many regions in Nigeria, parallel local organisations and vigilante groups have proved far more effective in combating crime. Whilst we recognise the danger of untrained citizens, without defined structures or commands acting outside the structures of law to enforce law and order; the police, pending the creation of independent state police commands must recognise the need to show greater understanding and appreciation of the useful and positive role that the OPC, the Egbesu, the Bakassi boys and other vigilante groups could play in the effective maintenance of law and order. In truth, the 'folk hero' status of these groups is as a result of the failing of the police. The police is well advised to see how the efforts of various vigilante groups can be harnessed in combating the intolerably high level of crime in the country.[31]

Even Islamic scholars have joined in. Dr. Is-haq Akintola, of the Lagos State University said the Nigeria Police had failed completely. He lamented that the crime wave had soared to such an extent that people now lived in perpetual fear. Islam, he said, supported OPC and Bakassi Boys so long as they would not go beyond fighting crime. He added that the Quoran stated that 'anybody who sees evil should use his hand to change it.'[32]

But though vigilantes may have improved the protection of people from physical violence or the threat of it and are widely popular, there has been a price in terms of democracy. There are a number of areas where their activities give cause for concern.

Diminishing Accountability

The provision of so important a service as policing in a democracy should be subject to systematic auditing and evaluation. Yet too often the vigilante services, even though officially regulated by local state law, are less than transparent. In the name of defending personal security and community interests, much escapes careful scrutiny. Currently vigilante services are, at best, loosely controlled by national and state law, at worse they commonly act outside of the law.

In Anambra the Governor has been inclined to turn a blind eye to the breaking of the law by the AVS, so long as 'the job is done.' He has also been adamant in defending the illegal means they have used (such as carrying weapons, which is forbidden by the state legislation), so long as the security ends are met. The case of the extrajudicial killing of Eddie Okeke was indefensible and the Governor might have been expected to immediately call the AVS to account for it. Instead, his actions demonstrated that they were above the law; they were to be defended not prosecuted. The local police argued that a man had been 'unwholesomely murdered' and those that murdered him should be brought to justice 'no matter how highly placed, nobody is above the law, be it Anambra State Vigilante Services or Bakassi or whatever name they are called, they will all be arrested and be charged for murder and tried for such offence'.[33] At the national level the Inspector-General of Police, angered that the local police command did not do enough to halt the extrajudicial killing of the prophet, ordered the removal of the state police commissioner and the arrest of the AVS treasurer, Emmanuel Udegbunam. With the existence of the Bakassi Boys under threat from this police campaign, and with over 10,000 angry traders storming the state capital to protest and threatening to make the state ungovernable, the Governor rushed to Abuja to defend their (and his) cause. President Obasanjo reiterated that the AVS had to work within the state law. Yet even he would not demand their being brought under strict accountability to the state and federal government and ordered the release of the AVS treasurer. Public order and political support were as much factors as accountability. Meanwhile the Governor simply made some bland statement about co-operation with the police:

> The President, myself and I.G.[Inspector General of Police] have agreed that the police and the Bakassi should work together...I think the essence is that the government must give priority to the police who have the traditional role of law enforcement. If there is a vigilante and we make a case for continuation of the vigilante, their role should be to support the police and to operate within the law that is already passed in Anambra State...Nobody is talking about disbandment of Bakassi in Anambra. In all my discussion with the President last night the issue didn't arise, he was only asking me to ensure that the

people operate within the law and that is what I decide to do myself. Law is law and nobody should be above the law.[34]

Only following the accusations of the murder of Okonkwo, the local chairman of the All People's Party, did the Governor yield to pressure to make the Bakassi Boys more accountable. In a radio and television broadcast on 12 March 2001, he promised to reorganise the service, bringing in a new executive committee that would include a top civil servant, a representative of the commissioner of police, a traditional ruler, a town union president and the chairman of the security committee of the house. It is envisaged that this will ensure that the AVS will stick to its functions as laid down in its founding charter, although the committee will still be chaired by the Governor's adviser on security matters.[35]

It remains to be seen whether these reforms are substantial or cosmetic. The general point is still true, however, that vigilante services in Anambra as elsewhere are, at best, loosely controlled by national and state law, and at worse they commonly act outside of the law.

Delegitimising the Federal State

The formation of the Bakassi Boys has proved to be more than a popular anti-crime measure. It has triggered a vigorous debate in Nigeria on policing and brought to the fore a power struggle between the federal and state levels of government.[36] Ironically, local security action, which claims it supplements and strengthens the legitimacy of the national police and the Federal state, may actually have a contrary effect. The Anambra State has faced a suspicious and sometimes hostile Federal government over the AVS. Confronted with the Federal government's early attempts to use the Mobile Police to close down the Bakassi Boys for fear it was an ethnic militia, the Governor set out firmly his case that security matters in the state were *his* prerogative and that in this area he was not going to be directed by the centre:

> I want to make this point very clear, the constitution makes the Governor the chief security officer of the state, not the Inspector-General, not the Commissioner of Police, not even the President. The president is in charge of all of us, all the states, but when it comes to Anambra State, I am in charge in terms of security... And I made it clear, that if the mobile police give too much trouble to the vigilante group, I will withdraw the mobile people. I will tell the President I don't need them. I will have to tell the president what I want in Anambra State.[37]

Anambra State Vigilante Service 141

As far as Mbadinuju is concerned, therefore, the Bakassi Boys are untouchable. His political support base meant he could adopt no other position. The situation puts the Federal Government in a predicament. On the one hand it does not want to be seen to be opposing any genuine popular moves to stem the rising crime. To be seen to hinder state and citizen anti-crime initiatives, when even the Federal Government itself admits that the Nigeria Police cannot cope, would be political suicide. In addition, Mbadinuju is a member of Obasanjo's PDP and one who has argued for Obasanjo's second term of office as opposed to seeking an Igbo president through an Igbo dominated party, as suggested by many political figures in the south-east. On the other hand, Nigeria has waited so long for an era of constitutionalism that they are determined to insist on the primacy of the rule of law. It does not want to encourage centrifugal forces at a time when it is trying to regain legitimacy for the centre after years of misrule have discredited it. Nor does it want to allow regional militias to arise that could be instruments in the hands of regional politicians, or worse, could become secessionist armies. Their ambivalence is represented in official statements that speak both positively and negatively. Thus, during the first lady's visit to Anambra State in late November 2000, she commended the Bakassi Boys' efforts[38] and the Minister of Police Affairs, Major-General David Jemibewon, has also expressed qualified support:

> The law recognises self effort in protecting yourself and your property…It will be ridiculous if your house is burgled and you sit at home hoping for the police to come and ask if your house is burgled or if someone slaps you, will you say until I report to the police, I will not slap the man back?[39]

He has, however, warned that the laws of the land must be respected: 'all I can say is that; don't take the laws into your hands; but the law allows for self defence'.[40] The delicate balance also characterised Nigeria's first ever National Security Retreat in August 2001, called to consider ways to tackle the rising crime wave. The final statement was careful to acknowledge that the anti-crime initiatives of some state governments reflected, 'the widespread desire to acquire for all Nigerians the key dividends of democracy'. Nevertheless they noted that such security organisations had 'inherent tendencies to further endanger Nigerians to the extent that they did not conform strictly with the relevant constitutional provisions.'[41]

It does not help the federal state's uncertainty that the Anambra State will give no unequivocal assurance that the AVS will not be allowed to become in time a state police force, in effect taking over from the federal police. Rather, Anambra state insists, like other states, that should a state police force be formed, it would not thereby be a threat to Nigerian national unity. Only a few months after Nigeria's democratisation, some state governors were talking of state police, whilst at the Second Southern Governors Forum in Enugu in January 2001, there was a quite explicit call for the establishment of state police. From their point of view they have found fulfilling their constitutional responsibility for maintaining peace and order in their states very difficult, when the only police force they have available takes its orders solely from Abuja.[42]

A state police force is perhaps a long-term ambition, but in the medium term Anambra has its sights on other roles for its Vigilante Service. Buoyed up by the success, as they see it, of the current vigilante policing, the state government has revealed that it has plans to expand their remit to include the protection of public facilities such as the installations of the National Electric Power Authority and pipelines belonging to the Nigerian National Petroleum Corporation.[43] By putting the AVS expansion in these terms, the Anambra state hope to forestall criticism, since the Federal government has suffered notorious lapses of security associated with these installations over recent years. Nevertheless, with the Northern Governors insisting that the demand for state police is unconstitutional and dangerous, it may be seen from Abuja as the thin end of the wedge.

As the tension between the centre and the state has been left, there is a situation in which a quasi-official militia currently competes with the Nigeria Police and, indeed, with the criminal justice system, to deter, arrest and punish those deemed criminals. The reality is that the Federal state is *not* having the last word on who may use force and under what conditions.

The Marginalisation of the Federal Police

The Nigeria Police, not surprisingly, has been wary of the vigilante groups from their inauguration, both because they share the Federal government's fear of the break up of the nation and from self-interest, in that the groups encroach on their own field of duties. In the face of criticism, police authorities are usually quick to claim that the high crime levels are due to inadequate police funding and low force levels.

The former Inspector General of Police, Alhaji Ibrahim Coomassie, has articulated publicly the Nigeria Police position towards the vigilante services. He has warned that the use of vigilante groups by state governments as an alternative to the police threatens the functions of the police and could also be used as an instrument of oppression. 'State police will be used by their masters as political thugs during campaigns against their opponents instead of being used for the state or public interest'.[44] His argument is based on the events of 1987, when the Federal Government ordered all police officers from the ranks of Constable to Superintendent to return to their states of origin. They became ethnic champions in their areas and were allegedly involved in various ethnic rioting across the country. By contrast, he argues that the Nigeria Police is a unifying force and that the solution to the rising crime is for the Federal Government to equip more fully the national force.

As mentioned before, the first response of the Nigeria Police to the Bakassi Boys in Anambra was to seek to remove them by drafting in a large force of the Mobile Police. It was not a welcome move to the inhabitants of Anambra. As one local correspondent to a newspaper observed:

> It is a wonder that the Police Inspector General just remembered to send down the mobile policemen after the Bakassi Boys when he never deemed it fit to do so to check the hideous robberies and murders a few weeks ago. In fact, the question that should be raised by the Igbo is why he has deemed it fit to tackle Bakassi Boys instead of robbers and murderers and why has he not sent the same mobile policemen after the OPC?[45]

Nor were residents impressed to see the return of police roadblocks and the collection of tolls and bribes, which the Governor had only recently outlawed. There followed negotiation and an understanding was reached between the police and the state authorities that allowed the vigilante services to be maintained so long as they acted in the capacity of supporting the police rather than superseding them. 'There is no conflict at all', announced the Governor:

> The vigilante are here to support the police in the area of law enforcement. The police will guide them as to the norms and how they should operate. But anybody saying that they will not operate at all is looking for trouble with me.[46]

From the beginning, the state authorities and the AVS have been keen to highlight joint operations against armed robbers. Their own official version of their relationship with the police is that it is 'cordial', though they admit it has fluctuated with the three changes in the Commissioner of Police in one year. Okoye, the AVS chairman, confided that when the latest Commissioner of Police was sent:

> Some unscrupulous police officers deceived him into believing that what we're doing is not right... I am advising [him] not to listen to these unpatriotic policemen who are annoyed that they are not making money from the traders because if there are no crimes, police won't make money.[47]

He was in no doubt as to why the former Commissioner of Police, 'one of the best police commissioners the state has ever had', had been removed. 'They went to the Inspector-General of Police to tell lies to him.'[48]

Under the surface, however, the resentment of the police in the state has been simmering. As the success of the Bakassi Boys was trumpeted, so people were making unfavourable contrasts with what the police had achieved before their arrival. The police have watched their credibility undermined and their roles by-passed. Inevitably, they have sought to look for every opportunity (some would say, have created opportunities) to so seriously discredit their rivals that they would be closed down. The alleged cases of AVS involvement in bank robbery, extrajudicial murder and political murder in 2000/2001 have been fully exploited by them and statements from them have been increasingly assertive. Thus the Assistant Inspector General of Police, in charge of the newly created Zone 9, told state police commissioners of Imo, Enugu, Abia and Anambra in January 2001 that he was ready to work with vigilante groups as long as they operated under the rule of law. Yet he warned that the command would not accommodate any group that arrogated to itself the position of a parallel body without any legal backing to operate.[49] Again, in June 2001 the Anambra State police commissioner handed down a public warning to the AVS that the rule of law must be obeyed. Though he said the Nigeria police was willing to work with any organisation whose aims and objectives were in line with the maintenance of law and order, he made it quite clear that they would no longer tolerate deviations from the original AVS code of conduct:

> The police will not hesitate to deal ruthlessly with a situation where an innocent citizen or citizens in general are arrested and treated as criminals without recourse to proper police investigation and prosecution... In our attempts to protect lives and property, it is important not to sacrifice the rule of law, which is one of the vital pillars of democracy, for the transient gains of cheap popularity.[50]

The struggle for who is to provide an efficient and incorrupt policing service in the state is openly engaged. Bakassi still maintain the support of the Governor ('AVS cannot and will never be banned'),[51] the Local

Government, the traders and the majority of the citizens of the state; but it is in danger of losing the crucial support of the federal Government under pressure from the police and federal politicians. Its presence creates rivalry not cooperation.

Inequality of Treatment

To secure legal-civil equality, liberal democracy, *inter alia*, provides for an equal right of access to the legal process and also an equal right to just adjudication of law. These rights are irrespective of ethnicity, gender, class, age, religion, or residence. This is already under strain with the introduction of Sharia law in 12 northern states. Such organisations as the AVS only exacerbate this. The nature of its services means that they can offer no equality of accessibility or adjudication across the state. The availability of their guarding and protection services within the state is not on offer outside the state. Further, in cases where the vigilante services undertake adjudication, there are inevitably serious concerns about standards of investigation, scrutiny of evidence, the sanctions available and a consistency of treatment for citizens. Amidst stories of earnestness to eradicate crime are others of hasty verdicts, presumption of guilt, torture, violence and intimidation.

The AVS, like all local anti-crime groups, tends to promote an underclass of citizens. The discourse is of 'undesirable elements' and of those 'hoodlums' who act in a 'sub-human' way. Society must be 'sanitized' and 'cleansed' of such by any means available, since they have forfeited their human rights. The AVS responses to them have been guilty of discarding lawful and humane procedures of investigation, detention, trial and punishment. This violence continues with apparent impunity since its 'victims' are the 'dangerous classes' of criminals who do not deserve protection. Thus the Governor of Anambra retorted to accusations of neglecting human rights with:

> Somebody is telling me about human rights? I can't understand it. If these armed robbers have human rights, we, law-abiding citizens also should enjoy our human right. But for them to keep killing us, and now we are defending ourselves and you are telling me human rights – human right of an armed robber – Hmmm – this is funny.[52]

Or again, in response to human rights groups who criticised him for the methods of crime control used, he replied: 'the methods may be crude but the armed robbers themselves were also crude and they too employed crude methods, so let the pot not call the kettle black.'[53] It is a justice of tit for tat.

Where violence and lawlessness by criminal *and* anti-crime groups prevails, it promotes atomisation, self-interest and brutalisation. People are readily branded as 'enemies' on the basis of their location or ethnicity, irrespective of their true practices. For example, the Head of Security in Anambra State came close to branding all the inhabitants of two settlements east of Onitsha as criminals when he said:

> We look forward to the total cleansing of the state of armed, violent robberies. We have decided to go to their den, make a big shed at Umuleri and Umuoba Anam and we shall take back our communities from criminals. I urged all citizens of Umuleri and Umuoba Anam to pack their bags and baggage and get to return to their villages.[54]

Of the same communities the police openly speak of them as ones which 'breed armed robbers'. Such labelling, whether of communities or individuals, can only undermine the equality of treatment expected in a democracy.[55]

An Escalation of Violence

The Bakassi Boys are a relatively young organisation, so it is impossible to assess the full implications of their arrival in Anambra state. Nevertheless there are potential concerns beyond what has already emerged. Violence breeds violence and so it can be expected that as citizens call on other armed individuals for protection, criminals will undertake their activity prepared to meet defensive violence with violence. Few would deny that the more extensive the carrying of instruments of coercion, the harder to control their responsible use. The vigilante service frequently allows its agents to carry instruments of coercion; there are very few restraints at all. The end justifies the means in their logic. So far the evidence is that the armed AVS has dissuaded robbers from activity, or even driven them away from the state. But there is the danger that they might return more heavily armed. The clearest case in Anambra was when 30 armed robbers stormed the house of the Supervisor of the vigilante group near the capital Awka. They killed his two wives and burnt his property and cars, apparently in revenge for the assault the man had been leading on the crime gangs of the Aguleri-Umeleri area. In the shoot out with the vigilantes that ended the assault, 22 were killed.[56] Even if an escalation does not occur, the expulsion of armed robbers from Anambra has only relocated the problem rather than solving it. In an interview, the Commissioner of Police of Enugu state acknowledged that an increase of crime in the state might have been due to the Bakassi Boys in neighbouring Anambra flushing out criminals. 'Some of the armed robbers escaped to neighbouring states, including Enugu'.[57] Certainly the notorious Derico gang fled Anambra and relocated in Lagos, causing havoc by its raids on the large electronics market.[58] Apparent solutions to violent crime may only be displacing violence.

Related to these concerns is anxiety as to whether the Bakassi Boys will evolve into an ethnic militia, aggravating ethnic tension that killed at least 2000 people in the year 2000 in attacks and reprisal attacks. The aversion to the outsider and the readiness to make the outsider the scapegoat for all social ills, has long been observed. In the light of the violence against the Hausa in 2000 associated with the OPC in Lagos, and APC attacks on people on the basis of their ethnicity, the Bakassi Boys were initially perceived to be just another ethnic militant group. So far, the Bakassi Boys have avoided the temptation and have stuck to their war against criminals of whatever class or ethnicity. In the Governor's words:

> It is an error to categorise the Bakassi Boys with such other groups as OPC in the west or APC in the north as the case may be. These other ones are ethnic motivated groups - ethnic cleansing organisations. But, Bakassi is a defensive mechanism to defend the people from the attack of armed robbers.[59]

They certainly claim to be multi-racial. In an interview, the Head of Security Services, Anambra State, claimed that the Bakassi Boys had 'a Yoruba man' and a 'Hausa man' working for them and that some of the leaders 'were from Ogoni in Rivers State and other parts of the Eastern States'.[60] Yet their association with a specifically Igbo separatist organisation such as the Movement for the Actualisation of the Sovereign State of Biafra (MASSOB), must be cause for concern. In neighbouring states it is apparent that the Bakassi Boys have already become involved in a political programme, taking it well beyond its original goals. A large proportion of the thousands that witnessed the MASSOB leader raise the Biafran flag and redeclare Biafra in Aba, Abia state, in May 2000, were Bakassi Boys.[61] They also worked with MASSOB in December 2000 when there was an excessive escalation of petrol pump prices in Abia and Imo states. They marched together from one filling station to another, with a multitude of buyers trailing behind them, to confront garage owners and to force them to lower prices to government approved rates.[62] Only time will show whether they will provoke and promote more violence than they curtail by their use of unrestrained force.

Conclusion

For a long time in Anambra there was remarkably little debate about the Bakassi Boys. Mbadinuju had been elected to the governorship of the newly created state in 1999 on a 'law and order' ticket and he sustained his support by its effectiveness in eradicating armed robberies. As far as the traders of Onitsha market are concerned he was a saviour of a once crime ridden city. 'He is a man of magic' says Vincent Obi, chairman of the Onitsha Main Market Amalgamated Traders Union.[63] But increasingly critical voices are being heard within the state that the Bakassi Boys are getting out of control. Sensing that the tide of popularity might have begun to turn, political rivals have sought to make political capital out of these concerns. Some members of the State Assembly have petitioned Abuja claiming that the AVS is undertaking extrajudicial murders. All are said to have been well connected with members of the federal establishment. Mbadinuju, therefore, has been forced on the defensive and has presented the legislators' move as threatening the 'peace' that had been achieved by the Bakassi Boys. He told the Onitsha traders: 'I want you to know that there are detractors, who are hell-bent on destabilising the state government. It is now up to you to guard and protect the state because you have no other.'[64]

More principled criticism has come from people like Chukwuemeka Odumegwu-Ojukwu the Igbo leader and the south-east members of the House of Representatives. Both have urged that security outfits, though not necessarily wrong, should be carefully controlled so that political and personal vendettas do not take place.[65] Up until now the Bakassi Boys have received widespread support for their policy that the end justifies the means. Though this is not likely to change at the popular level, they are likely to come under increasing pressure from the political leaders that they need as patrons, to act more circumspectly. Whether they will heed this restraint or mutate into a popular militia movement or even into a criminal gang, remains to be seen.

Notes

1 *Post Express*, Lagos, 16 October, 2000.
2 *This Day*, Lagos, 21 June, 2001; see also, 'Lagos under Robbers' Siege', *P.M. News*, Lagos, 18 June, 2001; 'Robbers Kill 400 in 6 months', *Post Express*, 5 July, 2001.
3 *The News*, Lagos, 16 April, 2001.
4 *Post Express*, 22 July, 2000.
5 In April 2001 three policemen stopped a bus at a road block; seeing they were carrying more than naira 1.4million, they diverted their bus to a nearby school and set light to it

with the intention of killing all five traders, although in the event only three died. *Panafrican News Agency*, 3 April, 2001.
6   *Vanguard*, 7 February, 2001.
7   *The News*, 16 April, 2001; for other examples of police collusion with criminals see *Guardian*, Lagos, 21 November, 2000.
8   *Post Express*, 17 July, 2000.
9   *Post Express*, 17 July, 2000.
10 *Post Express*, 1 February, 2001.
11 *Post Express*, 1 February, 2001.
12 *Post Express*, 29 July, 2000.
13 *Post Express*, 24 July, 2000.
14 Allegedly paying them naira 100,000 per month – *Africa Policy Information Centre*, www.africapolicy.org, accessed 26 February, 2001.
15 *Post Express*, 29 July, 2000.
16 *Post Express*, 29 July, 2000.
17 *Newswatch*, Lagos, 18 September, 2000.
18 *Post* Express, 1 February, 2001.
19 *Vanguard*, Lagos, 16 December, 2000.
20 *Vanguard*, 2 December, 2000.
21 *P.M. News*, Lagos, 3 July, 2001.
22 *Newswatch*, 18 September, 2000.
23 *The News*, 23 July, 2001.
24 *Vanguard*, 2 December, 2000.
25 *Vanguard*, 12 November, 2001.
26 *Newswatch*, 18 September, 2000.
27 *Vanguard*, 9 September, 2000.
28 *Vanguard*, 25 May, 2001.
29 *Post Express*, 31 January, 2001.
30 *Post Express*, 20 November, 2000.
31 *This Day*, 1 October, 2000.
32 *Post Express*, 17 July, 2000.
33 *P.M. News*, Lagos, 13 November, 2000.
34 *Vanguard*, 27 November, 2000.
35 *Newswatch*, 2 April, 2001.
36 The federal-state power struggle is of course of long standing. In the late 1970s in revolved around the attempt of the centre, without any consultation, to appoint Presidential Liaison Officers to represent federal policies in each state. To the States, especially those with Governors not of the ruling party, this was seen as a serious threat to their patronage networks. During the same period there was specific controversy over the Nigeria Police. When Governors found themselves unable to enforce gambling tax regulations they considered establishing state police forces, although their plans were finally quashed.
37 *Post Express*, 29 July, 2000.
38 She praised the governor for his ability to curb crime in the State and noted particularly that the Bakassi Boys had reduced armed robbery. 'We are happy to note that you have restored peace to this state and have taken a stand against the criminal element who threatened the livelihood of the decent industrious people of Anambra state' *Newswatch*, 27 November, 2000).
39 *Post Express*, 17 July, 2000.

40 *Post Express*, 22 July, 2000.
41 *The Guardian*, 13 August, 2001.
42 As regards other non-police services in states to combat crime, in Akwa Ibom the Governor has directed all local government councils to establish or resuscitate all Neighbourhood Security Committees. They are to liaise with the police in law enforcement (*Vanguard Daily*, 18 December, 2000). In Yobe the Governor directed the state traditional council in November 2000 to mobilize their people to form vigilance groups to fight the menace of armed banditry (*Guardian*, 20 November, 2000). In Lagos State, despite the outlawing of the OPC, such has been the spate of armed robberies that there have been widespread calls for their redeployment. The Governor has hinted at his intention to draft them in, saying, 'If OPC is one of the options I won't throw away any option to step down on crime and control it.' The Federal government reacted strongly that their views on engaging ethnic militia to contain crime had not changed; it was wrong and dangerous (*This Day*, 21 June, 2001). Edo State has also announced plans to form a central vigilance committee. However, following excessive intimidation by a vigilante group in Offa and its environs in Kwara State, it was banned by the Governor.
43 *Post Express*, 1 February, 2001.
44 *Post Express*, 22 September, 2000.
45 *Post Express*, 24 July, 2000.
46 *Post Express*, 29 July, 2000.
47 *Vanguard*, 2 December, 2000.
48 ibid.
49 *This Day*, 14 January, 2001.
50 *Vanguard*, 8 June, 2001.
51 *Post Express*, 7 December, 2000.
52 *Post Express*, 29 July, 2000.
53 *Vanguard*, 5 January, 2001.
54 *Post Express*, 29 July, 2000.
55 *Vanguard*, 16 August, 2001.
56 *Vanguard*, 20 July, 2001. The same appears to be happening in the case of armed robberies in Lagos, where not just police but vigilante guards are being picked out and shot dead. In one incident there, armed robbers killed two members of the neighbourhood's vigilante group. One of the vigilante group was brutally macheted by the robbers who did not leave until they drove a nail into his skull. The other vigilante member's corpse was taken away by the robbers (*P.M. News*, 18 June, 2001).
57 *Tempo*, Lagos, 16 November, 2000.
58 *PM News*, 23 July, 2001.
59 *Post Express*, 29 July, 2000.
60 *Post Express*, 29 July, 2000.
61 *Africa Research Bulletin*, 37, 5, 2000, p.13979. MASSOB had formed originally in 1994 to contest the presidential election result, believing that Abiola had rightfully won it. Forced underground they became militant and on their re-emergence in 1999 they adopted a separatist programme and an anti-crime agenda that brought them into conflict both with the police and with non-Yoruba.
62 *Post Express*, 9 December, 2000.
63 *Newswatch*, 18 September, 2000.
64 *Vanguard*, 9 April, 2001.
65 *Newswatch*, 2 April, 2001.

PART IV
THE PEOPLE TAKE THE LAW INTO THEIR OWN HANDS

7 Vigilantes and Crime in South Africa

Crime in South Africa

Crime is notoriously difficult to quantify given the complexities behind how it is recorded and the problems are exacerbated by the South African Government's moratorium on the release of crime statistics in 2000 (ostensibly while the data system is revamped, although more likely because of the bad international press it was attracting). It is known, however, that the 20 most common serious crimes increased between 1994 and 1998, from 1,998,000 reported crimes, to 2,154,000. That is an 8 percent increase, though the population did rise 10 percent in that time (Crime Information Analysis Centre (CIAC) of South African Police Service (SAPS) figures, quoted in Schonteich, 2000b, p. 21).

During the first three years following the democratic transition of 1994, overall crime levels seemed to stabilise, but the latest evidence is that they have been rising since 1997, apart from murder and attempted murder, which were already at very high levels. Between 1994 and 1997 the average year-on-year increase in recorded crime was 3 percent, whereas between 1998 and 1999 it was 7 percent (Louw, 2001). Thus between 1994 and 1999 violent crime increased by 22 percent and property crime by 15 percent (Schonteich, 2000c). Some would say these increases are the inevitable result of social controls being relaxed, the growth of the illegitimate opportunity structure and discovery by marginalised people that there was to be no change in their standard of living (Kinnes, 2000, p. 1, 12).

Making comparisons with other countries is always problematic, given the differences that exist in the way crime is reported and recorded. Nevertheless, Interpol figures suggest that though South Africa has manageable levels of property crime, it has an extraordinary high level of violent crime. In 1998, South Africa had the highest recorded per capita murder rate in the Interpol annual report, with 59 recorded murders per 100,000. Similarly there were very high rates recorded of robbery and violent theft (208 per 100,000) and of serious assaults (550 per 100,000) (quoted in Masuku, 2001). CIAC also reported that, between January 1997 and March 1999, murders committed during attacks on farms were averaging 10 per month (CIAC, 1999).

A fuller picture of crime levels is revealed by crime surveys, which typically uncover some 60 percent more crime than that reported by official sources. A survey conducted by the Human Sciences Research Council (HSRC) November 1999, found that 20 percent of the respondents had been the victims of crime in the previous 12 months, a figure twice that of 1995. In the Province of Gauteng, victimisation was as high as 27 percent. In terms of racial differentiation, a survey of victims of crime over a twelve month period found that 16 percent of the black population, 39 percent of the white, 18 percent of the coloured and 32 percent of the Indian were affected. 'This would appear to represent more than a doubling of crime experiences during the last four years' (Humphries, 2000, p. 4).[1] In rural areas, the victimisation rate was found to be very similar to urban areas, with 57 percent saying they had been victims between July 1993 and July 1998 (Pelser, 2000).

Democratisation has also seen a considerable growth in international and organised crime. It had already taken advantage under apartheid of a police force that was focussing on political surveillance and control, and of South Africa's first world infrastructure of transport, telecommunications and banking. Now it was able to exploit an expanded illegitimate opportunity. Border controls were relaxed, international trade and travel grew, and the police were slow to reorganise and to acquire criminal investigation skills (Shaw, 1997; Gastrow, 1998; Gastrow, 1999; Kinnes, 2000). Figures for organised crime are far from accurate (SAPS only engaged in its first relatively accurate audit of criminal syndicates in the late 1990s), but earlier 'audits' suggested that organised crime syndicates in 1994 had 1,296 suspected members. This had increased to 1,903 suspects in at least 500 organised criminal groups by 1997 (Gastrow, 1999, p. 59). Over the last seven years these syndicates have grown in size, in their international links, in organisational complexity and in the sophistication of their weaponry. The syndicates specialise in the highjacking of cars and lorries, narcotics, illegal weapons and smuggled goods. According to informants and court trials, their success has in part been based on their penetration of the middle and senior echelons of the local and provincial governments and the police itself (Gastrow, 1998, pp. 36-47, 55-60).

Though this chapter addresses nation-wide problems, I intend to provide a provincial focus and shall draw many of my examples from my research in the Eastern Cape (see Baker, 2002). Figures for the Eastern Cape reveal high crime levels. The reported number of the 20 most serious crimes increased from 244,176 in 1994 to 255,474 in 1998, an increase of 4.6 percent. Reported murders in the same period, however, fell to 3,769 from the 1994 figure of 4,492 (CIAC figures, quoted in Schonteich, 2000b, p. 21). 19 percent of the Eastern Cape residents said they had been victims of crime in the previous twelve months (Humphries, 2000, p. 5). Figures for the largest metropolitan area in Eastern Cape, Port Elizabeth, show that between 1994 and 1999, vehicle theft, car hijacking and murder went down, but crimes that rose included rape (20 percent), aggravated robbery (14 percent), business burglary (16 percent), and residential burglary (34 percent). For recorded serious crimes, figures per 100,000 are high, namely 71 for murder, 232 for rape, 294 for aggravated burglary, 995 for residential burglary (Louw, 2001). Or in Grahamstown, a small city of 120,000 in Eastern Cape, between August 1999 and August 2000, monthly averages were 4 for murder, 8 for rape, 9 for robbery and 89 for housebreaking and theft.[2]

The Response of Vigilantism

Vigilantism is a category of non-state policing. It not only acts independently of the state police, but often does not co-operate with it and is prepared to break the law to achieve its goals of protection and investigation (or even trials and sentencing). It is characterised by reactive, *ad hoc* and often violent methods of control. According to Daniel Nina:

> Vigilantism will adopt either a crime or social order approach. In either case, it is linked directly to the use of physical force and intimidation at levels not normally used by the state. In the denial of the state as the guarantor of the social order, vigilantism will invoke an 'imagined order' that either existed in the past (in its decadent mode), or never existed but is desired (in its idealized mode)... Vigilantism appropriates state functions in a way that creates a parallel sovereign power that is unregulated (Nina, 2001).

In South Africa vigilantism is largely, though not exclusively, concentrated in the black community (Schonteich, 2000d, pp. 28-9). It is in some respects a continuation of, or a return to, an established culture of self-reliance. It echoes the traditional forms of village and clan protection and popular justice, which was when all policing was local, voluntary and discretionary. The assumption of policing responsibilities by the public authorities from communities is, of course, only a recent phenomenon. In South Africa it only took place in the latter half of the nineteenth century e.g. Cape Town in the 1850s, the Natal Mounted Police 1874 and the Transvaalsche Rijdende Politie 1881 (Schonteich, 1999, p. 14). The centralisation of the South African police force did not occur until 1913. Even then the policing was primarily urban, the rural areas being responsible for their own security.[3]

Vigilantism under Apartheid

Though all forms of non-state security slowly decreased during the first half of the twentieth century, as the size and influence of the state increased, even as late as 1972 the South African Police (SAP) was only 34,500 strong. Yet with the increasing security problems of the 1970s and 1980s, and the SAP focus on this, non-state policing once more came into its own. This affected both black and white neighbourhoods and caused both to depend more than ever on non-state policing for crime prevention and detection. Black neighbourhoods, however, had special needs. They were not just neglected by the SAP in terms of crime, but were positively harassed by them as part of the apartheid Government's counter insurgency strategy to restore 'normality' to ungovernable townships. This included patrols, house-to-house searches, roadblocks, monitoring of organisations and arrests. In addition the state provided arms covertly for local 'warlords' and anti-UDF militias (usually called 'vigilantes' in South Africa – See Haysom, 1989, 1990; Charney, 1991; Harris, 2001). They operated against individuals and groups opposed to apartheid and in turn often spurred anti-vigilantist groups against perceived collaborators with the regime (Brogden and Shearing, 1993, pp. 85-8; Haysom, 1989, pp. 188-99; 1990, pp. 63-82). Other self-styled self-defence units (SDUs) and self-protection units (SPUs) arose to fight off rival political militias, such as those associated with the ANC (African National Congress) and the IFP (Inkatha Freedom party) in KwaZulu-Natal (Shaw, 1995, pp. 41-2).

The apartheid years also saw a large number of autonomous groups arise to deal with township crime, frustrated that the SAP did so little to protect their residents or investigate crime. There were vigilante groups, street committees, the Makgotlas (a revival of customary courts with an ethnic base) and the Township People's Courts, which covered a range of procedures from responsible and orderly investigation with restrained punishments, to the summary violent justice of the Comrades and kangaroo courts (Seekings, 1992; Brogden and Shearing, 1993, pp. 143-165; Harris, 2001). Both black and white communities also had ready access to guns, either legally, on the black market or from the agents of their acknowledged political leaders.

The apartheid years, therefore, saw the establishment of a tradition by black and white communities of seeking their own forms of policing, in a context where the state offered very little and what was offered was seen as, at best, inadequate and, at worst, hostile, racist and illegitimate. But whereas the whites had the wealth to employ private security firms, the blacks more often had to rely on cheaper or voluntary methods.

Vigilantism since the Transition

If apartheid saw a black vigilantism focusing on political activity, since the democratic transition such activity has returned to focusing on social ordering and crime control. This may very often be crime as defined by the state, differing only in the use of violence, rather than the criminal justice system to address it. In a 'Code of Punishment' drafted by an Ivory Park People's Court, crimes and their punishments were set out formally. Adultery: 500 lashes for the man and banishment for the woman. Murder: necklacing [placing burning tyre round neck and shoulders] or execution at gunpoint. Rape: paraded naked before receiving 400 lashes or execution. Child Abuse : 380 lashes and banishment. Motor vehicle hijacking: Death for repeat offenders and lashes for first-timers. Theft: 50 lashes. Burglary: 200 lashes for first offence and if items not returned to owners, extra 300 lashes. Assault: 90 lashes. Assault by a man on his wife: 50 lashes. Contempt of court: an additional 40 lashes and a two-year banishment from the area (Minnaar, 1999, p. 30).

But the crimes may also be defined by the vigilante group in contradiction to the state, and include domestic disputes, sexuality and witchcraft. A report in 1998 told of a mob killing a woman in KwaMancinza, near Durban, with stones and sticks for disclosing that she was HIV positive. The vigilantes accused her of degrading her neighbourhood.[4] And Hills reports there were 300 witchcraft related murders between 1990 and 1999 in the Northern Province (Hills, 2000, p. 61).

The crime control element is fuelled by three processes. The first is a perceived increase in crime and in personal insecurity. Whatever the true rate of crime, as opposed to reported crime, the *perception* in South Africa is that it has increased. Surveys conducted by the HSRC have asked, 'how safe or unsafe do you personally feel most days?' In 1994 73 percent of respondents said they felt safe or very safe, while 16 percent felt unsafe or very unsafe. But by 2000 the number that felt safe or very safe had fallen to 44 percent, while 45 percent felt unsafe or very unsafe on most days. The results were similar between male and female respondents and across the ages, but there were racial differences. It showed just 36 percent of whites and 33 percent of Asians feeling secure, but 45 percent of blacks and 58 percent of coloureds. There was also a variation between provinces, so that the overall figure for perception of personal safety in the Province of Gaunteng was only 36 percent (Schonteich, 2001). Given that in 1999 33 percent of crimes reported to the police involved violence or the threat of violence, that at least 30 people are shot dead in South Africa every day and that there are more than 4 million registered firearms and millions more illegal guns, there is plenty to fuel these fears (Schonteich, 2000c).

The second factor drawing people to vigilantism (and other forms of non-state policing) is a perceived failure of the criminal justice system in general and of the police efficiency and effectiveness in particular. Indeed in a survey of 45 police priority areas nearly half thought it had deteriorated over the previous four years, although those who had had direct experience of the police were more positive (Pelser, 2000). The HSRC 1999 survey revealed that only 9 percent believed the Government 'has full control' over the crime situation, 49 percent believed it had 'large' or 'small' control, but 35 percent believed it was 'not in control' (Humphries, 2000, p. 2). Often this was a matter of an overstretched police. The Institute for Strategic Studies', *Rural Victims Survey 1998,* asked, 'how often do you see a police officer on duty in your village (or area). 34 percent said never, and 32 percent less than once a month. Further, they recorded very poor response rates to reported crime by the police. Concerning violent crimes the police took more than two days to arrive at the crime scene in 14 percent of cases and never responded 14 percent of the time. As regards reported stock theft, the most common rural crime, it took the police more than two days to appear in 8 percent of the cases and in 26 percent of the cases they made no appearance.

Not surprisingly the survey found that 66 percent of the victims of stock theft were dissatisfied with the service they received from the police, as were 45 percent of the victims of violent crime (Pelser, 2000). As regards the court system, particularly in the rural areas, court cases are not being dealt with because of shortages of court officials. According to the Department of Safety and Security's *In Service of Safety: white paper on safety and security*, '74 percent of the country's police stations were situated in the white suburbs or business districts' (quoted in Pelser, 2000, p. 58). The number of residents per police officer in 2000 ranged from 313 in Free State to 669 in Northern Province, with Eastern Cape at 462 (Schonteich, 2000b, p. 17). In the Pietersburg and Tzaneen districts, where vigilante groups are reported to be particularly strong, the head of the Northern Province Department of Justice has conceded that many prisoners are behind bars because rural courts cannot dispose of their cases:

> Prisoners who do not have money for bail have to stay in custody for long periods, and those who can afford bail also need their cases to be finalised, but they are not finalised because of a shortage of magistrates and prosecutors... The state witnesses are often disillusioned by the court's delays in settling cases and many cases may have to be dropped if a witness to a case is not found.[5]

Though the ratio in 1999 of 408 civilians to each police officer compares favourably with many developing countries, the number of officers has fallen by 14 percent between July 1995 and April 2000, from 143,800 to 124,160 (quoted in Schonteich, 2000a, p. 15). Grahamstown in the Eastern Cape illustrates how thin is the blue line. For its population of 120,000 it has four police officers on patrol duty at any given time and two response vehicles (although in the daytime it is effectively 19, counting detectives, public order police and the crime prevention unit). For all its apparent calm in the city centre, there are something like 600 cases per month of reported crime. As regards serious crime, between August 1999 and August 2000 monthly averages were four for murder, eight for rape, nine for robbery, 89 for housebreaking and theft, though reported crime overall is said to be down on 1999.[6]

Yet the problem of growing crime and perceived police ineffectiveness is not just a lack of police numbers. Despite the formal institutions of oversight (the Ministry of Safety and Security, National and Provincial Parliaments, the Municipalities and Local Community Police Forums) there are serious problems with lawless behaviour by the SAPS. In August 2000 there were more than 14,000 criminal cases against members of the SAPS before the courts or under investigation. More than 1,000 policemen have been charged with corruption since 1996. These include not just petty misdemeanors, but car theft, murder, rape and syndicate crimes such as hijackings.[7]

The third factor drawing people to vigilantism is an attraction to its criminal justice framework. There is a fundamental difference between the state criminal justice model based on a liberal and human rights approach and that which shapes vigilantism. Vigilantism upholds the values of compensatory justice, immediate justice and capital/corporal justice.

The 'restoration of material belongings,' or at least financial 'punishments' that exact compensation for damages/loss, is an important reason behind the support for vigilantism. Vigilantes in Mamelodi are successful, said one interviewee, because

> the police can't do nothing, even if maybe my property was stolen and the person was found guilty by the court, they don't get a way of compensation, they don't get back what was stolen or whatever damage was sustained...[but] if they take their case to the kangaroo court, judgment is passed and then people are paid back (Harris, 2001).

This ability to restore belongings and compensate victims is particularly attractive to communities where material possessions are scarce.

Many also value its immediacy, as opposed to the slow methodical process of the state courts that is designed to carefully examine the evidence of guilt and protect human rights. In particular, bail is seen as allowing criminals to return to their communities and flaunt their 'freedom', as well as to intimidate their victims and continue with criminal actions. It appears in their eyes to serve only the interests of criminals, rather than their victims and the community. When communities arrest somebody on the basis of rumour and hand them over to the police, they are incredulous when the police tell them they are required to release the suspect because there is insufficient evidence to hold them. Even when they are held and charged the process of formal justice is problematic because it delays punishment.

Finally there is widespread support for corporal and capital punishment as opposed to rehabilitative justice. An interviewee said:

When a person has hijacked a car and shot the driver, that person must be given the death penalty. There is no need for the government to imprison that kind of person, it's a waste of our money. He has killed, therefore, he must also be killed. I think the reason why we were against the death penalty during the days of apartheid, was mostly because black people were being hanged and for wrong reasons. But now we have a democratic government in place, I think the death penalty must be brought back (Harris, 2001).

Sometimes the punishment is quite literally meant to fit the crime, as in the case of castration for child rape (Minnaar, 1999, p. 8).

Support for the death penalty is widespread. A survey of 3,600 participants in 1998 found that 73 per cent 'maintained it was a mistake to take away the death penalty in South Africa, and only 14 per cent disagreed with it' (Pigou, Greenstein & Valji, 1998, p. vii). It was found that the abolition of the death penalty in 1994 was regarded as a mistake by a wide cross-section of South African society, across the political spectrum and racial divide (ibid, pp. 95-6).

In this climate where policing is seen as inefficient, ineffective and possibly corrupt, and where the judicial system is slow, 'soft' and at odds with the principles of justice held by many, it is inevitable that some will take the law into their own hands and mete out their own brand of punishment on those deemed guilty. Hence anti-crime groups, kangaroo courts and self-protection units have sprung up across the country (Thulare, 1996, p. 51; Shaw, 1995, pp. 41-2; Harris, 2001).

Formal Vigilante Groups

Though most vigilantes are small, loosely organised and sporadic, there are some large formal ones as well. The largest such vigilante group in South Africa is 'Mapogo a matamaga', formed in 1996 in the Northern Province. The group has become infamous for its sjambokking [whipping] and brutal assaults of alleged criminals. Initially concerned with protecting rural communities, it now also patrols the suburbs of Johannesburg and Pretoria. Its leaders claim 10,000 members in Gauteng and 40,000 in Northern Province and Mpumalanga. Its president says:

Naturally, as crime is escalating in all places, almost everyone wants to join Mapogo. They feel protected by us because of our approach to crime. The main thing that attracts members...is that we know how to deal with criminals. We believe in corporal punishment and that really works.[8]

They say their investigations are effective because they work with the community members. Members call Mapogo, recount the incident of crime and name the suspect. Thereafter Mapogo track down the alleged offender, demand the stolen goods back and then hand out the punishment. There is rarely a chance for the suspect to defend themselves and investigation into the allegation is rudimentary. In the early days suspects would be handed over to the police but this practice largely ceased after police released a number of suspects (von Schnitzler, 2001). The 'medicine' used 'to cure suspects of their bad ways', is arbitrary and dependent on the individual Mapogo members. According to the President: 'At times Mapogo get very furious and they cannot control themselves. Especially if they are confronted with a hardened criminal... what do you expect from them? They can even kill you' (von Schnitzler, 2001). They include acts of severe violence such as murder, kidnappings, criminal injury, malicious damage to property, theft, robbery and sabotage. In one incident in November 2000 near Komatipoort, five armed members of Mapogo confronted two Mozambicans and accused them of stealing a pistol and some cables. They were severely whipped, kicked and punched. One subsequently died of his injuries.[9] In another incident a Groblersdal shopkeeper was beaten with sjamboks leaving him with a fractured arm after Mapogo stormed into his shop and found computers stolen from one of their members. The attack was fully justified according to the regional Mapogo chairman:

> We gave him medicine. Nobody can steal from our members and escape. We give every suspect medicine in the hope it will cure them of theft and criminal activity...The justice system in this country is very soft on criminals.[10]

In investigating the murder of a Mapogo member in December 2000 in Hazyview, four Mapogo members impersonated police officers and led away the chief suspect. He was subsequently thrown to crocodiles in the Kruger National Park.[11] Such methods show a scant regard for humanity, let alone the legal process.

Another well-known vigilante group is 'People Against Gangsterism and Drugs' (PAGAD), based largely in Cape Town. Concern about local gang killings in Cape Town had reached such a point by 1994 that an influential anti-crime group representing 30 communities was formed. It worked within the law using marches and demonstrations, both to condemn gang violence and to protest against police policies that were perceived as racist for their failure to allocate adequate resources to the black and coloured communities and their poor response to (if not complicity with) the organised crime. In 1996 they were overtaken by PAGAD, a group that felt no constraint to work within the law. It began with a series of widely publicised punishments and assassinations of drug dealers. It particularly hit the Hard Livings gang, with its boss, Rashaad Staggie, being publicly murdered in August 1996 during a PAGAD demonstration outside his Cape Flats home. Subsequent court proceedings have revealed the gang was making R100,000 a day selling drugs.[12] Following ultimatums to them to leave the area or face 'the mandate of the people', PAGAD launched bomb attacks on most of the leading drug dealers. Within two years they had executed 30 gang leaders and drug dealers and had seriously decimated the gangs, although not without precipitating reprisals from the newly allied gangs (Kinnes, 2000, p. 37). Over time PAGAD attacks shifted to police officers, police stations (for weapons) and businesses that refused to make 'donations.' By June 1998 they appeared to adopt an Islamist anti-West agenda and to switch their attention to Western capitalist targets, if the spate of bomb attacks in Cape Town (18 between June 1998 and August 2000) is correctly attributed to them (Hough, 2000).

Not all vigilantes are urban-based. Operating in the Eastern Cape, Gauteng and Transkei, is Umfela, an anti-stock theft vigilante group. They, too, highlight how vigilante activities can slide into criminality. In June 1999 hitmen, dispatched from the organisation ostensibly to deal with cattle rustling, attacked a homestead near Tsolo. In all likelihood it was really part of an ongoing Tsolo-Qumbu conflict. They surrounded the homestead with armed men and set light to it. Only the intervention of the village neighbourhood watch prevented the death of the occupants, although in the subsequent shootout four attackers and one villager died.[13]

Not all vigilante groups are predominantly black. As an example of white vigilantism, it was reported that in KwaZulu-Natal employees of a private farm protection organisation (including police reservists), working with the SAPS and SADF, had engaged in a string of attacks on farm labourers, leaving two dead and sixteen badly injured. The assaults were against those suspected of housebreaking and holding illegal weapons.[14]

Informal Vigilante Groups

Most vigilantes are far smaller and less well organised than Mapogo and PAGAD, although the same predilection for violence and corporal punishment characterizes them. Though fines and lashings are used, a significant proportion of vigilante punishments end in death following necklacing, stoning, shooting, beating with sjamboks, stabbing and machetting.

In the shadow of PAGAD, but maintaining a separate identity, is the group found in Guguletu, a township in Cape Town. Its own action against criminals has included physical assaults against alleged murderers, rapists, thieves and sometimes parading them naked down the streets of the township (Nina, 2001). There are regular reports, too, of vigilantes in the city townships stabbing and 'necklacing' thieves in mob assaults. One report reads:

> In the past fortnight, seven people have been killed by vigilantes. Last week a suspected thief was murdered by a mob in Johannesburg. And three young men were killed in Primville, Soweto, for stealing 20 chairs from a church...Primville's people are unrepentant. They say they will necklace all criminals they catch. On Tuesday, a mob in Indanda, Durban, killed two of four men they said tried to rob a woman...The sister [of the robber] heard people shouting 'Die you dog, die', and found several men and a woman leaning over her brother stabbing him in the throat and stomach. The killers ran past her, laughing, as police arrived. Paramedics had to be protected by police and soldiers when stones and bottles were thrown by locals wanting to finish off all the suspected robbers.[15]

It was reported in 2000, at Mamelodi, a Pretoria township, that more than 22 kangaroo courts were operating in the area. The kangaroo courts, according to the Community Police Forum representative, 'hand out fines ranging from R20 to R30,000 against offenders. If you fail to pay you know you will be in trouble and you will get little help from the police' They are assaulted and sometimes killed and witnesses are intimidated into silence.[16]

According to Schonteich, vigilante activity in the Eastern Cape was more likely to result in violence than in a peaceful resolution:

> In the majority of the cases, the victims of vigilante activity were beaten (55 percent), killed or shot (18 percent). In 10 percent of the cases, the victims were banished from the area, forced out of their village, or taken to the police (7 percent). Victims of vigilante activity in the urban areas and small towns were more likely to be beaten than rural victims who stood the greatest chance of being shot or killed (Schonteich, 2000b, p. 50).

Typical incidents reported in the Eastern Cape included a man accused in October 2000 of housebreaking and rape, who was beaten to death by locals at Lujecweni.[17] Again, residents in Walmer Township, Port

Elizabeth, banded together to seize four youths accused of robbery and the stabbing to death of an old man. They were so badly beaten with pangas, spades and knives, that one 14 year old died.[18] The following week they seized another three youths accused of theft and gave them a severe beating. Significantly, residents excused their action in both instances on their lack of confidence in the criminal justice system. The murdered boy, for instance, had had murder charges against him dropped after he had turned State witness and he had been granted bail.[19]

Schonteich's research found that although overall only 39 percent of Eastern Cape residents said there had been an incident of vigilante activity in their community, there was a higher reporting of it among black respondents. Whilst 75 percent of white and coloured respondents said that no acts of vigilantism had ever taken place in their communities, only half of blacks 'could say with certainty that no act of vigilantism had taken place in their community, with 20 percent saying there had and 31 percent being unsure' (Schonteich, 2000b, p. 50).

In the Eastern Cape city of Grahamstown this same racial pattern is apparent. There had been several groups operating in the townships during the apartheid era, but after 1994 the principal one was the 'Anti-Crime Committee' (ACC). This organised street patrols and investigated cases brought to it of theft, rape and the like by the community. Their Organiser said that they were able to establish the 'guilty party' through the use of informers, who would not have given evidence to the police because of their negative attitudes towards them developed over the apartheid era. The ACC would then confront the suspect and use 'persuasion' to get them to hand back the goods and money, although it was not explained to what degree the persuasion went.[20] Some suspects were handed over to the SAPS, but it seems others were given community sanctions. Schonteich's black focus group in Grahamstown alleged that suspects were only apprehended if they could be identified and if there was strong evidence against them, such as the stolen item being found in their possession. In the case of rape it was alleged that the victim had to obtain a medical certificate to show she was raped (Schonteich, 2000b, pp. 52-3). In 1996 the ACC had a serious leadership split, some saying it was over accusations of officials taking monies and goods for their own use, some saying that the leadership was perpetuating itself in power, and others saying it was a rift over allegiance to the ANC and UDM. Since then, township residents report that other more informal groups (street and area committees) operate as investigators, tribunals and judges. The SAPS admit to being aware of at least two informal groups in the townships. One group summoned an alleged rapist of a 15 year old girl to a community meeting eight days after the incident to defend the charge and probably face whipping (although it was admitted by one interviewee that some such criminals are 'shot'). On twice failing to attend, the angry community members tore down his wattle and daub house.[21]

With this evidence of widespread use of vigilantism in South Africa, what are the consequences on state policing, the rule of law and the institutionalising of democratic processes? It is to these considerations that the next section turns.

The Democratic Impact

Challenges to the Rule of Law

Currently vigilantism acts outside of the law and competes with the SAPS and the criminal justice system to deter, arrest and punish criminals according to their own law. The state is not having the last word on who may use force and under what conditions. As a result there has been widespread denunciation of autonomous groups by authorities at the national and provincial level with, for example, the Minister of Safety and Security visiting townships with the specific intention of seeing local vigilantism dismantled.

Nevertheless, this official position does not fully capture the attitudes of many South African people. Disrespect for state law and the state police has a long history in South Africa that has not yet dissipated. Though some of the new institutions and laws have gained respect, citizens still reserve the right to choose which laws of the state to obey and when. The good news for democrats is that survey results consistently show large support for democracy. The HSRC found in 1999 that 74 per cent agreed that democracy was preferable to any other system of government. Similarly, in 1997 56.3 per cent thought that 'even when things don't work, democracy is always the best' (quoted in Mattes and Thiel, 1999, p. 128).

The bad news is that 36.4 per cent think 'it might be better to ignore the law and solve problems immediately, rather than wait for a legal solution' and 30.2 per cent that 'it is not necessary to obey the laws of the government that I did not vote for' (Gibson and Gouws, 1997, p. 179). In terms of confidence in the legal system, 26.4 per cent of blacks said they had 'none at all' or 'not very much' (for whites the figure was 63.1 per cent) (Gibson and Gouws, 1997, p. 183). In other words, though support for democracy is very high, support for the rule of law is far from universal.

Schonteich found that 49 per cent of the residents of the Eastern Cape Province supported alternative or traditional forms of punishment such as peoples' courts, expulsion from villages and fines to be paid to the community leaders, or compensation to the victim. This support was especially pronounced among rural inhabitants (75 per cent, as opposed to 46 per cent for urban areas and 45 per cent for small towns) and also among black respondents (62 per cent, as opposed to 37 per cent for coloured and 38 per cent for white respondents). He found that such activities were justified by the respondents on the grounds of their effectiveness in ensuring offenders were punished, the support they leant traditional leaders and the efficiency with which they were able to access local information on crime (Schonteich, 2000b, pp. 45-7). Most local support appeared to come from the black/township dwellers, who argued that they preferred to see the community take the responsibility.

There is clearly a difference over what constitutes the rule of law. The state defines it in terms of conformity to the laws and formal judicial processes of the country, but many of the population define it in terms of ensuring that what their community deems criminality and disorder are punished and punished by the community without recourse to the state criminal justice system. It is clear that South African society is far from reaching a consensus about its attitude in principle towards vigilantism, the role of the courts and what should be the future policy. Not everything that is illegal is illegitimate. A state that purports to represent all, must persuade all its citizens that there should be one law for all and that the criminal justice system of the state should alone be responsible for determining crime and punishing the offender. It has to overcome a situation where some 20 per cent, at least of East Cape residents, who have never taken part in vigilante activity, are prepared to do so in certain circumstances (Schonteich, 2000d, p. 31). Without establishing a wider base of popular support, the state criminal justice system, a key institution in ensuring equality and human rights in a democracy, will be seriously weakened. If Diamond is correct that an 'overriding commitment to democratic proceduralism is a critical political cultural condition for democracy' (quoted in Gibson and Gouws, 1997, p. 188), then democracy cannot consolidate while vigilantism enjoys such levels of support.

Accountability

Non-state policing is engrained in every community of South Africa. It is ubiquitous to the point that few challenge its legitimacy, even if they criticise some of its practices. There are few in South Africa who would insist that the state be given a monopoly of all policing functions and that all non-state policing should be proscribed, with its units disbanded and/or absorbed into police reserves. Many would concede that the market can never ensure that there is equal provision and access (Thulare, 1996; Zwane, 1994; Shaw, 1995), but deficiencies in available resources,[22] training and institutionalised accountability for the SAPS make it impossible to contemplate them simply taking over non-state police roles in addition to their current responsibilities. For all the fine words of the South African Constitution asserting the right to 'freedom and security of person', the state is not yet in a position to provide that through the sole use of its own police force. Such is the current low priority given by the SAPS to the protection of property that few, including the SAPS themselves, would deny that non-state policing of whatever hue is seen as the best available deterrent and the fastest responder in time of emergency.

Though vigilante groups will continue to be outlawed, judging by conviction figures, little is likely to be done to bring them to an end. Between 1996 and 2000 there were 607 police charges against Mapogo members including 13 for murder, 19 for attempted murder, 23 for kidnapping, 221 for assault and 15 for theft and robbery (SAPS, quoted in Maepa, 2001). 63 of these came to court and of those, there were only 14 convictions. This is surely in part due to the reluctance of the public to give evidence against them for their illegal activities, for fear of reprisal. A similar situation prevails amongst the informal groups. The kangaroo courts and their punishments and killings in Mamelodi are well known to the police and yet, as of August 2000, no member had been arrested. This is in part because most residents are too afraid to lodge complaints or to act as witnesses. However there is also evidence that some police threaten complainants and witnesses and even forge their statements and signatures. 14 police have already been arrested in the area on charges of helping criminals, destroying evidence and accepting bribes.[23] The situation prevails, therefore, where although the vigilante groups cannot be said to act with impunity, they are certainly very rarely called to account. Their lawlessness is only minimally challenged.

Social Isolation Created by Non-State Policing

Few blacks can afford armed response guarding services, razor wire, or the 'gated communities' behind road booms and high walls patrolled by security guards that bar undesirable new residents and casual passers-by.[24] Instead they will continue to look to local level self-help groups and autonomous security groups. The difference in cost is not inconsiderable; armed response firms typically charge at least R3-4,000 p.a., resident street patrols cost around R650 p.a., and Mapogo's annual subscription is R50-165 (though farms and big businesses can be charged up to R10,000).

Though the security sought may have different levels of sophistication, legality and effectiveness, there is one feature that is becoming increasingly common to both black and white communities, namely, social isolation. Communities become wary of the stranger in a crime-ridden society and non-state policing is the method chosen by many for securing exclusion. 'No-go areas' keep the SAPS, opposition political groups and 'undesirables' from their streets in black townships. Yet when sections of society insulate themselves in this fashion, dialogue across political, class, and racial divides withers. Social exclusion and urban fragmentation is no basis for the sense of a common identity, which must be the foundation for South Africa's democracy. To many this development has echoes of the apartheid days of racial segregation that were supposed to have been abandoned.

Undermining the Legitimacy of State Policing

The widespread use and support for non-state policing unavoidably undermines the legitimacy of the SAPS. Non-state policing in its various forms is becoming institutionalised in substantial sectors of South African society as the normal channel of criminal justice. This is particularly true in two contexts. First, where the SAPS stand back, either to allow 'natural' justice to take its course, as they did in the murder of gangland leader Rashaad Staggie in the Cape Flats, or in their failure to successfully prosecute criminal activity by local vigilantes. In such situations the state ceases to be seen as a credible guarantor of personal security.

The other area where non-state policing is becoming institutionalised is in the rural communities, again because of the absence of visible SAPS policing. Pelser et al. report that of 756 interviewed across the country in 1998, 7 percent said that their community made its own arrangements to protect itself, with 80 percent saying they thought this was an effective way of securing the area. The underlying cause of this use, or willingness to use, non-state policing, was dissatisfaction with the SAPS. Only 35 per cent of all respondents believed the SAPS could control crime in their area. The majority of rural respondents said the SAPS in their area were doing a poor job to control crime. Indeed, most rural respondents rarely, if ever, saw a SAPS official and with the scarcity of transport and telephones, had limited access to the SAPS (Pelser, 2000, pp. 37-8 and 60-3). A similar finding was reported from a survey of 971 KwaMashu residents. In this case nearly 60 per cent thought local people solved crimes better than the SAPS.[25] The danger of an irrelevant state police is that it can be extended to seeing the state itself as irrelevant. And why, people might ask, engage with a state that fails to offer such a basic service as personal security and when private initiatives are available?

Exacerbating Inequality

Another cause for concern is the degree to which the scale of vigilantism in South Africa might be exacerbating inequality. The nature of non-state policing means that it can offer no equality of accessibility and adjudication, and at times even denies people their legal and constitutional rights. Access to non-state policing services is uneven, depending on location and/or wealth. Discriminatory policing was the hallmark of the apartheid era by both private and public forces. Much has changed since 1994, but few would deny that race and politics (in the decisions regarding the allocation of security resources) still influence the availability of private and public policing. For community self-help groups it depends on local initiative and by no means all people are offered any provision at all. In practice, therefore, many citizens have no ready access to guarding and protecting services from vigilantes (or for that matter, the public sector). The right to freedom and security is not universally available. In cases where non-state policing undertakes adjudication, there are serious concerns about standards of investigation, scrutiny of evidence, the sanctions available and a consistency of treatment for citizens. Amidst stories of sincerity and earnestness are others of hasty verdicts, presumption of guilt and even 'courts' taken over by gangs or powerful local actors bent on extortion (Brogden and Shearing, 1993, pp. 162-3).

Beyond the discrimination of provision is the nurturing of attitudes of discrimination. Some vigilantism promotes an under-class of citizens. The discourse is of 'undesirable elements', 'illegal immigrants' and of those who act in a 'sub-human' way. They must be 'cleansed' from society by any means available since they have forfeited their rights. Responses to them have been guilty of discarding lawful and humane procedures of investigation, detention, trial and punishment. The impression at times is that this violence continues with impunity, since its 'victims' are the 'dangerous classes' of criminals who do not deserve protection. It is not a discourse that is confined to the vigilantes. Steve Tshwete, the Minister of Safety and Security appears to have adopted it from the vigilantes in an attempt to portray the Government as being as tough on crime as they are. He has spoken of tackling 'these scum the way a bulldog tackles a bone' (von Schnitzler, 2001). Such inequality of regard and treatment is the very opposite of democratic principles.

Escalation of the Use of Violence

A further cause for concern is the potential for some aspects of vigilantism to provoke a still wider use of violence. A mother told Harris that her son, who was badly beaten by a vigilante mob, openly sought revenge:

> He says he hates everything, he hates the police, he hates interviews. We went to a counselling session and he said to me: 'what am I going to do? Until I find myself a gun and go and fight back, otherwise what must I do?' (Harris, 2001).

South Africans are divided over the right of individuals to carry weapons or to use other means of physical force over others. The right to self-defence and/or citizen arrest has to be weighed against the right to individual protection from unreliable and hasty methods of justice that may use violence without adequately establishing guilt. Few would deny, however, that the more extensive the carrying of instruments of coercion, the harder to control their responsible use. It is well known that instruments of violence, especially knives and firearms, are widely owned in South Africa. Though often the firearms are illegal, it has to be admitted that it is very easy to obtain gun licences, even after recent legislation which raised the age of legal gun ownership from 18 to 21 (unless they are farmers, or have opened businesses), limited ownership to one gun for self defence (and four for hunting) and required renewal of the permits periodically. Four and a half million are registered and millions more are unregistered in a country with only a population of 43 million.

It is within this gun culture, where there are high levels of violent crime and where people want to protect themselves with weapons, that vigilantism operates. The killings by criminals of police and counter killings by vigilantes of criminals, seems a never ending circle. For instance, 173 police were murdered (114 while off duty) in the twelve month period ending June 2001.[26] Whilst between January 1999 and March 2000, 137 persons were killed by vigilantes.[27] Not surprisingly its agents use a variety of weapons with very few restraints. With the Government doing very little to tackle the ownership and use of firearms and other weapons generally, and their use by non-state policing groups in particular, they are freely used in the course of non-state policing with little supervision.

The use of force provokes counterforce. But as citizens arm themselves, or call on armed vigilantes for protection and revenge, the fear is that criminals will undertake their activity prepared to meet defensive violence with violence. As PAGAD members, for instance, paraded their Uzi submachine guns, Magnum revolvers and automatic rifles, the gangs of the Cape Flats formed a coalition to fight the vigilantes, and increased their organisational and weaponry sophistication to counter the common threat. One court case revealed that 'The Hard Livings' gang stole military-type weapons from a police armoury in a deliberate effort to match PAGAD. For democracy this is a dangerous spiral of violence.

Political Mobilisation

The escalating crime, the way the Government and police have failed to curtail it, and the lawless way non-state policing is responding, has become an issue taken up by the media and by political groups. Yet though a stronger more efficient public police appears to be high on the public's list of priorities requiring Government attention, there is no corresponding citizen action on the issue of greater control of non-state policing. Far from mobilisation on this issue, there is genuine uncertainty among the public as to what the government should do about vigilantism. No more that 35 percent of Schonteich's survey in the Eastern Cape thought that vigilantism was a criminal act or a form of illegal punishment and only 21 percent of blacks thought so (Schonteich 2000d, p. 28). There is evidently a widespread sympathy for non-state policing. The support is not just from those actively engaged in it, but from those outside. Thus the Eastern Province Herald began its leader on the beating to death of a thief by a vigilante group with:

> There will be much empathy with Walmer township residents who finally took the law into their own hands after youths robbed and mugged an old man...Vigilante action cannot be condoned, but their frustration with the system which keeps letting the people down is easy to understand... unsatisfactory as the violent results may be, there seems little alternative for these people while the government continues its soft-bellied approach to the problem.[28]

The ambivalence to vigilantism has been noticeable in all the political parties. With condemnation of vigilante activity has gone statements to the effect that it is understood in the light of the failures of the criminal justice system (von Schnitzler, 2001). Even the Government preferred to try to co-opt Mapogo in its early years and, to many, only came down strongly against it when in 1999 its leader became a candidate for the UDM. Political activity has thus often focused, not in mobilising against non-state policing, but in mobilising the support of those engaged in it. One explanation of the leadership split in the Anti-Crime Committee of Grahamstown in 1996 was that it was over the issue of its political allegiance, with the ANC unhappy at the popularity the UDM was achieving through the ACC being led by one of its members. However, when it emerged in 2001 that schools, clinics and regional government offices in Tzaneen had paid 'protection levies' to Mapogo in an attempt to prevent theft and vandalism, the ANC reconsidered their indifference. In February they issued an ultimatum ordering their members to resign from Mapogo.

PAGAD, too, has tried to harness its anti-crime supporters into a political movement with a wider agenda. By June 1998 it appeared to have adopted an Islamist anti-West agenda and switched its attention to Western capitalist targets. However, its adoption of an urban terrorist stance has lost it the sympathy it initially had from the media, business and some members of the government. Currently its support has reduced to certain elements of the Islamic community (Shaw, 1996, pp. 170-1). Strangely, therefore, the issue of vigilantism is not high on the policy agenda of mainstream or even minority parties. In this sense the party system is failing to listen to the reason why so many are prepared to participate in vigilante activities and/or condone its departure from the criminal justice system. Beyond periodic clampdowns on vigilante activity by the Ministry of Safety and Security, there needs to be a wider debate about a matter of evident public concern. Such a debate is part of what constitutes a healthy democracy.

Criminal Complicity

Not all 'vigilantism against crime' is what it purports to be. Instead, the crime-fighting banner can merely offer a 'legitimate' cover for personal revenge or criminal motives of personal gain. People can have a grudge against someone and can persuade an anti-crime group that the person is guilty of crime and needs punishing. Stories are common of accusations made out of jealousy or settling personal scores. One victim recounted: 'The person that actually came to burn my house doesn't have a house. It's jealousy' (Harris, 2001). Vigilante members have been charged over the last few years with murder, assault, robbery, stock theft, kidnapping, housebreaking and arson. This is clear-cut crime that exploits the crime-fighting justification offered by vigilante rhetoric. This cannot be reduced to consequences of 'fighting crime' alone:

> Factors of emotion, prejudice and personal dynamics greatly dilute the 'fighting crime' rubric of contemporary vigilantism. Additionally, the material rewards that accompany vigilante actions, whether in the form of 'service fees' charged by Mapogo a Mathamaga; 'payments' to kangaroo courts; or losing a house, belongings or cattle to the 'plaintiff', suggest motives beyond the pursuit of crime-fighting. Rather than seeking to eradicate crime, vigilantism in this vein is motivated by personal benefit and, in certain instances, by crime itself (Harris, 2001).

Additionally, self-gain is commonly cited as a motive for vigilantes themselves. They may benefit by charging for their 'services' or they may receive financial reward from their victims. One township resident complained:

> In one section, you'll find there's a group of about 10 or 20 people involved in [kangaroo courts] and they're benefiting because they are intimidating the people they are living amongst. They will go into a shebeen, demand free liquor, you know, maybe offer protection or demand protection fees... It's just a handful of people who are doing this and they don't enjoy the support of the community (Harris, 2001).

Rather than seeking to eradicate crime, some anti-crime groups are criminal themselves.

Conclusion

The issue of policing is but one measure of democratic progress, but it is not an insignificant one. In 1994 South Africa officially abandoned apartheid and embraced democratic constitutionalism. Seven years later the prevalence of non-state policing permits the continuance of authoritarian values and practices; divides communities on the basis of their ability to secure alternative policing for a failing state provision; and nurtures the view that the rule of law is more of an obstacle to maintaining social order than an effective guarantee of it.

Notes

1. The use here and elsewhere of racial categories does not imply that the author condones the apartheid racial divisions.
2. Interviews with Crime Analysis Officer for Grahamstown and with senior police officers, August 2000.
3. Also working within the framework of the Constitution and the law, but providing their own distinctive policing, are some of the tribal communities of the former homelands and elsewhere. 1,500 traditional courts are recognised in the Black Administration Act. Many have largely broken down as a result of the forces of modernisation and the discrediting of the traditional leaders due to their collaboration with the apartheid regime. In these circumstances, those found guilty in the traditional courts simply ignore the fines imposed. Others, however, have maintained a measure of authority over those living under the jurisdiction of a chief. In these situations arrests are made by tribal police and courts pass verdict on those who have disturbed the social order by their petty theft, fights, out of wedlock pregnancies, adultery and civil disputes. Though they police customary law, traditional leaders do so only within the spirit and objects of the Bill of Rights. (Zwane, 1994, p. 43; Stack, 1997, p. 23-4).
4. *Sunday Times*, 27 December, 1998.
5. *Mail & Guardian*, 23 October, 1998.
6. Interviews with Crime Analysis Officer for Grahamstown and with senior police officers August 2000. Figures for the Eastern Cape reveal high crime levels.
7. The *Mail & Guardian*, 18 August, 2000 reports: 'Last weekend's papers included stories of three Eastern Cape policemen who have been charged with culpable homicide…after allegedly running over and killing a teenager who was dragged behind a moving car; a man who was allegedly abducted, assaulted and buried alive by members of the East Rand murder and robbery unit; a juvenile who was illegally locked up in police cells with adult prisoners and killed; a 16 year old girl who is suing the police after being raped in police cells and infected with HIV by a police officer…; and a member of the police crime intelligence unit allegedly linked to a prostitution racket in Johannesburg.'
8. *Africa Research Bulletin*, 1, 2000.
9. African Eye News Service, 14 December, 2000.
10. *Sunday Times*, 13 December, 1998.
11. African Eye News Service, 15 January, 2001.
12. *Cape Argus*, 19 June, 2001.
13. *Dispatch*, 7 June, 1999.
14. *Mail & Guardian*, 8 September, 2000.
15. *The Star*, 2000.
16. *Mail & Guardian*, 11 August, 2000.
17. *Eastern Province Herald*, 3 October, 2000.
18. *Eastern Province Herald*, 3 October, 2000.
19. *Eastern Province Herald*, 6 October, 2000.
20. Interview with Organiser, 8 August, 2000.
21. *Eastern Province Herald*, 25 August, 2000, and interviews with Steven Crossman, journalist with East Cape News and with a neighbour who asked to be anonymous.
22. (38,000 additional officers are required for the force to perform effective crime prevention according to the National Commissioner. Current manpower is down from

141,000 in 1996 to 123,000 in 2001. Business Day (Johannesburg, 5 November, 2001).
23 *Mail & Guardian,* 11 August, 2000.
24 *Mail & Guardian,* 12 January, 2001.
25 *Africa Research Bulletin,* 5, 2000.
26 *Mail & Guardian,* 15 June, 2001; for the Eastern Cape police officers killed on duty numbered 15 in 1996; 18 in 1997; 20 in 1998; 22 in 1999; 26 in 2000, *East Cape News,* 26 July, 2001.
27 *2000/2001 South Africa Survey,* quoted in *Mail & Guardian,* 22 March, 2001.
28 *Eastern Province Herald,* 9 October, 2000.

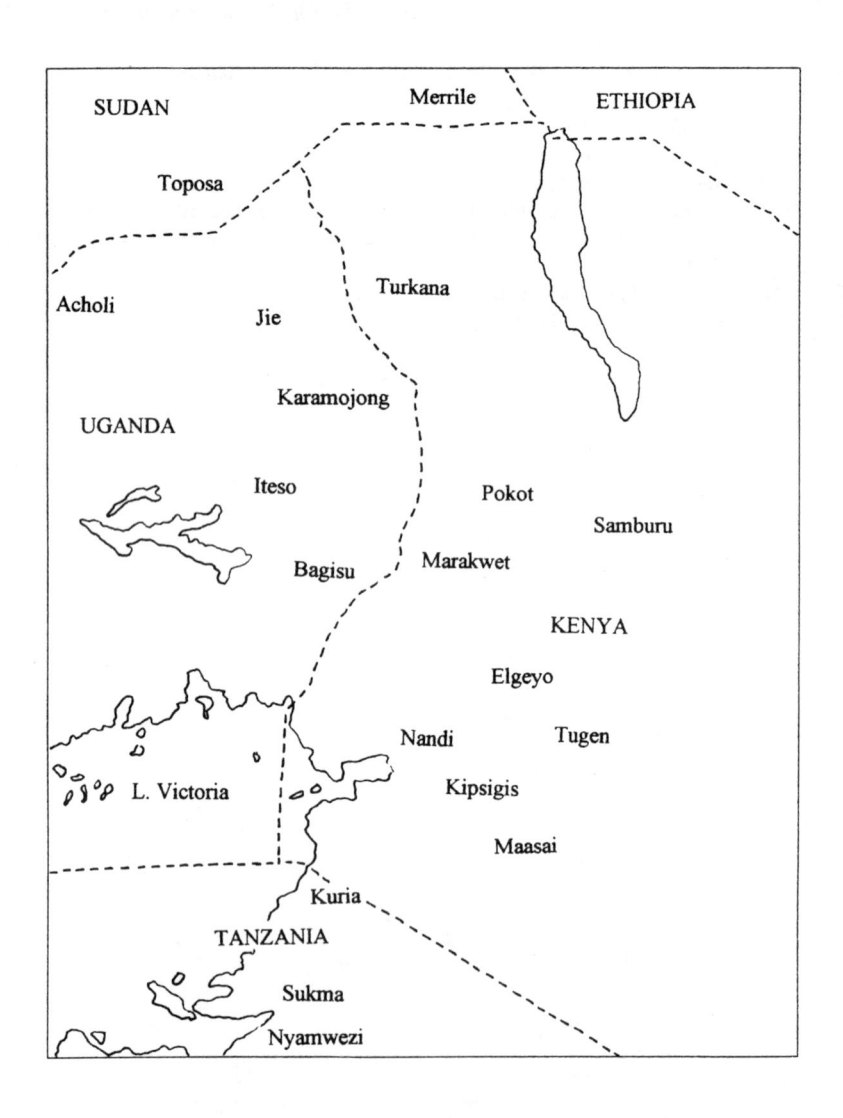

Figure 8.1 East African Pastoralists

8 East Africa's Vigilantes and Cattle Rustling

Across the grasslands of the eastern branch of the East African Rift Valley graze millions of head of cattle. For the estimated five million pastoralists of the region they are the chief source of wealth and are vital to the pastoralists' worldview, to the point that most 'cannot perceive their existence without cattle' (Fukui, 1994, 34). Nevertheless, the conditions in which they pursue their livelihood are harsh. Rain is frequently insufficient to provide sufficient pasture and water for the herds and overgrazing is further increased by the persistent encroachment of grazing land by ranches and game reserves. Even when grazing is available, it may be inaccessible because of fears concerning security. Conflicts with pastoralists from other communities are common in the search for grazing land during the long dry seasons, whilst the herds constitute an easy and profitable target for rustlers. For as long as memories can recall, it has been a feature of life in these areas that a minority have turned to raiding to supplement their income, to reconstitute herds after drought, to secure bride wealth, to demonstrate bravado and to wreak revenge on rival clans or tribes. Similarly the tradition is equally long of violently seizing back cattle and punishing the rustlers.

This chapter will focus on that part of the East African Rift Valley stretching from the north-western border of Kenya with Ethiopia, down the Kenya/Uganda borderlands and into north-west Tanzania, a belt some 1000 km long and 300 km wide. Among its principal people groups are the Turkana, Karamojong (with three important sub-groups, Matheniko, Pian and, Bokora), Jie, Kalenjin speakers (whose main divisions are the Pokot, Marakwet, Elgeyo, Tugen, Nandi, Kipsigis and Sebei), Samburu, Maasai, Kuria, Nyamwezi and Sukuma (see Figure 8.1). It is in these areas that hundreds die every year in raids that snatch tens of thousands of cattle.[1]

The scene at dusk in the village of Lolumupal in Karamoja, as described by two journalists, evokes the security concerns of many of the small settlements of East Africa's pastoralists:

Chatter and occasional laughter come from women and children in the small domed thatched huts, while half a dozen men settle down on hide mats around a fire at the edge of their own kraal. A large gourd of milk mixed with blood is passed around, and endless stories are swapped, nearly always of past fighting prowess and famous battles. The men keep their guns [AK47s slung over their shoulders] loaded, for tonight they are the guards and are only too aware of the dangers they, their families and their cattle constantly face. For cattle raiding is a way of life in Karamoja, and the possession of cattle a source of joy, wealth and respect, the only means of livelihood for the Karamojong (Errington and Lokiru, 1996).

The area has long been known for its absence of effective state-provided security since colonial days, owing to its marginality. 'The four corners region of the Ethiopian-Sudan-Ugandan-Kenyan border took on its marginal and interstitial status in large part because being maximally distant from the four centres of economic and political power around which the four states were formed' (Galaty and Bonte, 1991, p. 281). The colonial authorities of Uganda, Kenya and Tanganyika saw the pastoralists as not only difficult to administer, owing to their mobility and decentralised and fragmented political systems, but also as resistant to change and violent. Apart from pushing certain groups, like the Maasai, away from the land designated for white agriculture or game parks, they were largely ignored. Confinement to 'native reserves' or just the loss of gazing land, only promoted conflict between pastoralists over water and better pastures. Nor did granting approval for one group to use the grazing land traditionally used by another help relations, as for instance when the Pokot were given Karamojong grazing land (Azarya, 1996, pp. 60-3).

State policies towards the pastoralists changed little with independence. The new states of Kenya and Tanzania continued with the practice of allowing the pastoralists' land to be taken for agriculture or game reserves. Problems were further exacerbated by the severe drought across the whole region in the 1970s and mid 1980s, which wiped out entire herds. Many herders were forced to concentrate around towns, where grazing land could not sustain even those cattle that had survived. Inevitably the loss of livestock led to an increase in raids and counter-raids, as pastoralists tried to compensate for their losses (Azarya, 1996, pp. 75-85).

Cattle Rustling

Cattle rustling has been an evolving activity. Since 1900 it has undergone a number of significant transformations in the face of changing political pressures, technological innovations and market opportunities. The raids at the beginning of the twentieth century were large-scale affairs by groups of typically 40 to 60, using spears and arrows (though of exaggerated success – Waller, 1999, p.36). Most anthropologists attribute motives beyond that of acquiring or reacquiring cattle. They suggest the raids also involved the desire for prestige, retaliation, loot, young girls and even that they served to alleviate young men's rural boredom. Whatever the complexity of the motives, the raids were only undertaken after consultation with groups of elders, assessing the risk of retaliation and with the blessing of a local ritual leader. In other words, these raids clearly incurred a high degree of community culpability. Interestingly, in the Western Highlands of Kenya it has been observed that Kalenjin attitudes towards stock theft were differentiated. On the one hand there were cattle 'raids' on 'outsiders', that is on Europeans or other Africans (including other sections of the Kalenjin); and on the other hand there were 'thefts' from fellow section members (Anderson, 1986, p. 400). The moral distinction between the two was only too apparent from the social response. There were no sanctions against cattle raiders, but the strongest public curse and social ostracism against cattle thieves. In the eyes of the Kalenjin, raiding benefited the whole community, since younger members could acquire stock without the need for redistribution by the community. Even the British colonial officials were ambivalent about the raiding of other pastoralists. One report of 1905 spoke of how they 'worried that banning raiding at a time of particular stress in the pastoral economy might drive young men into permanent poverty and alienation, since they would not be able to accumulate enough to marry and become adults (Waller, 1999, p. 36). The large-scale raids were not, however, to last where white settlers were adversely affected. In Kenya from the 1920s they put pressure on the colonial authorities to take stern action.

Without such settler pressure in Uganda, cattle raiding stayed very much at stage one for a further 50 years. In Karamoja, write Mirzeler and Young,

> a purely pre-emptive administrative model prevailed...Full occupation and control was not necessary; insulation of the area from outside, restricting the gun trade, preventing raiding into the administered neighbouring zones, and limiting conflict within the region to a manageable level sufficed. A minimal

presence within the area would serve, mainly of police (Mirzeler and Young, 2000, p. 412).

Unable to successfully collect taxes, the authorities resorted to what amounted to raiding themselves, namely the confiscation of cattle to make up for the shortfall and for punitive reasons. The Karamojong were otherwise left to them and the area was declared a closed district that could only be entered with a permit.

In Kenya severe sentences against cattle rustling were introduced of 1-5 years imprisonment or heavy individual and community fines. As these began to bite in the 1920s, the large scale raids in the Kalenjin and Maasai areas began to slacken. For the first time young Maasai grew up without raiding and went in search of employment, especially as herders on the white farms where they sought payment in cattle (Waller, 1999, p. 37). Those who persisted in stock theft developed new strategies, particularly opportunist theft of cattle carelessly herded near their own stock. Though this form of theft entailed a minimal degree of community involvement, the Kenyan authorities, in their efforts to change public attitudes, still levied collective punishment. The effect, however, was not to change the pastoralists' morality, but only to encourage greater efforts to avoid detection. From the late 1920s onwards, therefore, stock theft in Western Kenya became prominent and, at least among the Kalenjin, increasingly the prerogative of organised crime.[2] Stolen cattle were now distributed over large distances by large multi-ethnic gangs. Their activities were made easier by the fact that, generally speaking, though chiefs were prepared to act against thieves from beyond their community, they protected those within the community by silence. The rule of law was their own, not that of the state.

Even without colonial pressure, the drift from traditional raiding patterns and cultural practice to one concerned more with the market and criminal acquisition, was apparent. The same process of transformation from local elder-endorsed raids to enlarge the community's herds, to organised criminal enterprises aimed at outside sales, is also noted elsewhere. Thus among the Kuria of north-west Tanzania/south-west Kenya, raiding ceased to be about the desire for prestige or retaliation. 'Kuria cattle raiders are in it for the money and have been for approximately the past 80 years' (Fleisher, 1999, p. 238).

In Karamoja, a Commission for the new independent Ugandan Government wrote in 1961 of the region as a primitive and lawless district. In its own words:

We are not dealing with mean and cowardly thieves who know that what they are doing is morally wrong and is not admired by the society they live in; we are dealing with determined brave warriors who will stop at nothing to achieve their aim (quoted in Mirzeler and Young, 2000, p. 415).

The Ugandan police response in the 1960s to the frequent cattle raids was completely ineffectual. They would interview the victims and fill out forms before ever venturing to pursue the raiders and if they did catch their prey they were often outgunned. It took the army under Amin's control to reduce the raiding using brutal methods. But having caught and killed the raiders they then sold the cattle for their own profit! Little wonder that the people began to make homemade guns or steal police guns to construct their own policing (Quam, 1997, pp. 4-5)

Raiding entered a still further predatory and violent stage with the arrival of large numbers of cheap semi-automatic weapons, like the AK47, into the rural districts from the late 1970s. The weapons were the bi-product of the insurgencies and civil wars of the African savannah (Chad, Mali, Ethiopia, Sudan, Somalia, Uganda, Rwanda, Burundi, Zimbabwe and Mozambique). In Uganda's case the Karamojong obtained large supplies of arms after sacking the well-stocked Moroto armoury abandoned by the fleeing army of Idi Amin in 1979. There is also the continuing availability of arms from Sudan via the rebel group, the SPLA. Arms markets currently thrive across the border in Sudan and Karamojong can still purchase an automatic rifle for 150,000 U.Shillings (£15) and a bullet for 200 (20p) according to one NGO.[3] Ugandan Government sources estimated that in 1998 there were 30-40,000 automatic weapons in the hands of the Karamojong and related pastoral communities.[4] Once armed, the Karamojong made devastating large scale raids on their neighbours, the Iteso and Dodoth, to replenish their heavy losses of cattle in the 1979 drought. Again in 1987 they began raiding the Acholi and had reduced their cattle numbers from 300,000 to 5,000 by 1997, 'compelling Acholi to abandon oxen cultivation in favour of donkeys' (Mirzeler and Young, 2000, p. 417). 'The guns' as one Karamojong describes them, 'were like maddened wild animals; the lions and leopards of Karamojo, out of control and man eaters' (Errington and Lokiro, 1996).

The fall of Amin even affected the Kuria community in north-west Tanzania, since they constituted 50 percent of the Tanzanian army that had invaded Uganda. The war resulted in a flood of smuggled military weapons into the area. This in turn led to 'a dramatic intensification of cattle raiding and instigated the precipitous decline of the Tarime District

[Tanzania] cattle herd that continues unabated to this day' (Fleisher, 1999, p. 249).

Over the last century, therefore, there has been an escalation in the degree of violence involved in cattle rustling. From raids using spears and arrows to seize small numbers of cattle with only occasional deaths, there are now open large-scale raids where firepower is the principal means of securing success. Raids take thousands of head of cattle and in the process whole village populations may be slaughtered. But the change is more than one of scale and weapon sophistication. Hendrickson and his colleagues describe this shift as one from redistributive to predatory forms of raiding. The former is essentially an internal conflict, involving actors practising the same activity. When livestock are seized, they still remain within the local/regional pastoral system and in a sense it merely redistributes resources within it. But the predatory form is an external activity, in that it involves not just the pastoralists, but entrepreneurs and others in the market economy. The raiding, therefore, is not just violent and involving large numbers of animals, but it is uni-directional – aimed at external markets – and therefore much more destructive than the earlier form (Hendrickson, 1996, p. 22).

Raiding and Revenge

Conflicts over cattle may have distinct beginnings, but usually the initiators of the conflict are lost in history and cattle raiding has become institutionalised against perceived enemies. Cattle raiding is under-reported and when it is it is usually large scale massacres and/or raids from across international borders. Below is presented a summary of the reported major incidents in the last few years. As will be seen, differentiating what is rustling and what is vigilante revenge is problematic.

Turkana

The Turkana of north-west Kenya number about 300,000, of whom about 21,000 are pastoralists. The number of pastoralists is still falling as years of sparse rainfall in the late 1990s have led to many selling their livestock and becoming almost completely dependent on relief food.[5] The pressure to support livestock on the limited grazing and water points of the region is the source of more or less constant conflict between the Turkana and their neighbours, the Pokot of Kenya, the Merrile of Ethiopia and the Toposa of

Sudan. In early 1999 the Turkana raided Pokot villages and stole hundreds of Pokot livestock, allegedly in retaliation for an earlier attack by the Pokot. In retaliation the Pokot launched a savage attack in March 1999 that left 100 dead, including 28 women (raped before being shot) and 15 children under 12. 300 head of cattle were taken, before the Turkana, assisted by homeguards, managed to counter attack, kill 14 of the raiders and recover all the livestock.[6] More recently, in August 2001, 7,000 cattle were seized by 300 armed Pokot in a raid that left six Turkana dead.[7]

As regards the frequent conflicts between the Turkana and the Merrile, the current cycle of tit for tat raids goes back to October 1999. Turkana armed cattle raiders attacked Merrile herdsmen grazing in Kenya and stole more than 400 head of cattle. In a revenge attack in February 2000, heavily armed Merrile attacked Turkana villages in the Kokuro district. Some 80 people were killed, 45 Turkana and 35 raiders.[8] The clashes with the Toposa have been less frequent, but even so, in two Toposa raids in September 2001, 100 head of cattle were stolen, though in the ensuing gun battles 10 Toposa and 10 Turkana were killed.[9] Raiding is also undertaken across the Uganda border among the Karamojong, such as those in November 2001 when two were killed and 50 cattle stolen. In this context of persistent raiding it is hardly surprising that a survey in the 1990s found that as many as 17 percent of the Turkana herds were raided animals (Broch-Due, 1999, p. 85).

Karamojong

Across the Kenyan border to the west of the Turkana, live some 370,000 Karamojong. Of the three important sub-groups, the Matheniko, the Pian, and the Bokora, it is the Bokora who have been the most persistent cattle raiders. They have been so heavily involved in cattle raiding that cattle rearing has virtually ceased in much of the northern Acholi districts of Uganda.

In a Bokora attack on a village of the Matheniko people in September 1999, raiders stole hundreds of heads of cattle, leaving between 100 and 400 killed (mainly children, women and the elderly). The raid was said to be in revenge for a similar raid on Bokora livestock in July 1999.[10] A year later, in July 2000, another large raid took place on seven villages, 35 km south of Moutu. 100 Bokora raiders attacked and wounded many, leaving some dead and drove away thousands of cattle. The villagers have never been attacked before. It is thought they may have been chosen since they were mainly Baptist church followers and known not to be armed. In addition, with a Ugandan Government disarmament programme about to begin, the Bokora may have reasoned that they needed to attack before they had to hand in their weapons. The villagers say the army did nothing to get the cattle back, further emphasising in their minds the need to take action themselves to deal with rustling.[11]

Outside their own ethnic group, the Karamojong raiding on the neighbouring agro-pastoralists, the Iteso, has been particularly destructive in the last few years. Between January and October 2001 some 54 raids were carried out, forcing some 38 percent, or 88,000, of the Iteso to take refuge in 58 government camps in Katakwi and Kapchorwa districts. Not only are the camps themselves suffering from shortages of food and medicine and inadequate sanitation but, of course, Government development programmes in the area have been severely hindered and services such as electricity are in short supply.[12] Even the camps, supposedly under the protection of the Local Defence Units, have been attacked and the cattle have been stolen.[13] The tragedy is that the raids were spurred on not only by food shortages in Karamoja, but by the Government issue of weapons to a Karamojong 'home guard' so that they could defend themselves against raids from the Pokot of Kenya.

The Karamojong are quick to defend what they see as their traditional grazing land from intruders, knowing that the state security forces are neither aware of the intrusions or in a position to do very much about it. When Pokot herders went into Uganda to graze their cattle in February 2000, they were attacked by the Karamojong, leaving 100 dead and 40 injured.[14] Similarly, more than 70 Turkana herders who had entered Uganda from Kenya were killed and 10,000 head of cattle stolen on 11 June 2000 when the Karamojong attacked them at Kasile in Kotido District.[15] Though peace initiatives amongst the Karamojong have not been totally in vain, it is evident that raiding and counter-raiding is still the occupation of some herders.

Kalenjin

The Kalenjin largely occupy the land to the south of the Turkana in Kenya. Of their main divisions, it is the Pokot and the Marakwet that have been principally involved in cattle raiding, whilst on the Uganda-Kenya border Pokot raiders have long engaged in violent cattle raids against the Karamojong. Following peace efforts by the Karamoja Initiative for Sustainable Peace, there was a lull, but it was short lived. In February 1999 two attacks in Karamoja left 48 Matheniko herdsmen and eight Pokot dead and 11 seriously injured. The raiders seized 3,000 head of Matheniko cattle.[16]

In April 1998, 500 Marakwet attacked a Kenyan police post in West Pokot and having killed two policemen went on to steal hundreds of Pokot cattle. Provoked by persistent attacks by the Marakwet, the Pokot retaliated. In October 1999, between 800 and 1,000 Pokot raiders attacked Tot Centre in Marakwet, killing 11 people. Again in October 2001, another major cattle raid by Pokot against the Marakwet took place in the Tot Division, during which about 50 Marakwet were massacred.[17] Such cattle raids between Pokot and Marakwet communities recent years have led to the displacement of entire communities and hundreds of lives have been lost. Inevitably such action has hampered development in the north west of Kenya.

Kuria

Among the Kuria there is frequent conflict over cattle raiding with the Luo, although in north western Tanzania, Fleisher found that most of the cattle raiding was done within the tribe and followed the modern pattern of organised and often violent crime for securing meat for butchers in Tanzania or Kenya (1999, p. 242). Four to ten men, abetted by accomplices in the target village, usually carry out the raiding. 'If they are caught in the act they are liable to be shot or beaten or hacked to death' (Fleisher, 1999, p. 241). Some perpetrators are apprehended by the criminal justice system and a number are jailed. But the men persisted, since it was a sure way of earning easy money to spend on clothes, beer, women, or to put aside for bridewealth cattle (currently down to 12 cattle per bride) for themselves and their siblings. 'The life of a cattle thief is to sell cows, go to bars and drink beer!' said one interviewee to Fleisher (1999, p. 243). A striking feature of his study is the prevalence of raiding despite its risks. In a single village of 2,232 people he was able to identify 66 men as cattle raiders, that is as much as 21 percent of the male population aged 20 to 39. The same village experienced the death of three raiders and one defender during his 19-month fieldwork 1994-96.

State Security Response

The East African states have always sought a monopoly in policing and punishing cattle rustling, but apart from their lack of capacity or political legitimacy in these more remote areas, they have actually eroded the judicial powers of local chiefs who were in the best position to tackle it. In addition, they have been hampered by the fact that several of the groups involved in cattle rustling straddle international borders and therefore intergovernmental co-operation is required. This showed little signs of taking place until the Second International Pastoralists Communities Harmonisation Initiative for the Horn of Africa Countries. The conference, held in May 2001, aimed at finding ways of initiating peace and development among all the rival groups.[18] Development is obviously crucial, since many are involved in cattle theft for lack of alternative economic activities. Up until now, however, governments have left development and peace initiatives to NGOs and churches and have pursued a more reactive and security orientated programme.

In Kenya there has been an Anti-Stock Theft Unit within the Kenya Police Force since President Kenyatta's day. Currently, following the accusation that their protection has been inadequate to stop hostilities turning to warfare between the Turkana and the Merrile, Toposa and Karamojong, the Kenyan authorities have increased the police and military presence in Turkana and on the border with Ethiopia, Sudan and Uganda. In addition, the Turkana were organised into a mini-self-defence force by being drafted into the Kenya Police Reserves and issued with AK47s. The Kenyan Government, however, seems uncertain about the benefits of community self-policing. In March 2001 it also armed the Pokot so that they could protect themselves against 'foreign aggression', following a spate of armed attacks from Uganda.[19] Yet a month later they were calling on the Pokot to surrender illegal firearms, although President Moi's offer of an amnesty in the Tot district met with little success – they were not prepared to hand in weapons until the Ugandan Karamojong disarmed. Indeed, the mayor of Kapenguria said in May 2001 that it would be disastrous whilst the Karamojong used their weapons 'like walking sticks.' His startling proposal was for a barrier like the Berlin Wall to be erected from Katikomor to Nauyapong to separate the Pokot and Karamojong. His proposal provoked the Local District Commissioner to say that if arms were not surrendered voluntarily, the Kenyan Government would seize the estimated 10,000 illegal firearms in Pokot hands when the amnesty expired.[20] The surrender did not happen and so the Government announced at the 2001 Conference of the International Pastoralists Communities that it would begin disarming the Pokot and other pastoral groups on the Uganda border.[21] The plan is to do this in synchronisation with the Ugandan Government's disarming of the Karamojong, so that neither side will be left at a disadvantage. The immediate effect, however, was not to promote a sense of security, but to cause residents of Baringo East to flee their homes for the hills. As they understood it, a crackdown on cattle rustling would mean harassment by the police.[22]

In the South West of Kenya, the Nyanza Provincial Commissioner has been sceptical about securing peace through forcible disarmament. He has argued for official armed vigilantes. In September 2000 he ordered Kuria District residents to form vigilante groups to arrest and punish criminal suspects, particularly where cattle rustling is prevalent. The move, however, was opposed by the Law Society of Kenya as being illegal and likely to encourage such vigilantes to turn to preying on the very people they were supposed to protect. In their view, also, such groups are prone to misuse by politicians to settle scores unrelated to security. Their alternative proposal was for villages to be encouraged to build police posts on a Harambee [local self-help organisation] basis, with the Government supplementing the efforts by supplying personnel and armaments.[23]

The same uncertainty as to the right approach of the state to cattle rustling is evident in Uganda. There the authorities, keen to stop the LRA northern rebellion spreading eastwards, were initially disinclined to take away weapons from the Karamojong. Instead they chose to rely on the police and an army-run militia (Local Defence Unit, LDU) of 1,000 per county. The latter were given basic military training and were paid 10,000 Ugandan Shillings a month. The assumption was that when cattle were stolen in Turkana and Pokot raids, their return would be negotiated, not fought over. Only if they were not returned within the given time was the army to be called in to confiscate them (Errington and Lokiru, 1996). Initially the militia brought about a dramatic declined in the raiding, but because the system failed to take weapons out of the hands of the Karamojong, it ultimately failed. The Karamojong resumed raiding their neighbours, the Iteso, in contravention of the law requiring them to leave guns at the local police station before entering Iteso lands. By the end of 1999 even the 'home guards' had become instruments of cattle raiding, along with rape, abduction of women and killings. In one notorious incident a sub-county LDU commander led 200 Karamojong on an attack on a camp of internally displaced Iteso, overcame the LDU unit, killed 17 people and stole 500 cattle.[24]

Initially the Ugandan Government response to Karomojong attacks was not to disarm them, but to arm vulnerable groups such as the Iteso, who were being driven from their villages into protected camps. From March 2000, it reinforced its police (principally the Anti Stock Theft Unit), sought to set up LDUs of 150 or so armed men across the Iteso/Karamojong border and sent army personnel into the area who pursued cattle raiders with their helicopters![25]

Only in January 2001 did the Government finally concede that the policy of tolerating the holding of arms by the Karamojong was a mistake. The new policy was to be one of voluntary disarmament, with 7,000 troops being deployed to seal off the Karamojong and to disarm them by September 2001.[26] By November, however, only 720 troops had been deployed, little disarmament had taken place and the raids continued. Museveni, under increasing criticism, was forced to announce a new full-scale disarmament in which the Karamojong were to be offered corrugated iron sheets for housing and ploughs and oxen for cultivation if illegal guns were surrendered.[27] In addition, at the instigation of the Ugandan Government, NGOs are attaching pacification conditions on their relief quotas.[28] Thus with stick and carrot the Ugandan Government hoped to bring weapon holding, cattle raiding and revenge attacks to an end and the signs by the end of 2001 were that it might well work. By early December 7,000 of the estimated 40,000 illegal weapons had been handed in, although the 60 LDUs being deployed across the region and along the Kenyan and Sudan borders were being manned by Karamojong pastoralists.

Local Vigilante Organisations

It has been mentioned already that the national and provincial administrations have at various times considered 'approved' vigilantes as a solution to cattle rustling. Stolen cattle could be identified and the return of the cattle could follow peaceful adjudication rather than violence. Currently the security response of the states has been judged by the victims of cattle raiding as quite inadequate in terms of preventing it or in bringing the perpetrators to justice. Not surprisingly herders that have lost cattle prefer to bypass the law and official channels and undertake spontaneous and violent retaliatory raids, both to recover their animals and to render summary justice to those they deem responsible.

Occasionally there have been attempts to put such grass roots security provisions on a more formal basis. Accounts of the details of how rural communities have organised vigilante groups against crime in general and cattle rustling in particular are few, but revealing. The fullest accounts come from the 1960s among the Bagisu of Uganda, the 1980s among the

Nyamwezi and Sukuma of Tanzania and the early 1990s among the Karamojong.

Bagisu Vigilantism

For the Bagisu of the Mount Elgon area of eastern Uganda in the 1960s, the dilemma was how to control serious crimes against the person (in their minds, primarily theft and witchcraft) in a context where state law enforcement had been transferred from local chiefs to distant and alien magistrates' courts and far away police posts (Heald, 1998). Given the impotence of the state in the rural areas, gangs arose that used intimidation, curfews, 'trials', and murder to eradicate the criminals, and ran protection rackets for the villagers. It was 'a local form of self assertion', an attempt, largely successful, 'to establish a viable parallel apparatus of social control in the community' (Heald, 1998, p. 252). They enjoyed both the support of local leaders and chiefs and the connivance of the police. The later were too under-resourced to stamp them out and so often preferred to work with them so as to forestall lynch-law and to effect arrests. By the late 1960s, however, some of the vigilante groups were co-opted by the ruling party and its local strong men to intimidate and terrorise rival political candidates, and by the 1980s were largely incorporated into the peoples' militia organised to protect the rural areas against the incursions of the civil war.

Tanzanian Vigilantism

More specifically targeted against cattle rustling were the village vigilante groups that arose in the early 1980s in rural north-western Tanzania amongst the Nyamwezi and Sukuma (Abrahams, 1987). In part, the spontaneous appearance of these village groups, armed with bows and arrows, that sought the culprits and frequently enforced a fitting punishment, was meeting the perceived failure of the state. The police were seen as under-resourced, inept and, worse still, possibly in collusion with the criminals. But beyond state inadequacy, there was a rejection of state values in determining what was criminal, in defining conclusive evidence, in fixing punishment, and even in the method of protection used by law enforcers. For the vigilantes, crime included witchcraft; evidence of guilt could be obtained from divination; punishment carried out by the groups themselves could range from social ostracism and fines of cattle to exile or even death; and the vigilantes frequently used traditional medicines to protect themselves from harm when they went after thieves.

The organisation was simple but effective:

> Every man, young or old, had to be equipped with bow and arrows and with a gourd-stem whistle which was to be blown in emergencies. If a theft was committed, a hue and cry was raised and the thieves were to be followed by the young men of the village concerned. The whistles would alert the members of neighbouring villages who would in turn alert others in the same way (Abrahams, 1987, pp. 181-2).

Though many villages established such groups, they were all independent, each with their own body of officers and membership subscription. Some of the armed rustlers were killed with poisoned arrows in the attempts to repossess the cattle (as were some of the vigilantes), others were brought back and tried in the vigilantes own 'courts.' Sometimes they were subject to torture and usually punished with fines of several head of cattle. More importantly, they had the effect of reducing violent crime, noticeably in the rural areas where they operated.

The Tanzanian state was intensely wary of these groups, although its official line was to praise them for their initiative, whilst insisting that they hand over suspects to the police and leave the determination of guilt and punishment to the courts. Ultimately the Tanzania state, like the Uganda state, used co-optation to neutralise the threat, formalising them in 1990 and announcing its intention to empower party cells and wards to form councils to legally deal with criminals. Not that these legal village militias were ineffective. Fleisher reported that cattle raiders he spoke to in the Kuria district of northwest Tanzania had felt the impact of the militia's crackdown that began there in 1994. As a result they were 'resting' from cattle raiding for a while. Many:

> move from cattle raiding to [gold] mining and back to cattle raiding again as their mining fortunes wax and wane and as efforts by the police or Sungusungu to crack down on cattle raiding, like the one that began in late 1994, take off with a vengeance and then, after administering scores of whippings and sending a few men to prison, run out of steam, their energies spent. 'Cattle thieving has stopped now [1995], but it will start again when the Sungusungu cools down', one cattle raider said. 'They can't stop the stealing', agreed another (Fleisher, 1999, pp.249-250).

Southern Karamojong Vigilantism

In 1992 such was the insecurity in southern Karamoja that the Moroto District Council decided to take the initiative and appointed a Secretary of Security to organise a force from among the Karamojong. They were required to own their own gun and more importantly to be recognised a local community leader. 10 men were appointed for each parish, with a total of 900 for the District. One innovative feature was that a few women were engaged as intelligence gatherers. They had hardly begun to organise when a headmaster was ambushed on the road and killed and the vigilantes were tasked with finding the killers. One of the three killers was finally tracked down, after a long pursuit, to a village. When he leapt out of his hiding place, shooting as he did, he was shot and killed. It was an important early success. In time they successfully secured the roads, something that the army had been unable to do, although the cattle raiding seemed to continue (Quam, 1997, pp. 6-7). As the effectiveness of the vigilantes was realised, some NGOs provided food and clothing for the organisation. The Government of Uganda, however, was uneasy with its independence and so in 1996 it was brought under the control of the army as Local Defence Units and subsequently expanded to 1,000 per county, 5,000 in Moroto District and 3,000 in Kotido District.

The Democratic Impact

Vigilantism in East Africa's pastoral communities means a wide variety of policing, from informal revenge raids, through formal self-policing initiatives, to government sponsored national militias. All are responses to the inability of state security to prevent, detect and prosecute cattle rustling. None of these groups is fully under the control of the state or abides completely with the rule of law. The availability of weapons and the absence or inadequacy of supervision means that responses to criminal and violent assaults by cattle rustlers are themselves criminal and violent and entail summary punishment on communities irrespective of whether the specific individuals that undertook the theft are the ones to suffer. With this degree of lawlessness amongst the cattle herders of Uganda, Kenya and Tanzania, there are clearly serious implications for their democracy.

The new regimes of the last dozen years, under the headline of 'democracy', have stressed political equality and participation, state accountability and the efficiency, and the provision of human rights, security and the rule of law for all citizens. Has the arrival of democracy changed anything in the experience of the pastoralists? Are the pastoralists of Africa, faced with violent cattle rustling, protected by the state, or at least protected to the same degree as citizens in the urban areas? Are their efforts to be involved in strategies of protection and/or arrest welcome or resisted? Do the vigilantes represent the wishes of the people or of the regime? Is the conduct of the vigilantes in their attempts to eradicate the problem within the parameters of human rights and political accountability?

The escalation of violence in tit for tat raids and counter raids has already been made sufficiently clear to warrant no further comment, but other issues are also worthy of consideration.

Resort to Violence rather than Negotiation

30 years of large scale violent cattle raids have made the resort to violence by its victims almost second nature. Eradicating this in favour of a culture that turns to negotiation first will be a slow process. There have been times when commentators have been too quick to conclude that new institutional forms can change things overnight. Thus the commentators were unduly optimistic in 1996, following the 1995 Peace Forum which brought together Karamojong leaders with NGOs, Ugandan Government officials and church representatives and set up a new official vigilante groups:

> cattle-grazing rights are being negotiated with neighbouring tribes... When cattle are stolen their return is now negotiated, not fought for... the near anarchy, gun law and vendetta killings of past years have been largely eradicated, and only a small amount of cattle raiding continues... (Errington and Lokiru, 1996)

The belief that the change was permanent and cause for 'quiet excitement and hope' proved misled. Instead of the gun becoming 'a symbol of pride and justice, not mayhem and murder', it took only a few years for it to become apparent that the resort to violence to rescue stolen cattle was not easily eradicated. More recently there have been fresh attempts in Uganda at negotiation and reconciliation between warring groups. NGOs and donors are backing peace and reconciliation projects (e.g. The Pokatusa peace initiative that incorporates an early warning and response programme and joint social activities such as drama and festivals) that endeavour to bring both sides together when there is an accusation of cattle rustling. However the persistence of the raids by the Karamojong have tended to undermine efforts so far and even many of those Itseo, who have previously been committed to reconciliation, now want to use arms. The same has been true between the Turkana and Jie. The Kotido District Administrator reported that the Turkana had long grazed their animals in the dry season in Jie sub-county and lived peacefully with the inhabitants. However, with persistent Turkana raids the local people were becoming increasingly hostile and meetings the DA had called for both sides to meet to resolve the problems had been shunned.[29]

Just how difficult negotiation is, is revealed in an incident that happened in July 2001 in Gilgal district, in the Rift Valley Province of Kenya. A Maasai invasion of farmland during the dry season, and subsequent cattle thefts, left six dead. At a peace meeting convened by the local people and presided over by the District Officer, Kikuyu farmers and Maasai herdsmen confronted one another. The herdsmen argued that the whole of the Rift Valley Province belonged to the Kalenjin, Turkana, Maasai and Samburu. They needed the land to graze their cattle and, in the words of one of the participants, 'we urge you to keep quiet and allow us to graze otherwise blood will be spilled'. On the other side, a local MP accused the pastoralists of destroying water pipes and grazing their animals on farms that did not belong to them. He called on the Provincial administration to enforce the Trespass Act against the pastoralists. His speech was cut short, however, when herdsmen started shouting and jumping in the air and two policemen cocked their guns at them to restrain them.[30] As discussions like these founder, groups resort to their violent vigilante methods in what they see as the most effective recourse for victims of cattle rustlers.

Social Polarisation

The large scale raids of the Karamojong in the 1980s, armed with their newly acquired AK47s, exacerbated antagonism towards them. It left their neighbours, the Iteso, largely without cattle to conduct the cultivation of their crops. As a result, there arose a new animosity towards the Karamojong. In one incident Iteso 'violently evicted those Karamojong who had settled in their area, detained several thousand at Soroti vehicle park without food or shelter, and for a time blocked relief food shipments to Karamoja through their region' (Mirzeler and Young, 2000, p. 417). And following the attack of 200 Karamojong (Pian) raiders on a camp for the internally displaced in September 2001, during which 15 were killed and 500 cattle stolen, there were fresh outbreaks of anti-Karamojong hostility. Eight Karamojong (Bokora) merchants were killed by an angry mob which barricaded the main road in Katakwi town and ambushed a bus on which they were travelling.[31] Inevitably Karamojong were threatening to storm Katakwi district in search of the killers if the army did not make a speedy arrest.

The same racial animosity towards the Karamojong arose in Acholiland after the Acholi lost all but 5,000 of their 300,000 cattle herd to Karamojong raids between 1985 and 1997. Similarly, the Bagisu in Butandiga subcounty sought to expel all Karamojong from Gisu in 1998 after a lethal cattle raid that left 20 dead and three girls abducted. They angrily asked why the Government was arming the Karamojong rather than protecting local populations.[32]

Similar tension is found elsewhere. The tendency in Samburu district to blame the Turkana for all cattle raiding has created so much animosity between the two groups that it has been reported that there is an ongoing campaign to evict all Turkana from the district. Certainly Samburus openly insult Turkana when the two communities meet in communal grazing areas and it is alleged that the Samburu County Council openly discriminates against the Turkana when recruiting.[33] Such ethnic tensions arising from raiding and counter-raiding endanger democratic institutions where there are heterogeneous compositions.

Unequal Justice

As raiding and counter-raiding has become more violent, those with access to weapons emerge as the 'winners'. They can defend themselves and mount retaliatory raids. Those with access only to traditional weapons are now much more vulnerable. Equality could be secured through universally arming the pastoralists, as the Governments of Kenya and Uganda did in the case of the Pokot and the Karamojong, but this has been found to only promote further cattle theft. The use of violent means of policing also discriminates against women who do not normally have access to weapons. As dependents, they have often been sent away from troubled districts to live with relatives in camps or urban areas (Hendrickson et al., 1996, p.24). In these situations they are much more susceptible to food scarcity. Likewise, with the increasing scale of the attacks and criminalisation of the operation, whole groups of herders can be affected, thus denying the chance for individual families to receive help from their neighbours. On the other hand, efforts at disarmament are dogged by fears that those who hand their weapons in first will also be put at a disadvantage. A disarmament that does not include everybody is as destructive of justice as an armament that is partial. Even a monopoly of the weapons of violence in the hands of the security forces of the state might not solve all the problems immediately. An investigation by the National Council of Churches in Kenya in 1999 found that, 'in times of conflicts, the security personnel sometimes fight alongside their ethnic communities instead of keeping peace impartially'.[34]

Mobilisation of Political Opposition

In chapter four it was noted that support for Museveni's Movement was very low in Northern Uganda because of the perception that the Acholi were at best marginal to the Government's policies. In north-eastern Uganda among the Karamojong, however, there has been longstanding support of the majority for the President. Is this a contradiction? Shouldn't the pastoralists be disillusioned that the Government has not stopped cattle raiding and has tried to prevent their vigilantes from revenge raids? The paradox resolves itself in part around the issue of guns. Up to shortly before the Presidential election of 2000, the Ugandan Government was still issuing guns to the Karamojong who joined the militias and was paying them 20,000 Shillings a month to fight cattle raiding. In addition, it had allowed the Karamojong (alone in Uganda) to carry guns since 1989. This might not amount to development (and after years of promises there are still no watering dams for cattle or tarmacked roads in the whole region), but it is interpreted in Karamoja as helping them to help themselves – a doctrine close to their hearts. It was no accident that during the election rumours went around that Besigye, the rival presidential candidate, would change things for the worse: 'We were told that if Besigye passes he will take away our guns and will persecute the warriors' one elder reported.[35] Others were warned that following a Besigye victory the UPDF would no longer protect them if they raided the Iteso or Bagisu. One group of Karamojong leaders even regarded Museveni as the best President because he was the weakest president ever. Doing nothing to curb violence, he thus condoned cattle rustling and revenge attacks. It is ironic that soon after Museveni received his 96.2 percent support from the region, it was he who introduced a disarmament programme.

But support for Museveni by no means implies that all are happy with the conduct of the Government in tackling raiding and the out of control vigilantes. The Iteso community in particular is incensed that so many are having to live in ill-protected and unhealthy camps because the Karamojong raiders are not being stopped. They expressed their dissatisfaction not by voting for non-Movement MPs in the parliamentary election, but by replacing nine 'non-performers' with nine who have taken a much more critical line of the executive in parliament. The pressure of the Teso parliamentary group was such as to cause the Internal Affairs Ministry to undertake an on-the-spot investigation of the problems facing the area. When the Minister presented the report in Parliament, she came under heavy criticism for the stalled disarmament process and the 'casual handling' of the 80,000 internally displaced by the raids.[36] Nor is this likely to be the end of the vocal criticism of the Government over this crisis. The Ugandan Parliament has now established a sub-committee into the crisis that has summoned the Defence Minister, Minister of State for Security and Minister of State for Karamoja to answer its questions. At last the people who are victims of raiders and vigilantes feel their voice is heard in the Ugandan parliament and in the national debates.

The ineffectiveness of the Kenyan Government to tackle the lawlessness of northwest Kenya might have been expected to provide the opportunity for opposition politicians to exploit the situation and campaign for peace and peaceful solutions to the interminable violent raiding and counter-raiding. However, the Turkana and Kalenjin region is a stronghold of the ruling party, KANU and opposition rallies and events are regularly disrupted by party supporters that constitute the state's own version of lawless policing. As a result, even though many cattle herders are bitter that they have lost cattle and the state has done nothing to help them, the opposition are an unknown quantity that few would choose to support. The problem of Government inactivity may go even deeper, as reports have emerged that even when raiders have been gathering over several days in the bush to get ready to launch a raid or counter raid, the district commissioners have claimed to know nothing about it. It would appear that KANU is not prepared to crack down on the illegal activities of their supporters, if this should mean the risk of antagonising them. (Jenkins, 1997). Far from the raiders and counter-raiders being the cause of mobilisation against their activities, the evidence suggests that in Kenya politicians sometimes play a crucial role in promoting violence and lawlessness. There are reports that politicians have been encouraging communities to set up vigilante groups and have issued ultimatums to rival ethnic communities to return stolen animals or face violent reprisals. One report claims that racial animosity has been fuelled by 'sensational statements by politicians in Samburu District', especially since the 1997 general election campaign.[37] Likewise the NCCK charges that politicians 'have no qualms inciting their constituents against other tribes' based on racist arguments.[38]

Adverse Exploitation of Lawless Environment

The endemic armed raiding and counter raiding has created a gun culture, a gun market and general lawlessness in which criminality flourishes. The cattle rustling requires guns on both sides, but those holding guns for policing activities are readily tempted to use them for other purposes such as highway robberies. For young men it is a ready way to purchase western goods and to indulge in social activity among their peers

Even security forces sent to enforce the law have at times seized the opportunities to exploit the insecure situation. In addition to the sale of arms and ammunition[39] there has been criminal activity by the army. Thus a UPDF officer and a deputy Chief Administrative Officer were arrested in May 2001 in connection with confiscating 18 cattle on transit and an unspecified amount of money. Further arrests were made in July 2001 of the Commander of the Anti-Stock Theft unit in Karamoja and three others charged with embezzling funds meant for Karamojong vigilantes attached to the Unit.[40] Previously the army had been accused of confiscating thousands of cattle in a punitive mission for Karamojong attacks. The cattle were said to have been sold to local markets.[41]

Conclusion

Some readers may be unhappy at the way much of this chapter has conflated cattle rustling and vigilantist responses to it. There may indeed once have been a clear distinction between crime and policing responses. But when vigilantes resort to the same practices and abuses as cattle raiders and show equal disregard for international human rights, national law and even communal mores, then the distinction blurs. This chapter, then, far from being unaligned with the rest of the book, in fact shows the fullest development of lawless policing. The causes, consequences and solutions of lawless policing and crime become identical. General lawlessness and violence is the final product of unrestrained lawless policing.

Notes

1. For the period July 1999 to June 2000 it is estimated that in the course of cattle raids there were 420 deaths and 49,500 cattle stolen or killed. Action by Churches Together, www.act-intl.org/news.
2. There is no hard evidence for the existence of professional stock rings in Maasailand (Waller, 1999, p.48, fn. 56.)
3. 'Uganda Awash with Guns', www.Oxfam.org.uk, accessed 8 June, 2001.
4. *The Monitor*, Kampala, 5 April, 1998.
5. *IRIN*, 4 September, 2001.
6. The Weekly Review, 12 March, 1999.
7. *Africa Research Bulletin*, 36, 3, 1999, p. 13483; *The Nation*, Nairobi, 23 August, 2001.
8. *Africa Research Bulletin*, 37, 2, 2000, p. 13859.
9. *IRIN*, 26 September, 2001.
10. *Africa Research Bulletin*, 36, 9, 1999, p. 13703.
11. BBC World Service broadcast, Focus on Africa, 19 July, 2000.
12. *New Vision*, 24 June, 2001.
13. *IRIN*, 14 September, 2001.
14. *Africa Research Bulletin*, 37, 2, 2000, p. 13875.
15. *Africa Research Bulletin*, 6, 2000, p. 14004.
16. *Africa Research Bulletin*, 36, 2, 1999, p. 13448.
17. *The Nation*, 6 May, 2001.
18. *The Monitor*, 28 May, 2001.
19. *New Vision*, 26 March, 2001.
20. *New Vision*, 3 May, 2001.
21. *New Vision*, 28 May, 2001. However, there were reports that in December 2001 a junior minister had held illegal meetings in Uganda among the Pokot urging them to keep their arms and to cross over into Kenya (IRIN, 10 January, 2002).
22. *The Nation*, 30 May, 2001.
23. *The Nation*, 14 September, 2000.
24. *IRIN*, 24 September, 2001.
25. *Africa Research Bulletin*, 37, 3, 2000, p. 13919. In 1962 a patrol of Uganda troops, commanded by Idi Amin, sent by the British in NW Kenya to disarm Turkana raiders, tortured, brutalised and killed a number. The Governor of Kenya would have had him prosecuted. The Ugandan Governor, however, claimed it was politically unacceptable in the light of objections from Obote, the prospective PM, who had only one other African officer in the army apart from Amin).
26. *Africa Research Bulletin*, 38, 2, 2001, p. 14314.
27. *IRIN*, 11 December, 2001.
28. *New Vision*, 24 June, 2001.
29. *IRIN*, 3 October, 2001.
30. *The Nation*, 12 July, 2001.
31. *IRIN*, 20 September, 2001. A man with a megaphone had incited the people to attack and to go to a neighbouring NGO compound (Christian International Peace Service, December, 2001).
32. *The Monitor*, 15 May, 1998.
33. *East African*, 9 October, 2000.
34. NCCK, www.act-intl.org/news, accessed 19 November, 2001.
35. *The Monitor*, 28 March, 2001.

36 *The Monitor*, 16 August, 2001. It also became apparent from the Auditor General's report that the Ministry of Defence had diverted Shs 543m of the Shs 2bn released to finance the fight against cattle rustling and used it to buy old cars (*The Monitor*, 16 August, 2001).
37 *East African*, 9 October, 2000.
38 NCCK, 1999, www.act-intl.org/news, accessed 19 November, 2001.
39 Revealed by research by Action for Development of Local Communities and reported in IRIN, 11 December, 2001.
40 *New Vision*, 18 May, 2001; *IRIN*, 24 July, 2001.
41 *The Monitor*, 23 September, 1999. There are also credible accounts of soldiers abusing women in the Iteso camps (*The Monitor*, 16 August, 2001).

PART V
THE IMPLICATIONS FOR DEMOCRACY

9 Sustaining Democracy in a Context of Lawless Law Enforcement

This book has examined the contradiction that exists between formal democratic institutions and persistent lawless law enforcement. Amongst the heterogeneous arenas of power, democratic values of equality and human rights co-exist with authoritarian and disciplinarian ones of inequality, repression and brutality. The social forms of authoritarianism and disciplinarianism have survived the transition, both in state institutions and in the local and domestic networks of society. Consequently, it has proved an uphill task to achieve the pacification of social conflict through the universal application of the rule of law and the legal control of violence. The most egregious forms of human rights abuses under authoritarian rule may have been removed, but the nature of democracy reintroduced in Africa in the 1990s has failed to provide for *all* of its citizens the fundamental rights to security or redress for wrongs. These negative legacies are not, of course, unique to Africa. Writing of Brazilian society, Pinheiro observes: 'There are profound authoritarian strands that pervade not only politics but society' (Pinheiro, 1997, p. 264). Along the same lines, O'Donnell writes: 'The combination of extreme inequality and very authoritarian patterns of social relations [in Brazil] poses great difficulties in creating a more solid and open democracy (O'Donnell, quoted in Pinheiro, 1997). The new democratic regimes have been installed throughout the developing world, but they have not yet been able to realise all the requisites of full democracy because of the continuities with an authoritarian past. They are in limbo between the past and the present or rather, different elements of society are moving at different speeds in their adoption of democratic values and the rule of law. And amongst the slowest to change their values and practices are the law enforcers of the state and of local communities. To many of them the rule of law is actually an obstacle to maintaining social order. With states and local civic organisations lacking the capacity to bring such policing under full and effective accountability, their virtual impunity is assured and their adoption of consistent democratic values will be a slow and uncertain process.

In many accounts of the relationship between violence and response, the assumption is that the abuses are the work of the regime reacting to perceived threats by social groups. Yet the chapters of this book have detailed internal security agents at times acting independently, rather than as simply tools of the regime. They have their own reasons for using violence illegally towards those who are violent or who threaten violence and instability. These include revenge for violence done to them, authoritarian and disciplinarian shared values towards disorder, political pressure for 'quick results' and social discrimination. Both internal security agents and their political leaders are implicated in lawlessness.

If lawless law enforcement is likely to persist, what are the implications for the prospects of sustaining and institutionalising political democracy? To what degree will the process be stalled or even undermined, or is it that this area can be ring fenced as an issue to be addressed in time, but not impeding movement on other fronts? This chapter explores nine areas where problems are likely to arise. They are issues that are raised by both state and non-state agencies, which I believe justifies the incorporation of them together in the analysis of this book.

Popular Support for Democracy: Can it Sustain its Appeal?

In itself, lawless law enforcement is not likely to lessen support for democracy as the preferred political system. Surveys in Africa consistently show very high support for democracy, as opposed to the alternatives of one party rule and military rule that characterised the previous regimes (Bratton and Mattes, 2001).[1] Yet it should be carefully noted that, when African interviewees have been asked what they thought democracy meant, very many have defined it in terms of civil liberties and human rights. Thus Bratton and Mattes report that their survey of more than 10,000 respondents across six nations showed that people cited civil liberties and personal freedom more frequently than any other meaning (34 percent, compared with, for example, 24 percent for 'government by the people' and 11 percent for 'voting rights'). Ottemoeller, in a much smaller survey in Uganda, found 40 percent defining it in terms of government by the people and 38 percent in terms of various civil freedoms (Ottemoeller, 1998). At best, therefore, many will see a discrepancy between the civil freedoms that they define as democracy and that they support, and the lawless law enforcement that they experience. At worst, their support for political democracy may be undermined by their lack of satisfaction with it, as they understand it. Already satisfaction levels are down to the mid 50s in percentage terms, in countries like Malawi, Namibia and Ghana, and down to 15 percent in troubled Zimbabwe (Bratton and Mattes, 2001, p. 118). It may be true that years of official (and unofficial) oppression have bred a tolerance of abuse, which, coupled with the widespread ignorance on human rights and legal provision, means that abuses are rarely challenged in the rural areas. But overall, the African populations are in no doubt that their expectations of democratic rule by the state are not being realised and the possibility remains that support for political democracy, especially by those who define it in terms of civil liberties, could evaporate.

The conduct of law enforcers will surely not be exempted from negative reactions, if for no other reason than that it has such an immediate impact on levels of social order. Law enforcement agents are one of the first and principal contacts that ordinary citizens make with their political authorities. It is for many the point at which government (democratic or otherwise) is experienced on a daily basis, where rights won in pro-democracy demonstrations and passed in parliament are translated into practice. In this respect, non-state policing will differ from state policing, since it is not linked with political democracy in the same way. Its lawless conduct will undermine democracy more indirectly, as citizens are dissatisfied with the inability of the democratic state to curtail it. In both cases, it is unlikely that democracy can sustain unequivocal support whilst lawless law enforcement is as widespread as it is.

Retaliation: Do Victims Seek Revenge?

Democratic consolidation is about institutionalising democratic values and behaviour. It means reducing (if not removing) the attractiveness of using unlawful methods, especially by powerful actors such as the military, police and vigilante groups, as they pursue their own interests outside the democratic institutions. Unless security agents of the state or other political authorities abandon their lawlessness and give to citizens the respect commensurate with their definition of democracy, their victims will be tempted to resort to illegal methods themselves. In Apter's words, democracy 'requires a self-monitored self-restraint and a self-generating individual dignity' (Apter, 1997, p. 26). Yet the evidence is that political leaders and their security advisers, at the national and community levels, still instinctively react to outbreaks of lawlessness by rebels, organised crime and political opponents with illicit force and other contraventions of human rights in much the same way as their authoritarian predecessors. The unquestioned assumption is that counterforce deters and the more severe the counterforce, the less lawlessness will be committed. Yet this book has shown that the very reverse can be true. As Gurr observes:

> The most fundamental human responses to the use of force is counterforce. Force threatens and angers men, especially if they believe it to be illicit and unjust. Threatened they try to defend themselves; angered they want to retaliate. Regimes facing armed rebellion usually regard compromise as evidence of weakness and devote additional resources to military retaliation. The presumption justifying counterforce is that it deters: the greater a regime's capacity for force and the more severe the sanctions it imposes on dissidents, the less violence they will do. This assumption is often a self-defeating fallacy. If a regime responds to the threat or use of force with greater force, the effect is likely to be an intensification of resistance: dissidents will resort to greater force (Gurr, 1970, p. 232).

Motivated by such reasons, law enforcement agencies have engaged in illegal and unjust violence that has often provoked violent responses in self-defence and retaliation. Each injury or death in East Africa at the hands of cattle vigilantes has provoked further raids. Likewise violence and human rights abuses in Uganda and Senegal at the hands of the army has led to rebel retaliation, which in turn provokes further abuses by the armies to revenge their losses. There seems no end to the assaults, ambushes and mines aimed at the combatants of both sides. Likewise, the determination to enlist intelligence information, or to prevent collaboration, promotes the use of intimidation, coercion, torture and executions by both sides. Despite occasional cease-fires, tit for tat attacks in the conflicts of northern Uganda and Casamance have been more or less continuous for fifteen or twenty years, leaving hundreds of fighters and civilians dead each year and many more homeless and destitute.

Coercion and extortion by policing agencies is usually more disseminated and makes less use of lethal firepower. The result is that though it generates opposition, the opposition is usually less intense and systematic. However, the same logic of violence and counter-violence prevails. In the case of the national police force of Mozambique, it has been seen that their illicit methods, particularly against RENAMO supporters, is part of the reason why certain elements in RENAMO were able to organise violent assaults against the police in November 2000 that left seven policemen dead. The brutal revenge of the police was the result.

As regards the more informal and loosely controlled Anambra State Vigilante Services in Nigeria, the evidence presented suggests that their uninhibited violence has deterred armed robbery in the short period of its existence, but there may already be signs that criminals are prepared to return, intent on meeting violence with violence. This is precisely what was seen to have occurred in South Africa in response to some of the non-state vigilante groups. As citizens armed themselves, so criminal gangs in the Cape Flats formed a coalition to fight the vigilantes, and increased their organisational and weaponry sophistication to counter the common threat. The impact on democracy, when law enforcement goes beyond the law in its use of force, is an escalation of violence, and the very opposite of respect for human rights and the law that are key elements in establishing democratic values.

Non-Violent Settlements: Is Their Employment Undermined?

Not only does the resort to illicit violence and other practices by law enforcers provoke counter-violence, but simultaneously it undermines democratic values that call for resolving conflict with the minimal use of force and where appropriate, by negotiation. If law enforcement shows no regard for the law, there is little inducement for citizens to seek change through legal, democratic and non-violent means. This is certainly the case with the pastoralists of East Africa and of the city mobs across Africa who beat or lynch and burn thieves in their communities. As they see it, there is no other channel for seeking redress, other than violence. And in the case of insurgencies, both sides tend to interpret the other side's readiness to use violence as meaning that there is no prospect of a negotiated settlement. They become so locked into using violence that they become deaf to alternatives or at least cynical about peace negotiations. This has certainly been the pattern in Uganda and Senegal, even in the face of growing peace movements led by the churches, women's groups and NGOs in both countries.

Few may doubt the relatively consistent support of the Ugandan and Senegalese governments for free political debate and public consultation, but both have been reticent to engage in genuine peace talks with insurgents, for all the evidence of years of neglect and underdevelopment in the conflict regions. Peace 'talks' have been held against a background of deep-seated government scepticism about the worth of negotiating with 'men of violence' and whilst simultaneously planning military operations. In both countries leaders in government, or certainly in the military, seem to have an unshakeable conviction that those that speak only in violence can be answered only in violence. When state security forces on the ground understand that that is the position of their masters, then the necessity for restraint and adhering strictly to the law is loosened. The repeated peace talks in both Uganda and Senegal have all failed, following renewed outbreaks of violence. It may be that these incidents were accidental, but it is just as likely that on both sides factions have sought to deliberately sabotage the negotiations that they have no faith in. The lesson drawn from the failure of lawless practices has not been, however, that the policy is flawed, but that it must be intensified. The evidence shows deeply embedded authoritarian attitudes in the ruling elite that have not yielded to new democratic ones. In as much as the democratisation is a top down process, this warns of a slow or incomplete consolidation. The very same pattern is visible among the East African pastoralists. Attempts by governments and NGOs to encourage groups to turn to negotiation have had only temporary success. Violent retaliation has been the practice since the arrival of the AK 47, for it appears to the herders to be the most effective means of settling disputes when violence has been experienced. There is clearly a contradiction between heralding the value of the new political parties as agents of non-violent mediation and negotiation in political matters at a national level, and the grass roots methods of conflict resolution. Until there is harmonisation, democracies must remain fragile.

Legitimacy: Are Law Enforcement Providers and Authorizers Harmed?

It is not just political scientists who argue that one of the best indicators of the basic character of a political regime is the nature of its policing (Bayley, 1969; Hills, 2000). The populations of northern Uganda, Casamance, Mozambique, Nigeria, the East African cattle belt and South Africa have also drawn their own conclusions. There seems little doubt that the lawless conduct of law enforcers towards the local inhabitants ensures that in some areas lawbreakers can count on the silence and toleration, if not support, of the local people. The ambivalence is captured well in a conversation held in Beira during the middle of Mozambique's civil war. A journalist asked a local whether it was likely that RENAMO 'bandits', who had slipped into the city to attend the Pope's open air mass, would be turned over to the police. 'Not necessarily. The police are not popular here'. 'Were the bandits popular then?' 'Not necessarily' (Finnegan, 1992, p. 102).

Fuelled by a RENAMO campaign against the Mozambique police for the violation of citizens' rights, the Mozambican public at the very least harbour suspicion, if not hostility, towards them. Even President Chissano has been forced to admit that when the public police act lawlessly the state itself, as their authorizer, is 'tarnished'.[2] Lawless law enforcement can delay the rule of law and in the process undermines the legitimacy of, and support for, the authorities.

The problem is not just one of creating ambivalence among members of the public towards lawbreaking. The severe treatment of those suspected of supporting or collaborating with the lawbreakers may only rouse sympathy for them, as the steady stream of recruits to the MFDC in Casamance demonstrates. On the other hand not all illegal policing is disapproved of or causes the providers and authorizers of policing to lose support and legitimacy. It has been seen that the Governor of Anambra state in Nigeria manages to head up a policing organisation that evidently breaks the law, without any apparent loss of support. The popularity of the Bakassi Boys, because of their success in combating crime, is so great that there appears to be little conscience about their lawless methods. On the contrary, they are enthusiastically cheered on in their public decapitations of alleged criminals. Meanwhile other Nigerian states are clamouring for them. Similar, if more divided, support is expressed for vigilante groups in South Africa. Some 62 percent of black residents in the Eastern Cape say they support alternative forms of punishment and only 21 percent of blacks thought that vigilantism was a criminal act (Schonteich, 2000d, p. 28).

It may be that an instrumental attitude to lawless law enforcement is widespread. If it fails to tackle crime and rebel groups, then the lawless methods are condemned by the public as evidence of the inadequacy of response. But if lawless policing 'works' and, perhaps more to the point, doesn't affect the 'innocent', then there is a willingness to turn a blind eye. This in itself tells us something about democratic consolidation in Africa. Though some of the new institutions and laws have gained respect, citizens still reserve the right to choose which and when to obey the laws of the state. In South Africa it was found that 36.4 percent think 'it might be better to ignore the law and solve problems immediately, rather than wait for a legal solution' and 30.2 percent that 'it is not necessary to obey the laws of the government that I did not vote for' (Gibson and Gouws, 1997, p. 179). In these circumstances, the legitimacy accorded those who break the law to enforce the law will be variable.

Transparency: Are the Facts Suppressed?

Establishing constitutionalism, respect for process and the protection of rights, are fundamental for sustaining democracy. Something so related to the process as law enforcement, must be subject to systematic auditing and evaluation. Yet too often law enforcement services (state and non-state) are less than transparent. In the name of defending personal, community and national interests, they assume a cloak of operational secrecy and, as a result, much escapes careful scrutiny. Indeed, much is conducted with minimal parliamentary or popular consultation and with restricted news information.

Lawlessness by security personnel leads to lawlessness by their authorizers. The latter will seek to cover up the excesses or grant immunity from prosecution if some of the unacceptable truth leaks out. The justification for this stratagem is usually in terms of preventing their forces from being discredited, morale being undermined, court space being given to hostile critics and the exacerbation of social/ethnic tension. They are also well aware that a single incident, where innocent victims are injured or killed, can devastate support and cause people to hate, or even fear, the law enforcers.

As has been shown, information about law enforcement is published and debated in the independent media of Uganda, Senegal, Mozambique, South Africa, Kenya and Nigeria. They have not been afraid to voice criticism of governments, security forces and vigilante groups. Nevertheless, all the authorities in charge of law enforcement considered in this book have sought to restrain criticism of their law enforcement agencies by news blackouts, straight denials and by intimidation of the media and prosecutions against them. In military conflict zones it is relatively easy to exclude journalists and suppress information. Without this facility, the leaders of the AVS in Anambra or the leaders of PAGAD and Mapogo in South Africa, simply deny that any illegal activity was by their authorisation or by their members. Indeed, the Governor of Anambra resorts to constant reassurances, in the face of overwhelming evidence to the contrary, that the AVS are fully co-operating with the national police.

In Uganda and Senegal, however, the state has been active in the suppression of information. Action against Ugandan journalists has included detention, arrests, prosecution for sedition and the publication of false news, and anonymous assaults, in an attempt to warn off journalists from negative reports. Similarly, Senegal, in addition to a policy of denial and restriction of information about troops in Casamance, uses the law to intimidate the press. Laws prohibit the expression of views that 'discredit' the State, disseminate 'false news', damage the army, or undermine public morale. Further, warnings have been issued that anyone threatening national unity, through the dissemination of separatist views, will be prosecuted for attempting to sabotage the peace negotiations.

As far as Mozambican Government action is concerned, there is far less attempt to manage the news. The problem in this case lies not with the authorizers, but with the providers. The police have shown considerable sensitivity, if not clear anger, to public criticism, and have used violence and detention to intimidate journalists from reporting abuses. The informal autonomous policing groups, of course, have far less incentive to suppress the truth, since much of their activity in the townships or in the cattle regions is not recorded, they are not accountable to the wider society and they believe that they have the full backing of their own local supporters. They may also have the confidence that any that may consider 'stirring up trouble' can be intimidated into silence. It is of no surprise that South African police investigations into extrajudicial killings and bombings by PAGAD met a wall of silence.

Wherever, therefore, lawless law enforcement exists, something of a cloud of smoke is produced in order to conceal it. It must evade the very law it says it is trying to uphold. It is hard to imagine that a society where such an attitude is prevalent will meet much success in holding political leaders to accountability and lawful conduct.

Accountability: Are Offenders Immune from Prosecution?

In their attempt to suppress the details of the abuses of security personnel, authorities in charge do all they can to prevent their coming to court, or to secure their acquittal in court. There is also the option in Senegal of diverting cases that arise from abuses by army personnel into the separate and secretive military court system that exists for members of the security forces. Yet even in the civilian courts, matters are not dealt with adequately. The current democratic constitutions of African states provide for an independent judiciary, but in practice magistrates and judges are vulnerable to political pressure from governments, due to (what they consider as) low pay, poor working conditions, and family and political ties. There is little other explanation for the failure of magistrates to investigate when prisoners appear before them with clear signs of ill treatment, as is reported in Senegal. Nor, for that matter, is much done to prosecute everyday vigilante brutality, save some publicity conscious trials of PAGAD leaders and some Mapogo activists in South Africa. In the same category of partial justice must also be placed the extraordinary lengths to which the Governor of Anambra state has personally gone to secure the release of his AVS operatives from Federal prosecution, using all his influence with the President to do so.

No doubt the political elite rationalise the bending of the rules and the tearing open of the judicial net to let some 'fish' through as part of the necessary evil to crush a worse evil. But inequality before law is an imperfect, if not impossible foundation on which to build democracy. It sets a dangerous precedent and is hardly likely to be popular with the victims of abuses by law enforcers or even with the wider public. One is reminded of the pleas, so often made in negotiated democratic transitions, for immunity for offenders under the previous regime. In Mozambique, for instance, the price of keeping RENAMO from returning to war was said to be the immunity of its troops from prosecution for war crimes. Commenting on the Spanish transition, Aguilar notes that, far from being beneficial, its very timidity may have produced a democracy that is mediocre and inferior in quality. She quotes Colomer, 'The virtues of the transition have become the vices of democracy' (Aguilar, 2001, p. 117). Failure of courage by political authorities to tackle those who hold the instruments of force and act in the name of law enforcement is understandable, but it is also unforgivable.

Intolerance: Do the Legitimising Discourses Promote Social Polarisation?

A noticeable feature of the accounts presented in this book is that, where law enforcement transgresses the legal boundaries, it frequently denigrates and criminalizes whole groups as part of its legitimising discourse. Membership of the 'lawless' group then becomes sufficient alone to warrant discrimination and the assumption of guilt and the justification of heavy-handed treatment. The effects, of course, are a vicious cycle of deviance amplification and the introduction of social antagonism into a polity that is supposed to be based on equality. People are divided by affiliations of race, ethnicity, religion, language and class, irrespective of actual conduct. And it is around these affiliations that victim groups and law and order groups are polarised.

In the cases of northern Uganda and Casamance and frequently in East African pastoralists societies, the conflict has been ethnicised. Hence discrimination and violence is used against civilians for no other reason than their ethnic identity. In the eyes of one side, the Acholi are viewed as

LRA terrorists or their supporters, whereas in the eyes of the other side, the army is made up almost entirely of westerners seeking revenge on the North. In the case of Senegal, the Diola are seen by the army as automatically sympathising with the MFDC rebels, whereas Diola themselves see the state as Wolof dominated and local non-Diola as collaborators, indifferent to the struggle for independence. With the Acholi and Diola so categorised by the state as 'enemies of the state', it is (and will be) extremely difficult to convince them that they have a part in the state. The same process of labelling is also seen in north-east Uganda and north-west Kenya, where cattle raiding is perceived in terms of the ethnic antagonism, whether it is Karamojong against the Pokot or the like.

In Nigeria and South Africa there is a more localised version of the same negative labelling taking place. The 'hoodlums' dens' of Anambra state are the two settlements, Umuleri and Umuoba Anam. If a whole community is deemed guilty, they have forfeited their civil rights. As long as their lawlessness is stopped, it little matters what means are used to achieve it, even if they are told to pack their bags and go back to their villages. Likewise, in South Africa 'undesirables' are kept away from the streets that vigilantes control by force.

Social generalisations both divide and polarise citizens and minimise the opportunities for dialogue across the social boundaries. It is not the basis for the consultation and inclusiveness that strengthens democracy.

Criminal Exploitation: Does Crime Thrive Under these Conditions?

Once the agents of law enforcement break the law in their dealings with lawbreakers, it is a short step for them to break the law in other respects. David Keen has argued that the label 'war' can be 'very useful for those who wish to promote certain kinds of violence' since it can confer a kind of legitimacy upon certain types of violence' (Keen, 2000, p. 19). The same is true of the pursuit of criminals and rebels. It can provide a cover for personal revenge, sexual abuse and economic exploitation. Further, when the general public sees that law enforcers pay little regard to the law, it is an open invitation for them to do likewise. What was conceived as simply bending the rules to improve law enforcement can end up opening the flood gates to general criminality, with criminals, police and opportunist groups seeking to take advantage of the disorder.

Regrettably the evidence is that this is what has happened in Uganda and Senegal. All ranks of the army appear to have adopted the 'plunder mentality' and exploited for their own profit the situation where the law is not upheld. They have undertaken protection rackets, looting, control of trade in scarce commodities, exploitation of labour, theft of international aid and rape. Little surprising that some will have an interest in perpetuating insecurity so as to sustain the alternative system of profit. The analyst is left with the dilemma of deciding whether security agents exploit civilians to further the campaign against lawlessness, or whether they further the campaign against lawlessness to exploit civilians. Keen's wry adaptation of Clausewitz rings true: 'War may be the continuation of economics by other means' (Keen, 2000, p. 27). The overall lawlessness of both armies has opened the door for other illicit activity and in both northern Uganda and Casamance there are reports of criminal activity in drugs, weapons dealing, smuggling, cattle raiding and the like becoming an overt element of economic life.

In Mozambique it may be common knowledge that the police can be bribed and that they have close contacts with organised crime, but equally depressing is the model that their conduct provides. As the young highway robber in Mozambique said, 'The police use guns all the time to make money. So can I!' In Anambra criminals have disguised themselves as the Bakassi Boys as a sure way of being able to extort goods successfully, whereas in South Africa both PAGAD and Mapogo have mutated from groups that seek to control crime to groups who at times carry out crime. The gap is small between protection and protection racket. So too is the use of instruments of coercion to ward off armed raiders and to become an armed raider. It has already been recorded how in East Africa there is little difference between cattle raiders and vigilantes – the two roles being almost inter-changeable. When law enforcement and law breaking merge, it is impossible to construct the rule of law.

Mobilisation: Has the Subject Become a Political Issue?

The degree to which political opposition mobilises around the issue of how law enforcement is conducted is a measure of how democracy is working. Received wisdom argues that the only guarantee that a government will remain democratic is the presence of a lively and effective opposition. For democracy to be sustained, it is said, there needs to be not just party competition offering viable alternative governments, but opposition that is effective at keeping national and local government alert in terms of accountability and integrity.

Neither in Uganda or Senegal has there been an aggregation of opposition support around a single political party representing Acholi or

Casamance demands for an end of abuses by security forces and social and economic justice. Nevertheless, the lawless actions of the armies in their handling of the insurgencies has entered the national political debate and, to a degree more evident in northern Uganda than Casamance, has become a focus for mobilising opposition. In Uganda, the Acholi may not have formed (or have been allowed to form) an opposition party, but their voice is represented in Parliament by the Acholi parliamentary group. They have been vocal, along with human rights groups, in calling for serious peace negotiations with the LRA, to the point of securing from a reluctant Government the Amnesty Bill 2000. Certainly part of the reason for the large support for the political opposition in the north during the 1996 and 2001 Presidential and Parliamentary elections was due to the UPDF's failure to defeat the LRA and their abuses in the camps and countryside. In Senegal, the voice of the marginalised region has been much more muted, with only minor parties showing any serious interest in representing Casamance or Diola interests.

It is in Mozambique that the most encouraging signs are taking place in terms of effective opposition to lawless law enforcement. The press has long campaigned to see the police reformed and was sufficiently strident to bring about in 1995 the removal of the Minister of the Interior, the prosecution of police officers for torture and the rousing of a Parliament Commission to investigating police corruption. The campaign received a considerable boost from the violent over-reaction of the police to the violent protests of RENAMO supporters in November 2000. This gave RENAMO the opportunity to launch a serious campaign, not just against the police, but also against the Government, whom they accused of instigating the police violence. The criticism reached even higher levels of public support following the murder, also in November 2000, of Carlos Cardoso, perhaps Mozambique's best known newspaper editor and a fearless critic of corruption. There was a huge national outcry over his murder, in the belief that it was linked to the elite corruption and police complicity that he was about to expose. There is a real sense, at least amongst the educated population, that the press is the champion of freedom and scourge of corruption. The current momentum is such that it is unlikely that police practices will ever be the same again and the evidence is that the Government is now serious about ensuring that the truth comes out and that the guilty (police or otherwise) are prosecuted. It appears that the police reform that did not happen at the transition and would never have happened at the initiative of the political class, may actually happen as a result of this popular roots pressure.

There may be an intriguing parallel here with Japan. If Katzenstein's analysis is correct, cultural norms of internal security and law in Japan changed dramatically in the 1950s, but not as a result of the military defeat in 1945 and American occupation. Neither of those events could by themselves have achieved the transformation from norms of police violence and repression to norms of low violence and tolerance for open political debate. Rather, in his view, the change emerged from intense conflicts in the parliament, the factories and the streets between the Government and its opponents. In those conflicts the ground rule came to be established that the police would not fire on unarmed demonstrators, whatever the provocation. At the same time the police (at least at the leadership level) learnt that restrained tactics do not lead to social collapse (Katzenstein, 1996). In other words, policing norms are more likely to change as a result of sharp contestation and historical contingency, than as the result of regime change and institutional reform.

The bitter battle may have begun in Mozambique, but it has yet to take place in Senegal and Uganda. The same is true of South Africa. The escalating crime, the way the Government and police have failed to curtail it, and the way non-state policing is responding, certainly receives widespread coverage in the South African media. Yet though the media presentation of the vigilantes has been negative, it has failed to rouse public opinion or to put pressure on the vigilantes. Rather, there is notable sympathy with their frustration with the national police, even though their violent methods bring criticism. But if those opposed to vigilantism have failed in their mobilisation in South Africa, so have the other side. PAGAD's efforts to harness its anti-crime supporters into an Islamist political movement has had only limited success. In Anambra state the opposition to the ruling party in the state legislature have certainly tried to make political capital out of the abuses of the Bakassi Boys, but so far with little success. The vigilantes are still too popular for any large scale opposition to develop. What people oppose is not all illegal law enforcement, but that which targets those deemed innocent. When it successfully targets the 'guilty', it is not likely to attract strong opposition.

In the Final Analysis

There can be little doubt that policing and law enforcement is a key diagnostic test of the health of a democracy. As Bayley and Shearing put it, 'The governance of security is both an indicator of the quality of political life and a major determinant of it' (2001). Across a whole array of areas its control, or lack of it, impinges on many issues pertaining to democracy. The practices related in this book constitute many potential dangers to the sustaining and deepening of democracy. How law enforcement conducts itself, especially in the early years of a democracy's life, has a profound impact on levels of social order, the experience of human and civil rights, and the degree to which the rule of law as a principle of self-restraint and compliance takes root within the citizenry. Political democracy is fairly robust. It can survive social disorder, particularly if that disorder is confined to one area of the country; and it can continue in its formal institutions even when there are human rights abuses, as long as those abuses are not systematic and gross. But if the rule of law is disregarded, particularly if that is by the very persons who are charged with upholding it, it is much more ominous for democracy. This is because the rule of law is a spider's web; to tear a part tends to destroy the whole. Laws may be broken by individuals or sometimes by groups acting together, but the law itself stands. The rule of law, however, is a communal principle, which makes its damage less visible but more insidious. The citizens of Kampala, Dakar, Maputo, Cape Town, Nairobi and Onitsha may be able to point to elected leaders, functioning parliaments, opposition press, freedom of assembly, an independent judiciary and the like, even as the rule of law is slowly breaking down. What is the critical mass of people who feel no internal restraint to abide by democratically determined binding rules, so that democracy fails? No one is sure. But most would agree that when law enforcement is commonly unrestrained by the law, it is a bad sign.

The rule of law may not be the guarantee of liberty, but it is a necessary condition of it. The task is to ensure that policing is based on justice, equality and respect for human rights. Yet if this proved difficult when the government was the authorizer and provider of policing services, it will be much harder in the new environment of multiple authorizers and providers and with the state not holding the monopoly of the instruments of coercion. Democratic states may see no other alternative but to share policing with other authorizers and providers, but few would want them to lose the responsibility for it. This requires not just state regulation, which is relatively cost free, but training and auditing which demands a degree of financial commitment which many African states will find hard to meet. However, the price of not making law enforcement lawful may be even higher for the future of the state, democracy and society.

In Africa's new democracies citizens are choosing who makes the laws, but still have little influence on how they are applied and who may use force to do so. For some years to come it appears that the fight against lawlessness will often be conducted lawlessly.

Notes

1. The Human Sciences Research Council found in South Africa, in 1999, that 74 per cent agreed that democracy was preferable to any other system of government. Similarly, in 1997, 56.3 per cent of South Africans thought that, 'even when things don't work, democracy is always the best' (quoted in Mattes and Thiel, 1999, p. 128).
2. Panafrican News Agency, 7 December, 2000.

Bibliography

Abbink, J. (2000), 'Violence and the Crisis of Conciliation; Suri, Dizi and the State in South-West Ethiopia', *Africa*, vol. 70, pp. 527-50.

Abrahams, R. (1987), 'Sungusungu: Village Vigilante Groups in Tanzania', *African Affairs*, vol. 86, pp. 176-96.

Aguilar, P. (2001), 'Justice, Politics and Memory in the Spanish Transition' in A. Brito, C. Gonzalez-Enriquex and P. Anguilar, *The Politics of Memory: Transitional Justice in Democratizing Societies*, Oxford University Press, Oxford.

Almond, G. and Verba, S. (1963), *The Civic Culture: Political Attitudes and Democracy in Five Nations*, Princeton University Press, Princeton.

Alpers, E. (1984), 'To Seek a Better Life: The Implication of Migration from Mozambique to Tanganyika for Class Formation and Political Behaviour', *Canadian Journal of African Studies*, vol. 18, pp. 367-88.

Amnesty International, (1998), *Senegal: Climate of Terror in Casamance*, AI Index: AFR 49/01/98.

Amnesty International, (1998b), *Mozambique: Human Rights and the police*, AI Index: AFR 41/01/98.

Amnesty International, (1999a), News release, 17 March, 1999.

Amnesty International, (1999b), *Uganda Breaking the Circle: Protecting Human Rights in the Northern War Zone*, London.

Amnesty International, (2000a), 'Human Rights and the Police', AFR 41/002/00.

Amnesty International, (2000b), 'Mozambique: Suspected Extra-judicial Executions', AFR 41/02/00, May 2000.

Amnesty International, (2000a), 'Mozambique Torture', AFR 41/01/00, May 2000.

Anderson, D. (1986), 'Stock Theft and Moral Economy in Colonial Kenya', *Africa*, vol. 56, pp. 399-415.

Apter, D. (1997), 'Political Violence in Analytical Perspective', in D. Apter (ed), *The Legitimization of Violence*, UNRISD and Macmillan, Basingstoke.

Azarya, V. (1996), *Nomads and the State in Africa: The Political Roots of Marginality*, Avebury, Aldershot.

Baker, B. (2000), *Escape from Domination in Africa: Political Disengagement and its Consequences*, James Currey, Oxford.

Baker, B. (2002), 'Living with Non-state Policing in South Africa: the Issues and Dilemmas', *Journal of Modern African Studies*, vol. 40.

Bayart, J., Ellis, S. and Hibou, B. (1999), *The Criminalization of the State in Africa*, James Currey, Oxford.

Bayley, D. (1969), *The Police and Political Development in India*, Princeton University Press, Princeton.

Bayley, D. and Shearing, D. (2001), *The New Structure of Policing: Description Conceptualization and Research Agenda*, U.S. Department of Justice, Office of Justice Programs, National Institute of Justice, available at www.ncjrs.org.

Behrend, H. (1998a), 'War in Northern Uganda', in C. Clapham, *African Guerrillas*, James Currey, Oxford, pp. 107-18.
Behrend, H. (1998b), 'The Holy Spirit Movement's New World: Discourse and Development in the North of Uganda', in H. Hansen and M. Twaddle (eds), *Developing Uganda*, James Currey, Oxford, pp. 245-54.
Behrend, H. (1999c), *Alice Lakwena and the Holy Spirits*, James Currey, Oxford.
Berlin, I. (1958), *Two Concepts of Liberty*, Oxford University Press, Oxford.
Bienart, B. (1962), 'The Rule of Law', *Acta Judica*, vol. 99, pp. 109-35.
Bratton, M. and Van de Walle, N. (1997), *Democratic Experiments in Africa: Transitions in Comparative Perspective*, Cambridge University Press, Cambridge.
Bratton, M. (1997), 'Deciphering Africa's Divergent Transitions', *Political Science Quarterly*, vol. 112, pp. 67-93.
Bratton, M. and Mattes, R. (2001), 'Africans' Surprising Universalism', *Journal of Democracy*, vol. 12, pp. 107-21.
Bratton, M. and Lambright, G. (2001), 'Uganda's Referendum: The Silent Boycott', *African Affairs*, vol. 100, pp. 429-52.
Brewer, J. (1994), *Black and Blue: Policing in South Africa*, Clarendon Press, Oxford.
Broch-Due, V. (1999), 'Remembered Cattle, Forgotten people: The Morality of Exchange and the Exclusion of the Turkana Poor', in D. Anderson and V. Broch-Due (eds), *The Poor Are Not Us*, James Currey, Oxford.
Brodeur, J-P. (1999), 'Comments on Chevigny', in J. Mendez, G. O'Donnell and P. Pinheiro (eds), *The (Un)Rule of Law and the Underprivileged in Latin America*, University of Notre Dame Press, Notre Dame, pp. 71-86.
Brogden, M. and Shearing, C. (1993), *Policing for a New South Africa*, Routledge, London.
Callaghy, T. (1994), 'Africa: Back to the Future?', *Journal of Democracy*, vol. 5, pp. 133-45.
Chabal, P. (1992), *Power in Africa*, Macmillan, Basingstoke.
Chandler, D. (2000), 'International Justice', *New Left Review*, Nov/Dec, pp. 55-68.
Charney, C. (1991), 'Vigilantes, Clientelism and the South African State', *Transformation*, 16, pp. 1-28.
Chazan, N. (1988), 'Ghana: Problems of Governance and the Emergence of Civil Society', in L. Diamond, J. Lintz, and S. Lipset (1988), (eds), *Democracy in Developing Countries: Africa*, Lynne Rienner, Boulder.
Chazan, N. (1994), 'Between Liberalism and Statism: African Political Cultures and Democracy', in L. Diamond, (ed), *Political Culture and Democracy in Developing Countries*, Lynne Rienner, Boulder.
Christiano, T. (1996), *The Rule of Many: Fundamental Issues in Democratic Theory*, Westview Press, Boulder.
Clapham, C. (1998), 'Introduction: Analysing African Insurgencies', in C. Clapham (ed), *African Guerrillas*, James Currey, Oxford.
Collier, R. (1982), *Regimes in Tropical Africa 1945-75*, University of California Press, Berkeley.
Coulon, C. (1988), 'Senegal: The Development and Fragility of Semidemocracy', in L. Diamond, J. Lintz, and S. Lipset (1988), (eds), *Democracy in Developing Countries: Africa*, Lynne Rienner, Boulder.
Crime Information Analysis Centre of the SAPS (1999), 'Attacks on Farms and Smallholdings 1/99', www.saps.org.za (accessed 03/05/01).
Crowder, M. (1987), 'Whose Dream Was it Anyway? Twenty-Five Years of African Independence', *African Affairs*, vol. 86, pp. 7-24.

Da Costa, P. (1993), 'Casamance Quandary', *Africa Report*, March/April.
Darbon, D. (1984), 'Le Cultualisme bas – Casamancais', *Politique Africaine*, vol. 14, pp. 125-8.
Davenport, C. (2000), 'Introduction', in C. Davenport (ed), *Paths to State Repression: Human Rights Violations and Contentious Politics*, Rowman and Littlefield, Lanham, pp. 1-24.
Diamond, L. (ed), (1994), *Political Culture and Democracy in Developing Countries*, Lynne Rienner, Boulder.
Diamond, L., Lintz, J., Lipset, S. (eds), (1988), *Democracy in Developing Countries: Africa*, Lynne Rienner, Boulder.
Diamond, L. and Plattner, M. (eds) (1999), *Democratization in Africa*, John Hopkins University, Baltimore.
Diaw, A. and Diouf, M. (1998), 'Ethnic Group Versus Nation: Identity Discourses in Senegal', in O. Nnoli (ed), *Ethnic Conflicts in Africa*, CODESRIA, Dakar.
Dicey, A. (1960), *Introduction to the Law of the Constitution*, E. Wade (ed), 10th edition, Macmillan, London.
Doom, R. and Vlassenroot, K. (1999), 'Kony's Message: A New Koine? The Lord's Resistance Army in Northern Uganda', *African Affairs*, vol. 98, pp. 5-36.
Dykman, A. (2000), 'The Reintegration of the Casamance Region into Senegalese Society', SAIS Studies on Senegal, Johns, Hopkins University, available at www.sais-jhu.edu.
Ehrenreich, R. (1998), 'The Stories We Must Tell: Ugandan Children and the Atrocities of the Lord's Resistance Army', *Africa Today*, vol. 45, pp. 79-102.
Errington, S and Lokiru, P. (1996), 'Taming the Gun', *BBC, Focus on Africa*, April-June, www.bbc.co.uk/worldservice/africa, accessed 11.06.01.
Evans, M. (2000), 'Briefing: Senegal: Wade and the Casamance Dossier', *African Affairs*, vol. 99, pp. 649-58.
Finnegan, W. (1992), *A Complicated War: The Harrowing of Mozambique*, University of California Press, Berkeley.
Fisk, R. (1990), *Pity the Nation: Lebanon at War*, Andre Deutsch, London.
Fleisher, M. (1999), 'Cattle Raiding and Household Demography among the Kuria of Tanzania', *Africa*, vol. 69, pp.238-55.
Freedom House, (yearly) *Freedom in the World: The Annual Survey of Political Rights and Civil Liberties*, Freedom House, New York.
Fukui, K. (1994), 'Conflict and Ethnic Interaction: The Mela and their Neighbours', in K. Fukui and J. Markakis (eds), James Currey, London.
Fuller, L. (revised edition 1969), *The Morality of Law*, Yale University Press, Yale.
Galaty, J. and Bonte, P. (1991), 'The Current Realities of African pastoralists', in J. Galaty and P. Bonte (eds), *Warriors and Traders: Pastoralism in Africa*, Westview, Boulder, pp.267-92.
Gastrow, P. (1998), *Organised Crime in South Africa*, Monograph Series, No. 28. Institute of Strategic Studies, Pretoria.
Gastrow, P. (1999), 'Main Trends in the Development of South Africa's Organised Crime', *African Security Review*, vol. 8, pp.58-69.
Gibson, J. and Gouws, A. (1997), 'Support for the Rule of the Law in the Emerging South African Democracy', *International Social Science Journal*, vol. 152, pp. 173-92.
Gurr, T. (1970), *Why Men Rebel*, Princeton University Press, Princeton.
Hamber, B. (1999), 'Have no doubt, it is fear in the land: an explanation of the continuing cycles of violence in South Africa', paper presented at the Centre for the Study of Violence and Reconciliation Seminar, 27 May, 1999.

Hanlon, J. (1991), *Mozambique: Who Calls the Shots*, James Currey, London.
Hanlon, J. (1996), *Peace Without Profit: How the IMF Blocks Rebuilding in Mozambique*, James Currey, Oxford.
Harris, B. (2001), *"As for Violent Crime that's our Daily Bread": Vigilante Violence During South Africa's Period of Transition*, Centre for the Study of Violence and Reconciliation, Violence and Transition Series, Vol. 1.
Hargreaves, J. (1988), *Decolonizaton in Africa*, Longman, Harlow.
Hayek, F. (1976), *The Road to Serfdom*, Routledge and Kegan, London.
Haysom, N. (1989), 'Vigilantes and Militarisation of South Africa', in J. Cock and L. Nathan, (eds), *War and Society: The Militarisation of South Africa*, David Philip, Cape Town.
Haysom, N. (1990), 'Vigilantism and the Policing of African Townships: Manufacturing Violent Stability', in D. Hansson and D. van Zyl Smit, *Towards Justice?: Crime and State Control in South Africa*, Oxford University Press, Cape Town.
Heald, S. (1998), *Controlling Anger: The Anthropology of Gisu Violence*, James Currey, Oxford.
Held, D. (1995), *Democracy and the Global Order*, Cambridge University Press, Cambridge.
Hendrickson, D., Mearns, R. and Armon, J. (1996), 'Livestock Raiding Among the Pastoral Turkana of Kenya: Redistribution, Predation and the Links to Famine', *IDS Bulletin*, vol. 27, pp.17-30.
Hills, A. (2000), *Policing in Africa: Internal Security and the Limits of Liberalization*, Lynne Rienner, Boulder.
Hochschild, A. (1999), *King Leopold's Ghost*, Macmillan, London.
Hough, M. (2000), 'Urban Terror in South Africa: A New Wave?', *Terrorism and Political Violence*, vol. 12, pp. 67-75.
Howe, H. (2000), 'African Private Security', *Conflict Trends*, June, pp. 22-4.
Human Rights Watch, (1997), *Scars of Death*, Human Rights Watch, New York.
Human Rights Watch, (1999), *Hostile to Democracy: the Movement System and Political Repression in Uganda*, Human Rights Watch, New York.
Human Rights Watch, (2001), *World Report 2001*.
Humphries, R. (2000), 'Crime and Confidence: Voters' Perceptions of Crime', *Needbank ISS Crime Index*, vol. 4, pp.1-6.
Inkeles, A. (1961), 'National Characters and Modern Political Systems' in F. Hsu (ed), *Psychological Anthropology: Approaches to Culture and Personality*, Dorsey Press, Homewood.
Jacobs, T. and Suleman, F. (1999), *Breaking the Silence: A Profile of Domestic Violence in Women Attending a Community Health Centre*, Health Systems Trust, www.hst.org.za.
Jenkins, C. (1997), 'Guns Spread to Halt Kenyan Cattle Rustling', 1 December, 1997, *BBC Broadcast, From Our Own Correspondent*.
Johnston, L. (1992), *The Rebirth of Private Policing*, Routledge, London.
Joseph, R. (1998), 'Africa, 1990-1997: From *Abertura* to Closure', *Journal of Democracy*, vol. 9, pp. 3-17.
Joseph, R. (ed) (1999), *State, Conflict, and Democracy in Africa*, Lynne Rienner, Boulder.
Kamrava, M. (1993), *Politics and Society in the Third World*, Routledge, London.
Kaplan, R. (1994), 'The Coming Anarchy: How Scarcity, Crime, Overpopulation, and Disease are Rapidly Destroying the Social Fabric of our Planet', *Atlantic Monthly*, February.

Bibliography 225

Katzenstein, P. (1996), *Cultural Norms and National Security: Police and Military in Postwar Japan*, Cornell University Press, Ithaca.

Keen, D. (2000), 'Incentives and Disincentives for Violence', in M. Berdal and D. Malone (eds), *Greed and Grievance: Economic Agendas in Civil Wars*, Lynne Rienner, Boulder.

Kinnes, I. (2000), *From Urban Street Gangs to Criminal Empires: the Changing Face of Gangs in the Western Cape*, Monograph Series, No. 48, Institute of Strategic Studies, Pretoria.

Kriegel, B. (1995), *The State and the Rule of Law*, Princeton University Press, Princeton.

Lambert, M. (1998), 'Violence and the War of Words: Ethnicity v. Nationalism in the Casamance', *Africa*, vol. 68, pp. 585-603.

Linares, O. (1992), *Power, Prayer and Production: The Jola of Casamance, Senegal*, Cambridge University Press, Cambridge.

Louw, A. (2001), 'City Crime Trends', *Needbank ISS Crime Index*, vol. 5, available online at www.isi.co.za?Publications/Crimeindex.

Luckham, R. (1998), 'The Military, Militarisation and Democratisation in Africa', in E. Hutchful and A. Bathily (eds), *The Military and Militarism in Africa*, CODESRIA, Dakar.

Maepa, T. (2001), 'Out of Hand? Government's Response to Vigilantism'?', *Needbank ISS Crime Index*, vol. 5, available online at www.isi.co.za?Publications/Crimeindex.

Maloba, W. (1993), *Mau Mau and Kenya*, Indiana University Press, Bloomington.

Mamdani, M. (1996), *Citizen and Subject: Contemporary Africa and the Legacy of Late Colonialism*, David Phillips.

Masuku, S. (2001), 'South Africa: World Crime Capital?', *Needbank ISS Crime Index*, vol. 5, available online at www.isi.co.za?Publications/Crimeindex.

Mathews, A. (1986), *Freedom, State Security and the Rule of Law: Dilemmas of the Apartheid Society*, Juta, Cape Town.

Mattes, R. and Thiele, H. (1999), 'Consolidation and Public Opinion in South Africa', in L. Diamond and M. Plattner, *Democratization in Africa*, Johns Hopkins University Press, Baltimore.

Mbembe, A. (1990), 'Democratization and Social Movements in Africa', *Africa Demos*, November, pp. 1-9

McLean, I. (ed), (1996), *Oxford Concise Dictionary of Politics*, Oxford University Press, Oxford.

Mendez, J., O'Donnell, G. and Pinheiro, P. (eds), (1999), *The (Un)Rule of Law and the Underprivileged in Latin America*, University of Notre Dame Press, Notre Dame.

Mereleman, R. (1991), *Partial Visions: Culture and Politics in Britain, Canada and the United States*, University of Wisconsin, Madison.

Michelman, F. (1998), 'Law's Republic', *Yale Law Journal*, vol. 97, pp. 1493-1537.

Minnaar, A. (1999), 'The New Vigilantism in Post-April 1994 South Africa: Crime Prevention or an Expression of Lawlessness?', Paper presented at the CRIMSA International Conference: crime prevention in the new millennium, Arendsnes, Cintsa East, East London, 25-28 May 1999.

Mirzeler, M and Young, C. (2000), 'Pastoral Politics in the Northeast Periphery in Uganda: AK-47 as Change Agent', *Journal of Modern African Studies*, vol. 38, pp.407-29.

Monteiro, O. (1999), 'Governance and Decentralization', in B. Ferraz and B. Munslow (ed), *Sustainable Development in Mozambique*, James Currey, Oxford.

Muthoga, L. (1997), 'Is there a Justification for Corporal Punishment?', *Wajibu*, vol. 12, available online at www.peacelink.it/wajibu.

Newitt, M. (1981), *Portugal in Africa: The Last Hundred Years*, Hurst, London.
Nina, D. (2001), '*Dirty Harry* is Back: Vigilantism in South Africa – The (Re)emergence of "Good" and "Bad" Community', www.iss.co.za, accessed 14.1.2001.
O'Donnell, G. (1996), 'Delegative Democracy', in L. Diamond and M. Plattner (eds), *The Global Resurgence of Democracy*, Johns Hopkins University Press, Baltimore.
O'Donnell, G. (1999), 'Polyarchies and the (Un)Rule of Law in Latin America: A Partial Conclusion', in J. Mendez, G. O'Donnell and P. Pinheiro (eds), *The (Un)Rule of Law and the Underprivileged in Latin America*, University of Notre Dame Press, Notre Dame, pp. 303-37.
Odunjinrin, O. (1993), 'Wife Battering in Nigeria', *International Journal of Gynaecology & Obstetrics*, vol. 41, pp. 159-64
Ottaway, M. (ed), (1997), *Democracy in Africa: The Hard Road Ahead*, Lynne Rienner, Boulder.
Ottemoeller, D. (1998), 'Popular Perceptions of Democracy: Elections and Attitudes in Uganda', *Comparative Political Studies*, vol. 31, pp. 98-124.
Oxfam/Sayer, G. (2000a), 'It is the Rebels who Bring us Hunger: Displaced families Sheltering in Kitgum Mission', internal report on Kitgum Water and Sanitation Project, Kitgum Food Security Project, 01/06/2000, Oxfam.
Oxfam/Sayer, G. (2000b), 'A Forgotten War: the Destruction of the Acholi in Northern Uganda', internal report on Kitgum Water and Sanitation Project, Kitgum Food Security Project, 01/06/2000, Oxfam.
Oxfam/Sayer, G. and Leggett, I. (2000c), 'The Acholi Religious Leaders Peace Initiative: interview with Monsignor Matthew Ojara', internal report on Kitgum Water and Sanitation Project, Kitgum Food Security Project, 21/06/2000, Oxfam.
Oxfam/Sayer, G. (2000d), 'Pandwong Primary School, Kitgum: Teaching in a War Zone', internal report on Kitgum Water and Sanitation Project, Kitgum Food Security Project, 21/06/2000, Oxfam.
Oxfam/Sayer, G. (2000e), 'The LRA Robs the Children of their Humanity: the Experience of Three Children Abducted into the LRA', internal report on Kitgum Water and Sanitation Project, Kitgum Food Security Project, 24/06/2000, Oxfam.
Paye, M. and Diop, M. (1998), 'The Army and Political Power in Senegal', in E. Hutchful and A. Bathily (eds), *The Military and Militarism in Africa*, CODESRIA, Dakar.
Pelser, E. (2001), 'A Critical Distance: Public Perceptions and the Police Service', *Needbank ISS Crime Index*, vol. 5, available on www.isi.co.za/Publications/Crimeindex
Pelser, E., Louw, A. and Ntuli, S. (2000), *Poor Safety: Crime and Policing in South Africa's Rural Areas*, Monograph Series, No. 47, Institute of Strategic Studies, Pretoria.
Pettit, P. (1999), *Republicanism: A Theory of Freedom and Government*, Oxford University Press, Oxford.
Pigou, P., Greenstein, R. and Valji, N. (1998), *Assessing Knowledge of Human Rights Among the General Population and Selected Target Groups*, (Braamfontein: Community Agency for Social Enquiry).
Pinheiro, P. (1997), 'Popular Responses to State-Sponsored Violence in Brazil', in D. Chalmers et al. (eds), *The New Politics of Inequality in Latin America*, Oxford University Press, Oxford.
Pirouet, L. (1994), 'H R issues in Museveni's Uganda' in H. Hansen and M. Twaddle (eds), *Changing Uganda*, James Currey, London.
Przeworski, A. (1995), *Sustainable Democracy*, Cambridge University Press, Cambridge.
Quam, M. (1997), 'Creating Peace in an Armed Society: Karamoja, Uganda, 1996', *African Studies Quarterly*, 1, available at www.africa.ufl.edu/asq.

Radin, M. (1989), 'Reconsidering the Rule of Law', *Boston University Law Review*, vol. 4, pp. 781-819.
Rawls, J. (1971), *A Theory of Justice*, Oxford University Press, Oxford.
Raz, J. (1977), 'The Rule of Law and its Virtue', *Law Quarterly Review*, vol. 93, pp. 195-211.
Reiner, R. (1985), *The Politics of the Police*, Wheatsheaf, Brighton.
Rodley, N. (1999), 'Torture and Conditions of Detention in Latin America' in J. Mendez, G. O'Donnell, and P. Pinheiro (eds), *The (Un)Rule of Law and the Underprivileged in Latin America*, University of Notre Dame Press, Notre Dame.
Rose, R. and Shin, D. (2001), 'Democratization Bbackwards: The Problem of Third-Wave Democracies', *British Journal of Political Science*, vol. 31, pp. 331-54.
Rothchild, D. and Chazan, N. (1988), (eds), *The Precarious Balance: State and Society in Africa*, Westview Press, Boulder.
Rousseau, J. (1973), *The Social Contract*, Dent, London.
Rule, S. (2001), 'Declining Turnout in Southern African Elections: Disillusionment or Normality', paper presented for ECPR Conference, Canterbury, September 2001.
Ruth, S. (1980), 'The Dynamics of Patriarchy', in S. Ruth (ed), *Issues in Feminism*, Houghton-Mifflin, Boston.
Sandbrook, R. (1993), *The Politics of Africa's Economic Recovery*, Cambridge University Press, Cambridge.
Sangmpam, S. (1994), *Pseudocapitalism and the Overpoliticized State: In Search of a Theory of the Third World State: The Case of Zaire*, Avebury, Aldershot.
Scharf, W. (2001), *Police Reform and Crime Prevention in Post-Conflict Transitions. Learning from the South African and Mozambican Experience*, accessed, www.um.dk/upload/english/DP3cScharf
Schatzberg, M. (1993), 'Power, Legitimacy and Democratisation in Africa', *Africa*, vol. 63, pp. 445-61.
Schmidt, E. (1992), *Peasants, Traders, and Wives: Shona Women in the History of Zimbabwe, 1870-1939*, Heinemann, Portsmouth.
Schonteich, M. (1999), *Unshackling the Crime Fighters: Increasing Private Sector Involvement in South Africa's Justice System*, South Africa Institute of Race Relations, Johannesburg.
Schonteich, M. (2000a), 'The Thin Blue Line: Police Resources in the Provinces', *Needbank ISS Crime Index*, vol. 4, pp. 15-20.
Schonteich, M. (2000b), *Justice Versus Retribution: Attitudes to Punishment in the Eastern Cape*, Monograph Series, No. 45, Institute of Strategic Studies, Pretoria.
Schonteich, M. (2000c), 'A Battle Lost? Violent Crime Trends in 1999', *Needbank ISS Crime Index*, vol. 4, available on www.isi.co.za/Publications/Crimeindex.
Schonteich, M. (2000d), *Justice Versus Retribution: Attitudes toPunishment in the Eastern Cape*, Monograph Series, No. 45, Institute of Strategic Studies, Pretoria.
Schonteich, M. (2001), 'Sleeping Soundly. Feelings of Safety: Based on Perceptions or Reality', *Needbank ISS Crime Index*, vol. 5, available on www.isi.co.za/Publications/Crimeindex.
Seekings, J. (1992), 'The Revival of People's Courts', in G. Moss and I. Obery eds., *South African Review 6: From 'Red Friday' to Codesa*, Ravan Press, Johannesburg, pp. 186-200.
Sekhonyane, M. (2000), 'Using Crime to Fight Crime: Tracking Vigilante Activity', *Needbank ISS Crime Index*, vol. 4, pp. 1-4.

Seleti, Y. (2000), 'The Public in the Exorcism of the Police in Mozambique: Challenges of Institutional Democratization', *Journal of Southern African Studies*, vol. 26, pp. 349-64.

Shaw, M. (1995), *'Partners in Crime'? Crime, Political Transition and Changing Forms of Policing Control*, Centre for Policy Studies, Johannesburg.

Shaw, M. (1996), 'South Africa: Crime in Transition; Terrorism and Political Violence', *Terrorism and Political Violence*, vol. 8, pp. 156-75.

Shaw, M. (1997), 'State Responses to Organized Crime in South Africa', *Transnational Organized Crime*, vol. 3, pp. 1-15.

Skinner, Q. (1998), *Liberty before Liberalism*, Cambridge University Press, Cambridge.

Stack, L. (1997), *Courting Disaster? Justice and South Africa's New Democracy*, Centre for Policy Studies, Johannesburg.

Tanner, M. (2000), 'Review Article: Will the State Bring *You* Back in? Policing and Democratization', *Comparative Politics*, vol. 33, pp. 101-24.

Thulare, P. (1996), 'Policing and security on the East Rand – Katorus area', *African Security Review*, vol. 5, reproduced in, *Double Take: A Collection of Material Written by CPS Researchers*, Centre for Policy Studies, Johannesburg.

Tilly, C. (1975), *The Formation of National States in Western Europe*, vol. 3, Princeton University Press, Princeton.

US Department of State (1998), Bureau of Democracy, Human Rights, and Labour, *1997 Country Reports on Human Rights Practices: Mozambique*.

US Department of State (1999), Bureau of Democracy, Human Rights, and Labour, *1998 Country Reports on Human Rights Practices: Mozambique*.

US Department of State (1999), Bureau of Democracy, Human Rights, and Labour, *1998 Country Reports on Human Rights Practices: Uganda*.

US Department of State (2000), Bureau of Democracy, Human Rights, and Labour, *1999 Country Reports on Human Rights Practices: Mozambique*.

US Department of State (2000), Bureau of Democracy, Human Rights, and Labour, *1999 Country Reports on Human Rights Practices: Uganda*.

US Department of State (2000), Bureau of Democracy, Human Rights, and Labour, *1999 Country Reports on Human Rights Practices: Senegal*.

US Department of State (2001), Bureau of Democracy, Human Rights, and Labour, *2000 Country Reports on Human Rights Practices: Mozambique*.

US Department of State (2001), Bureau of Democracy, Human Rights, and Labour, *2000 Country Reports on Human Rights Practices: Uganda*.

US Department of State (2001), Bureau of Democracy, Human Rights, and Labour, *2000 Country Reports on Human Rights Practices: Senegal*.

US Department of State (2002), Bureau of Democracy, Human Rights, and Labour, *2001 Country Reports on Human Rights Practices: Mozambique*.

Vail, L. and White, L. (1980), *Capitalism and Colonialism in Mozambique: a Study of Quelimane District*, Heinemann, London.

Vengroff, R. and Magala, M. (2001), 'Democratic Reform, Transition and Consolidation: Evidence from Senegal's 2000 Presidential Election', *Journal of Modern African Affairs*, vol. 39, pp. 129-62.

Villalon, L. and Huxtable, P. (eds) (1998), *The African State at a Critical Juncture: Between Regime Disintegration and Reconfiguration*, Lynne Rieinner, Boulder.

Vines, A. (2000), 'The Struggle Continues: Light Weapons Destruction in Mozambique', *Occasional papers on international security issues*, April 1998, Number 25, Department of War Studies, King's College, University of London, available on

www.basicint.org/bpaper25, accessed 13 December, 2000. An earlier version of this paper appeared in the *Journal of Southern African Studies*, vol. 24, 1998.
Von Schnitzler, A. et. al. (2001), *Guardian or Gangster? Mapogo a Mathamaga: A Case Study*, Centre for the Study of Violence and Reconciliation, Violence and Transition Series, Vol. 3.
Walker, G. (1988), *The Rule of Law: Foundation of Constitutional Democracy*, Melbourne University Press, Melbourne.
Waller, R. (1999), 'Pastoral Poverty in its Historical Perspective', in D. Anderson and V. Broch-Due (eds), *The Poor Are Not Us*, James Currey, Oxford.
Widner, J. (ed) (1994), *Economic Change and Political Liberalisation*, Johns Hopkins University Press, Baltimore.
Wilkinson, P. (1996), 'The Role of the Military in a Democratic Society', *Terrorism and Political Violence*, vol. 8, pp. 1-11.
Williams, R. (1981), 'Legitimate and Illegitimate Uses of Violence: A Review of Evidence and Ideas', in W. Gaylin, et al., (eds), *Violence and the Politics of Research*, Plenum, New York.
Wiseman, J. (1996), *The New Struggle for Democracy in Africa*, Ashgate, Brookfield.
Wood, K. and Jewkes, R. (1997), 'Violence, rape, and sexual coercion', *Gender & Development*, vol. 5, pp. 41-6.
Woods, J. (2000), *Mozambique: The CIVPOL Operation*, www.ndu.edu/inss/books/policing/ch5, accessed 13 December, 2000
Yoder, J. (1998), 'Good Government, Democratisation and Traditional African Political Philosophy: the example of the Kanyok of the Congo', *Journal of Modern African Studies*, vol. 36, pp. 485-507.
Young, C. (1994), 'In Search of Civil Society', in Harbeson, J., Rothchild, D., and Chazan, N. (eds), *Civil Society and the State in Africa*, Lynne Rienner, Boulder, pp. 33-50.
Young, C. (1988), 'The African Colonial State and its Political Legacy', in D. Rothchild and N. Chazan, N. (eds), *The Precarious Balance: State and Society in Africa*, Westview Press, Boulder.
Zolberg, A. (1992), 'The Specter of Anarchy: African States Verging on Dissolution', *Dissent*, vol. 39, pp. 303-11.
Zwane, P. (1994), 'The Need for Community Policing', *African Defence Review*, vol. 18, pp. 38-43.

Index

abductions 9, 57-8, 60, 64-5, 66, 70, 76, 83, 87, 92-3, 135-6, 176, 189, 196
accountability 12, 14, 19-24, 32, 48-50, 66, 71, 74, 103, 107-8, 117, 122, 132, 138-40, 168, 193-4, 206, 213, 216
Acholi 55-6, 59-60, 64-5, 67-9, 72-4, 77, 183, 185, 196-7, 214-17
army, *see* military
armed robbery 108-9, 129-35, 138, 143, 145-50, 209
arrest 12, 24, 40, 44, 61-2, 70, 74-5, 85, 87-9, 93, 96, 101, 111-16, 118, 120-21, 123, 126, 129, 134-7, 139, 142, 144, 156, 160, 166, 168, 171, 176, 189, 191, 194, 196, 199, 212
authoritarianism 16, 27-49, 64, 107-8, 175, 205-6, 208, 210

Bagisu 190-91, 196-7
banditry 9, 38, 47, 95, 100, 108, 110-1, 130-31, 150, 210
banishment 157, 164
Bayley, David 12-13, 210, 218
beating 9, 36-8, 42, 45, 57-8, 61-2, 64, 75, 83, 89-90, 107, 114-16, 118, 157, 161-4, 172
Belgian Congo, *see* Congo D.R.
Bokora 179, 185-6, 195
bribery, extortion 25, 30, 33, 44, 90, 112, 114, 118, 124, 129, 133, 136, 143, 163, 168, 170, 208, 216; *see also* corruption
Britain 32, 43-4, 181, 200
brutalisation 73, 146, 200

cattle raiding 28, 38, 42, 55, 63, 67, 83, 100, 158, 163, 174, 179-200, 208, 215-16
Chissano, President 111, 118, 124-5, 211
churches 14, 45, 65, 67-8, 77, 99, 130, 163, 185, 188, 194, 197, 209

civil war 32, 47, 72, 81, 107-9, 124, 183, 210
colonial rule 32, 39, 40-8, 124, 180-2
commercial, business interests 12-13, 32-3, 42-4, 68, 116, 120-122, 125, 131, 133, 163, 169, 173
confessions under torture 47, 62, 88-9, 114-15
Congo D.R. 35, 38, 42, 47, 60
corruption; *see also* bribery 24-5, 27, 31, 48, 108-9, 116, 118, 121-2, 124, 160, 217
courts, informal 9, 155-7, 160-62, 164, 166, 168, 170, 174, 191-2
crime gangs 39, 59, 110-11, 118, 130-31, 134-5, 146-8, 154, 159, 162, 169-72, 182, 191, 209
crime 9-12, 28, 30, 34-40, 46-7, 61, 107-11, 113-14, 116-18, 125, 129-36, 138-9, 141-50, 153-64, 166-75, 182, 187, 190-93, 199, 208-9, 211, 214016, 218
criminal complicity 48, 62, 111, 116-18, 130, 135-6, 149, 162, 173-4, 191, 217
criminal justice system 75, 102, 107, 123, 142, 157-160, 164, 166-7, 169, 172-3, 187
culture, security force 10, 30-31, 76, 123

democracy 18-25, 27-31, 34, 38, 46, 60, 65-7, 69-71, 73, 75-6, 90, 95, 98, 102-3, 118, 121-2, 124-5, 131, 137-8, 141, 144-6, 161, 166-7, 169-70, 172-4, 193, 196, 205-7, 209-10, 212-16, 219, 220
democratisation 27-8, 31, 34, 38, 40, 48-9, 64, 66, 108, 142, 152, 154, 157, 205-7, 210-11, 214, 219
detainees 9, 61-2, 87-9, 91-3, 110-15, 120, 134, 195
Diamacoune, Senghor 84, 89, 92-5
Diouf, President 82, 84, 92-3, 98-9, 103
disappearances 86-7, 96, 112

disarmament 84, 92, 107, 109, 186, 188-90, 196-8, 200
disciplinarianism 28-49, 205-6
discourse of violence, legitimist 69, 71, 94, 145, 170-171, 214
discrimination 10, 16-17, 23-5, 27, 59, 74, 101, 170, 196
displaced persons 42, 58, 63-4, 84, 92-4, 100, 187, 189, 195, 198

elections 22, 25, 27, 45-6, 49, 71, 79, 82, 84, 98-9, 115, 150, 197-8, 214, 217
equality 15, 16, 18-23, 27, 48-9, 66, 124, 145-6, 167, 170, 193, 196, 205, 214, 219
Ethiopia 28, 47, 68, 179-80, 183-4, 188
ethnic militia 33, 140-41, 147, 150
executions, extra-judicial 57, 61, 66-7, 85-7, 112-13, 134-7, 213

firearms, weapons 12, 28, 32, 33-4, 47, 55, 58, 67, 93, 100, 107-8, 110-12, 116-17, 119, 121, 135, 139, 154, 158, 163, 171-2, 183-4, 186, 188-90, 193, 196, 209, 216
France 89, 92

Gambia, The 81, 84-5, 92, 94, 103
governance 21, 218
guards, presidential 13, 32
Guinea-Bissau 47, 81-2, 84-5, 92, 94, 97, 100-111, 103-4

Hills, Alice 13-14, 33, 39, 48, 157, 210
HSMF, *see* LRA
human rights 11, 15, 17, 20-21, 23-4, 31-2, 34-8, 40, 48, 60-65, 73-4, 76, 85-6, 88, 93, 96, 102-3, 110-111, 117, 120, 124, 126, 134, 145, 160, 167, 170, 193-4, 199, 205-9, 212, 219

Igbo 130, 132, 141, 143, 147-8
immunity from prosecution and impunity 15, 33-4, 40, 73-5, 89, 96, 102-3, 108, 123-4, 139, 145, 168, 171, 206, 212, 214
immunity to violence 74
impartiality 17-18, 33, 102, 104, 133, 197

independence, political 39-40, 46-8, 81-4, 92, 95, 98, 101, 180, 182, 193, 215
insurgency 47-8, 55-60, 64-6, 69-72, 81-5, 90-91, 94, 99, 101-2, 156, 183, 209, 217
international law 9, 23, 75, 87
intimidation 24-5, 33, 66, 69, 71, 84, 97-8, 100, 114, 120-21, 132, 145, 150, 155, 160, 164, 174, 191, 208, 212-13
Islam 138, 163, 173, 218
Iteso, Teso 183, 186, 188-90, 195, 197-8, 201

Jie 179, 195
journalists 29, 70-71, 96-8, 117, 120-22, 129, 133, 176, 179, 210, 212-13; *see also* media; newspapers
judiciary, magistracy 14, 17-19, 22, 25, 30-31, 39, 43, 49, 82, 87-9, 94, 102, 113, 119, 136, 159, 161, 165, 167, 191, 213, 219

Kalenjin 179, 181-2, 186, 195, 198
Karamojong, Karamoja 179-83, 185-6, 188-91, 193-9, 215
Kenya 34, 37, 38, 39, 43-5, 77, 179-82, 184-90, 193, 195-8, 200, 212, 215
Kony, Joseph 56-7, 59-60, 62, 65, 67, 70, 77-9,
Kuria 179, 182-3, 187, 189, 192

labelling 11, 146, 215
Lakwena, Alice 56, 73, 76
law, rule of 11, 14-25, 27-9, 33-4, 39-40, 45, 48-9, 60, 73, 75, 119, 125, 141, 144, 165-7, 175, 182, 193, 205, 211, 216, 219
legal rights 17-24, 27, 48-9, 113, 145, 168, 170-71, 212
legislature, parliament, national assembly 11, 19-20, 22-5, 64-5, 68, 71-2, 96-9, 121-5, 132, 136, 148, 159, 197-8, 207, 212, 217-9
legitimacy 10-11, 17, 19-20, 28, 32-3, 36, 41, 45-6, 68-9, 71, 74, 94, 98, 101, 107-8, 124, 140-41, 153, 157, 167, 169, 174, 188, 210-11, 214-15
LRA 55-76
Maasai 179-80, 182, 195, 200

Mapogo 161-3, 168, 173-4, 212, 214, 216
Marakwet 179, 186-7
MASOB 147, 150
Matheniko 179, 185-7
Mbadinju, Governor of Adambra 131, 141, 148
media 27, 41, 48, 69, 95-7, 107, 120, 122-3, 172-3, 212, 218; *see also* journalists; press; radio; television
Merrile 184-5, 188
MFDC 82-6, 89, 91-5, 97-8, 100-103, 211, 215
military 9, 13-14, 30-32, 41-50, 55-73, 75, 82-103, 107-110, 116-17, 125, 130, 132, 183, 186, 188-90, 193, 196, 199-200, 206-9, 213, 215
militia 42, 50, 57, 60, 119, 140-42, 147-8, 150, 156, 189, 191-93, 197; *see also* non-state policing; vigilantes
minorities 15, 17, 24, 27, 94, 103
murder 45, 55, 68, 122-4, 134, 136, 139-40, 143-4, 148, 153-5, 157, 159, 162-4, 168-9, 172, 174, 176, 191, 194, 217
Museveni, President 55, 59-60, 64-5, 67-8, 71-3, 75, 77, 79, 190, 197

national assembly, *see* legislature
newspapers 30, 66, 68, 70, 73, 75, 86, 95-9, 114, 121-3, 133, 143, 154, 213, 217, 219,
news management 69, 94, 120
non-state policing 9, 12-14, 34, 155, 158, 167-172, 174, 207, 212, 218
NRA 55-7, 62-3, 70

Obasanjo, President 139, 141
OPC 130, 132, 137-8, 143, 147, 150

PAGAD 162-4, 172-3, 212-14, 216, 218
parliament, *see* legislature
parties, political 17, 27, 35, 71-4, 82, 84, 91-2, 98-100, 107, 109, 117, 119, 121-2, 124-5, 136, 140-41, 149, 156, 165, 173, 191, 198, 216-18; *see also* RENAMO

peace negotiations, settlements 34, 57, 59-60, 64-5, 67-8, 72, 74, 83, 85, 89, 91-5, 97, 99, 186, 188-9, 194-5, 209-10, 213, 217
plunder economy, war economy 72-3, 100, 215
Pokot 179-80, 184-9, 196, 200, 215
police 9-10, 12-14, 23-4, 30-44, 47-50, 49-50, 60, 77, 85, 87-9, 91, 102, 107, 126, 129-50, 153-6, 158-72, 175-7, 182-3, 187-92, 195, 207-8, 210-13, 215-18
politicians, MPs 33, 35, 46, 65, 68, 77, 100, 116, 141, 145, 189, 195, 197-8
press, *see* newspapers
prisoners 9, 62, 83, 88-90, 93, 102-3, 112, 114-15, 120-21, 134, 159-60, 175, 213
prosecutions 24-5, 33, 40, 45, 48, 70, 75, 87, 97, 102, 119, 122-3, 144, 159, 169, 193, 200, 212-13, 217; *see also* immunity
punishment, capital 37, 160
punishment, corporal 30, 36-8, 157, 160-61, 163
punishment, summary 11, 25, 33, 47, 157, 162, 168, 193

racism 27, 74, 101, 157, 162, 170, 196, 198
radio 55, 69, 95, 97, 118, 120, 122, 126, 140
rape 55, 57-8, 61-2, 108, 155, 157, 159, 160, 164-6, 176, 185, 189, 216
reconciliation 28, 68, 194-5
RENAMO 107-10, 113-15, 119, 121, 124, 208, 210, 214, 217
revenge 10, 28, 56-7, 88-9, 91, 115, 117, 125, 146, 171, 174, 179, 184-5, 190, 193, 197, 206-8, 215

Samburu 179, 195-6, 198
Schonteich, Martin 153, 155-6, 158-9, 164-7, 172, 211
self-policing, *see* militia; vigilantism
social polarisation 73, 101, 195, 214-15
SPLA 57, 59, 65, 77-8

Sudan 47, 57-9, 63, 65, 68, 78, 180, 183, 185, 188, 190
Sukuma 179, 191

Tanzania 37, 179-80, 182-4, 187, 191-3,
television 69, 95, 97, 119-20, 140
torture 9, 33, 45, 55, 57-8, 62, 66, 85, 87-9, 93, 102, 104, 107, 111-12, 114-15, 121-2, 124, 134, 145, 192, 200, 208, 217; *see also* beatings; rape;
training of security forces 34-5, 47-8, 60, 85, 108, 111, 117, 123, 125-6, 168, 189, 219
transparency 93, 139, 212
treason charges 57, 62, 75

Turkana 179, 184-6, 188-9, 195-6, 198, 200

victimisation 72, 121, 154
vigilantism 9, 13, 33, 36, 50, 119, 129-32, 135-40, 142-6, 150, 155-74, 184-95, 197-200, 207-9, 211-13, 215-16, 218; *see also* militia

Wade, President 83-5, 93, 97, 99, 103
warlord 32-3, 59, 117, 156
weapons, *see* firearms
witchcraft 56, 157, 191

Zaire, *see* Congo D.R.